Off the Record

Off the Record

THE TECHNOLOGY AND CULTURE
OF SOUND RECORDING IN AMERICA

DAVID MORTON

Rutgers University Press

New Brunswick, New Jersey, and London

Library of Congress Cataloging-in-Publication Data

Morton, David, 1964–
    Off the record : the technology and culture of sound recording in
America / David Morton.
        p. cm.
    Includes bibliographical references.
    ISBN 0-8135-2746-5 (cloth : alk. paper). — ISBN 0-8135-2747-3
(paper : alk. paper)
        1. Sound—Recording and reproducing—United States—Case studies.
    2. Sound recording industry—United States—Social aspects.
    I. Title.
    TK7881.4.M66   2000
    621.3899'3'0973—dc21   99-27914
                                                                        CIP

British Cataloging-in-Publication data for this book is available
from the British Library

Manufactured in the United States of America

To my mother and the memory of my father

CONTENTS

ILLUSTRATIONS

PREFACE

When I started this project, I did not know how it would end. Initially I sought the origins of a technology, sound recording, that seemed to have infused American society of the 1990s. As I would later learn, discovering the roots of recording technology did not explain why it had become ubiquitous in our culture. When I turned my attention to the implications of ubiquity, I realized that explaining the way a new technology becomes a part of daily life is even more difficult than uncovering its origins. The greatest task, however, has been to explain why an everyday technology is important. As a colleague once pointed out to me, "Air is ubiquitous, and it's certainly important in everyone's life, but it doesn't make interesting history." Such is the nature of writing history that sometimes the most important things make the least captivating of subjects. Fortunately, for many people sound recording holds a great deal of intrinsic interest, and I hope I have done justice to its history. I will feel that I will have succeeded if I can convince the general reader of the profound cultural and economic significance of a technology that has become so commonplace that its use is becoming almost as unremarkable as the presence of air. My hope is that by visiting a few of the many small places where Americans use sound recording, its importance today will become more evident.

The research for this project involved a large number of archives and libraries. Many people took the time to help me find the obscure material that has made all the difference. Doug Tarr, at the Edison National Historic Site, lent his considerable experience in Edison corporate records. Paul Israel of the Edison Papers Project at Rutgers University provided invaluable guidance regarding Thomas Edison's work. Bernard Finn and Elliot Sivowich of the National Museum of American History both steered me toward important archival sources. The West Virginia Historical Society in Springfield, the Wis-

xi

consisn Historical Society in Waukesha, the Library of Congress Folk Music Repository, and Ameritech Corporation generously donated their services to the project. Marc Regberg of the Venture Development Corporation and Samuel J. Kalow provided valuable information on office dictation equipment. Sheldon Hochheiser went beyond the call of duty several times to help find material in the AT&T archives. Special thanks goes to Janet Abbate, Amy Slaton, Pamela Laird, and Susan Schmidt Horning, who read parts of the manuscript. I would also thank the faculty and staff of the Auburn University Department of History, the School of History, Technology, and Society at the Georgia Institute of Technology, and my colleagues at the IEEE History Center and the Rutgers University Department of History.

Financial assistance for the cover design was generously provided by the IEEE History Center at Rutgers University.

Off the Record

Introduction

＋≍

Invention

$\mathcal{D}$uring the busy summer and fall of
1877, Thomas Edison and his team of tinkerers worked on dozens of projects, moving from one to another as new ideas struck them. Edison speculated that one of his gadgets, a device to record telegraph dots and dashes as they came over the line, might also be useful for recording the electrical messages of the telephone. For the first time, he realized, it might be possible to record and reproduce the human voice. In July, the telegraph recorder was modified so that it would respond to the voice, and Edison recorded the words, "Mary had a little lamb." After some more tinkering, Edison transmitted the news of this invention to the press, and *Scientific American* announced that the subscribers to Alexander Graham Bell's exciting new communication service would soon be to employ their telephones for serious business matters rather than just idle chat, since there could now be an exact record of their conversations.[1] He projected a confluence of these radically new inventions to accomplish a long-time goal of inventors; a system of instant, long-distance communication in which the voice could also be captured for later use. Further investigation showed that telephone recording was more difficult than anticipated, so Edison worked on a purely acoustic device, the "phonograph," in which a needle incised a groove on a wax-coated strip of paper. Scientific devices for tracing sound waves had been in existence for many years, but Edison aimed for something more; a machine that would not only record sound waves but reproduce them. In early December, Edison had one of his machinists construct a new model of the phonograph that used a sheet of tinfoil, wrapped around a metal cylinder, as the recording medium. The inventor bent over and shouted a few words into it, and to everyone's surprise

1

FIGURE 1. Edison's first tinfoil phonograph, 1877. U.S. Department of the Interior, National Park Service, Edison National Historic Site.

the phonograph worked the first time. Then, on December 7, 1877, at the offices of *Scientific American* magazine, he demonstrated a phonograph recording to the editors which "inquired as to our health, asked how we liked the phonograph, informed us that *it* was very well, and bid us a cordial good night."[2]

If in retrospect it seems like Edison had failed to rise to a momentous occasion in this choice of words, perhaps it is because the distance of a hundred years obscures the novelty of a machine that could talk. His words were not as impressive as the mighty "What hath God wrought?" used by Morse to demonstrate his telegraph years earlier, nor even as pragmatic as Bell's calling out to his assistant Mr. Watson. In any event, some inventors in the field of communication who followed Edison did even worse: Marconi's first transatlantic radio transmission would be simply the letter "s."

Americans greeted the phonograph as if it were a major scientific discovery, and the subsequent round of publicity for the phonograph made Edison a national hero. It was this invention that solidified Edison's "Wizard of Menlo Park" mystique, and the public's enthusiastic reception convinced him that the talking machine would amount to something big. Although he had created many inventions by 1878, Edison told a reporter that "this is my baby, and I expect it to grow up and be a big feller and support me in my old age."[3] But what would Americans do with the phonograph, especially since Edison himself was unable to build a practical telephone recorder? The specific commercial applications were still unknown. That same year he outlined his vision for the phonograph's future. What he initially conceived as a way to record telephone messages would now become a mechanical stenographer for businessmen, a talking book for the blind, an elocution instructor, a music box, a family album, a speaking toy, an announcing clock, an historical chronicler, a student's note-taker, and, perhaps with a little more work, a telephone recorder, too.[4] In other words, what Edison had first conceived narrowly as a telephone recorder for business he now predicted would become a more general-purpose enhancement or even replacement for many kinds of oral and written communication for business and personal purposes.

Edison's phonograph was soon joined by another fundamental invention that, while less successful initially, would come to assume great importance later. Just a few years after the introduction of the phonograph, an inventor named Oberlin Smith, who, like Edison, was working in New Jersey, conceived of a technology to record sound magnetically. His recorder captured the telephone's electrical output on the surface of a steel wire or tape, just as motion picture film captures the effects of light. Instead of light, Smith's recorder responded to magnetism, since steel will retain an "image" of any nearby magnetic field. The source of the magnetic field was the flow of electricity in a telephone wire, for every electrical flow emanates an invisible magnetic field. Smith disclosed his ideas in 1888, and they were picked up by the Danish inventor Valdemar Poulsen. He demonstrated his "telegraphone," recording on steel wire, tape, or disc to an enthusiastic audience at the 1900 exposition in Paris, and announced his intention to sell it as a telephone recorder, a dictating machine, a telephone-based broadcaster, and a "relay," or amplifier.[5]

Almost all of these applications would eventually play important roles in American history, becoming the basis of systems of entertainment, record-keeping, communication and surveillance. Like the technology of writing, sound recording proved to be remarkably versatile, with many different uses in business and industry, in the home, in schools, churches, and almost everywhere else. Sound recording was destined to become more important, commercially and socially, than even Edison imagined. The basic phonograph would soon be joined by other forms of sound recording, allowing even more technical variation and expanding the possibilities for this new technological system.

Users of sound recording gradually wove the technology into the social fabric, and in so doing transformed both. Edison's original phonograph was merely a clever parrot, or better yet, an aural mirror. The phonograph's lackluster sales soon made it clear that few Americans would be satisfied with

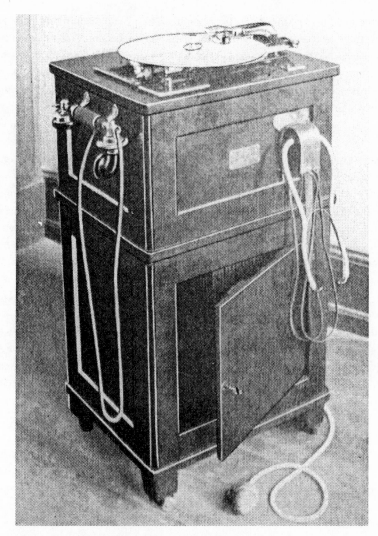

FIGURE 2. An early form of magnetic recording device, called the telegraphone, came in versions that could record on tape, wire, or disk. American Technical Publishers, Inc.

simply recording themselves. Instead, buyers rewarded those who used the phonograph to create a system for mass-produced entertainment, purchasing millions of records (or later tapes or compact discs) for their personal enjoyment.

While the word "record" has become virtually synonymous with music recordings, these represent only a single facet of sound recording's complex history. The title of this book suggests that it is possible to appreciate sound recording's long history as something much more than simply the story of mass-produced entertainment. It is time to reevaluate the history of recorded sound, to explore more of its history, and to include with the story of music on "records" the much wider history of sound recording in general.

On the heels of recorded musical entertainment came many other applications for recording, which neither Edison nor Poulsen could have predicted, such as its use in radio broadcasting, telephone service, and for various purposes in the home. With each new application came fundamentally new ideas about the meanings and purposes of recorded culture, reflected in the technology, the practices associated with making recordings, and the recordings themselves. For example, some of the inventors of new recording technologies strove to make recordings that preserved the desirable aesthetic qualities of the original sound, and hence render the recording process invisible to listeners, while others struggled to make recordings of sounds that could not otherwise be heard, and hence make the recording process obvious to listeners. The aesthetic aspects of the recording were almost irrelevant in other circumstances, where sound recording became a tool for interpersonal, two-way communication, combining the spontaneous, personal qualities of the voice with the time-storage capacity of ordinary writing. That such an astonishing variety of technologies with such different uses could emerge from one simple, original machine is indicative of the adaptability of recording, and also suggests that its importance in American society can only be appreciated by examining it from several different perspectives.

The aims of this book are to evaluate the history of sound recording technology, the business of making recordings and recorders, the relationship of technology to "practice," or the act of recording, and the significance of sound recording in American history. Understanding the history of both the hardware and the ways people used it is essential for understanding why any particular technology succeeded or failed in the marketplace, became a fixture in everyday life, or faded into obscurity. "Recording culture" encompasses the motivations for and outcomes of the act of recording; the relationships between the creators, promoters, and users of recording technology; and the interactions between people, recording machines, and recordings them-selves. Recording culture in America emerged not through the dictates of the technology itself but in complex ways that were contingent upon the actions of people. Every successful or persistent use of sound recording was the result of a two-way process of negotiation between the designers and users of a tech-nology, which sometimes favored one or the other's intentions or desires more heavily. Ultimately, though, the persistence of practice is determined by users or consumers, whose purchasing decisions spell commercial success or failure, and whose individual actions shape the form and function and new technologies, if sometimes only indirectly. Yet the definitions of the terms "users" and "consumers" vary under different circumstances. The "con-sumer" can not always be equated with some hypothesized, typical member of "the public." In reality, consumers or users of a technology operate at dif-ferent levels in the economy and in society, and exercise different levels of input into the technological development process. The purchasing decision of a manager acting on behalf of a company, for example, may have systemic effects throughout a firm or group of firms, with much greater social and eco-nomic significance than a decision by an individual to purchase a particular item for the home. Any analysis of the role of users in technological history has to account for these different types of consumers.

Starting with the basic technology of sound recording, a variety of inven-tors, companies, and consumers modified and reshaped the phonograph and its successors to create an equally complex mix of new technologies. Each of the case studies in this book emphasizes one aspect of the culture of recording and its relationship to new technology, at the same time telling the broader story of sound recording history in America. At the most general level, sound recording was an elaboration or outgrowth of existing forms of cul-ture, absorbing and reshaping existing culture to create the new practices of recording. The recording of music, for example, incorporated but reshaped the aims, conventions, economy, and social hierarchy that had already devel-oped around musical performance. Recording as a form of communication also enveloped and modified existing social structures. When recordings were used as a form of mass communication, for example, sound recording technology often became a medium within a medium that both facilitated exist-ing communications and offered something radically new. Another form of social practice that sound recording affected was labor, and this is particu-larly evident where the recorder was a production tool in business. As such, sound recording involved issues of skill, managerial imperative and gender relations. Only by defining culture broadly to include not only the traditional "high culture" but also other practices, beliefs, habits, and institutions of American society is it possible to analyze fully sound recording's rich history.

Recordings, Culture, and the Culture of Recording

One of the misconceptions that this book hopes to dispel is that the only important category of sound recording involves music. However, music is important, so to illustrate what I mean by "culture of recording" in familiar terms, I begin this study with a brief history of sound recording in the American record industry. Here it is possible to see quite clearly some of the relationships between musical culture, the act of recording as a distinct form of culture, recording technology and the record as a cultural artifact. The histories of music, listening, and the record are familiar territory for many historians. For scholars as diverse as Theodor Adorno, Walter Benjamin, Jacques Barzun, Marshall McLuhan, and Daniel Boorstin, to discuss a sound recording was to discuss commercially recorded music. The modern "culture industry" that Adorno criticized commodified and "preserved" culture in the form of music recordings. Barzun's understanding of recorded sound was similarly limited to music and the music record's alleged "effects" on experience. He perceived an America saturated with the music delivered by "the machine" and believed that Americans were in the midst of a cultural revolution rooted in music. Boorstin, on the other hand, saw recording technology's importance as making possible the "freezing" of performance, annihilating time and making the musical experience repeatable. These are all useful concepts, but none adequately captures the scope of recording's role in American history.[6]

There is more to the history of sound recording than just music, of course, but for the moment consider the relationships between musical culture and the technology of sound recording. Music making in the nineteenth century had its own traditions, practices, and technologies independent of recording. Not all of the musical performance was compatible with the phonograph. Specifically, it was unclear whether the whole of any musical performance could ever be captured on the phonograph. If the phonograph required modification to suit music, what kind of music should be the model? Further, in the nineteenth century performance was already established as a form of business enterprise; the newly formed record companies now sought to combine performance with the technology of the phonograph in a new form of business. What, then, was the relationship between music, performance, business, and technology?

From the perspective of the finished product, the record, many have argued that sound recordings have a cultural influence, but the reverse is also true; culture has an influence on the making of sound recordings.[7] One particularly important, recurring cultural influence has been "highbrow" ("serious" or "classical") music, owing to the high social status of symphonic and operatic music in American society. The repertoire, styles of performance, and the traditional relationship between audience and the music all found their way into the evolving culture of recording. At the same time, recording brought high culture music into the capitalist system of production. Despite considerable technological changes in recording technology over the last century, one of the most consistent features of the U.S. record industry has been its devotion to providing high culture music, despite the small economic rewards gained from recording and marketing it. Sales of popular music, not classical music, have been the major source of growth in the industry, so economic logic would dictate that recording technology should evolve somehow to suit popular music. However, during the formative years of the record industry, it was classical and other forms of highbrow music which proved surprisingly influential in fomenting technical change and shaping the practices associated with music recording studios. Only in the last thirty years have other forms of music come to influence the making of recordings in as profound a manner. In fact, one could argue that the capabilities of new recording technologies now have a stronger influence on popular music than ever before, but even so, highbrow culture is still a ponderous legacy.[8]

Sound Recording and Mass Communication

Business, culture, and recording technology also interact in commercial radio studios, where the act of recording is a step in the process of broadcasting. Recording and the use of recordings in American network radio from the 1920s to the 1950s was an activity dominated by a few powerful corporations.[9] The leaders of the powerful networks that dominated American radio during its first three decades perceived sound recording as a direct threat to their commercial viability. Network managers, aided by government policy makers, enforced rules that prevented most recording activity in radio, and convinced the public that "canned" programs were a second-rate form of entertainment. Today, however, much of every radio station's programming comes from recordings, even the parts that seem to be "live." The crumbling of the networks after 1948 stimulated the greater use of recording technology, but radio stations bought recorders and invented ways to use them that could preserve the live sound of radio. Because recordings on the radio continued to carry a stigma, both within the radio business and among the public, inventors, engineers, and radio station technicians labored to hide the use of recording technology from the audience. Thus the desire to broadcast live (or at least simulate a live broadcast) continued to influence radio practice long after network restrictions on recording were relaxed. Sound recording use in radio today is simultaneously the dominant source of radio content and one of the least apparent of radio's techniques. Through innovations in recording, most evidence of the process of radio has been neatly removed from the product.

Sound Recording and Labor

The commercial, cultural, and technological history of sound recording must also be interpreted in the context of labor history. Like any production process, the making of a recording involves technology plus work. In the context of business, the human side of this equation necessarily entails issues of labor and management. One of these labor contexts was the use of office dictation machines. Between the time of World War I and end of World War II, dictation equipment companies sold tens of thousands of dictation recorders to American companies, and managers in these companies successfully imposed the practice of office dictation on women and many lower-level male employees.[10] Equipment makers were much less successful in attracting higher-level managers and their secretaries to the device, despite considerable technical innovation and an intense marketing effort. Where corporate employees had the power to choose for themselves, as often as not they rejected machine dictation, because it was an unpleasant technology that threatened their skills and office social relations. Efforts to support the practices associated with machine dictation and stimulate voluntary adoption reveal how gender, power relations, and sound recording intersected in the office.

Even after a hundred years of promotion and technical change, office recording practice is not a part of normal business operations. Because it never truly displaced writing, the cultural aspects of machine dictation and their relationship to business imperatives, labor issues, and consumer desires are particularly visible. Dictation records themselves are not particularly important in this part of the story. They were the temporary and often pedestrian intermediate products in the process of correspondence production. This fact makes it easier to focus on the production process rather than the content of the records themselves, and makes the dictation recorder the ideal lens though which to examine the labor aspects of recording technology.

Sound Recording as Interpersonal Communication

The history of the dictation machine also crosses the middle ground between the "industrial" forms of sound recording, those in which the recorder acts as a gateway between culture bearers and a mass audience, and forms of recording more readily available to the average American consumer. While dictation equipment was used by a minority of office workers during the twentieth century, it was nonetheless the form of recording technology most widely known to Americans before 1945. Up to that time, the vast majority of Americans experienced recording technology only as consumers of records. The history of the telephone answering machine, on the other hand, demonstrates the way recording developed into an activity in which ordinary Americans participated. The answering machine is also an outstanding example of the way an invention takes twists and turns on a long path from conception to widespread diffusion. Although the answering machine dates to the nineteenth century, it has entered daily life for most Americans only since the 1980s. The lengthy delay between the answering machine's invention and its ubiquity is partly attributable to the resistance of the nearly monopolistic American telephone service provider, American Telephone & Telegraph, or AT&T. The company recognized demand for telephone answering devices but tried for many years to satisfy customers with live answering services. However, AT&T underestimated the appeal of telephone answering technology, and demand for the machines grew. The company responded by narrowly defining the functions of the recording machines it provided, with important long-term results for the machines and the ways we use them. With the removal of legal restrictions to their use and the blossoming of microelectronics technology, sales skyrocketed in the late 1970s. As millions of consumers bought or used these machines, several things happened. One is that, for the first time, most Americans could have the experience of making sound recordings themselves. Once they overcame their initial shyness or hostility, and became accustomed to the peculiarities of telephone recording "Ma Bell" style, they embraced the practices of making and leaving answering machine messages and even began to find new ways to use the machines. Between the late 1970s and the mid-1980s, consumers transformed the use of the answering machine from a rather utilitarian business machine to an important enhancement of the telephone system.[11] Answering machines in use today embody the legacy of AT&T's resistance (in the form of features built into the machines and generally unquestioned by users), while consumers have invented many of the most widespread practices associated with telephone recording. By transgressing the boundaries of functionality and proper use laid out for them by telephone companies and equipment manufacturers, ordinary consumers developed new ways to communicate via telephone, and in the process extended the utility of the answering machine. The history of the answering machine demonstrates several of the most important aspects of sound recording in the last fifty years; its diffusion to an ever-wider number of Americans, the ability of users to invent new uses for the machine, and the transition of sound recording from a tightly held communications monopoly to a more democratic form of interpersonal communication.

Sound Recording at Home

One pressing issue in the history of the answering machine is why ordinary people decided they wanted to make recordings of themselves or of others. Why, in other words, did the culture of telephone message recording emerge at all? This is also a central issue in the history of home tape recording since World War II. Edison's original phonograph was both a recorder and a reproducer, yet its capacity for recording soon atrophied and finally disappeared by the early 1900s, reflecting the lack of demand for machines with the ability to record at home. Home recording machines were available in the United States during every subsequent year, as one manufacturer after another tried to interest the public in making their own sound records in addition to simply consuming mass-produced ones. Americans disliked standing before the recording machine and hated the sounds of their own recorded voices even more. If they would not record themselves at the turn of the century, manufacturers speculated by the 1920s and '30s that perhaps they would record the radio or duplicate phonograph records. They did not. Even an exciting new technology like the tape recorder, introduced in the late 1940s, did not stimulate more than a small fraction of the American public to begin making recordings. Many who did buy tape recorders abandoned their use when the novelty of the experience wore off. Even though the technologies of home recording changed over the years, changes in practice and not merely technical changes were the true stimulus to the revival of home recording. A sustained culture of home recording emerged only after new technologies and cultural changes converged in the 1960s, establishing the tape recorder as a portable entertainment device and tape recording as a low-cost, personalized alternative to commercial records and radio. As the size and price of recorders diminished, as young Americans began listening to rock and roll, and as the suburbs and the automobile stimulated patterns of mobile music listening, greater numbers of people became home rerecordists of music albums and singles. The practice of home rerecording was growing rapidly in the late 1960s when the Philips Company introduced its "cassette," which proved to be a huge commercial success as a medium for both commercial records and those of the homemade sort. As record and electronics companies consider the next generation of home entertainment technology, the widespread and seemingly irrepressible practice of home recording looms like a dark cloud above their plans.

The case studies in this book illustrate the development of recording technology, the different meanings of the culture of sound recording, and the variety of contexts in which sound recording played a role in American history. The making of sound recordings is relevant to many areas of business, economic, cultural, gender, and labor history. The ways of—and motivations for—making sound recordings have played into events in American history as varied as the broadcast of the crash of the *Hindenburg*, the success of "The Chipmunks" musical group, and the outcome of the Watergate scandal. In an age when aural experience is increasingly mediated by recording technologies, it is important to understand what recordings are, why people make them, and how the technology for making them came to exist. For many reasons, recording technologies and the culture of recording are subjects worthy of study and long overdue for historical consideration.

Chapter 1

High Culture, High Fidelity, and the Making of Recordings in the American Record Industry

+⤝

John Philip Sousa, in his 1906 essay on the "menace of mechanical music," predicted a dire outcome for American culture, a deterioration of talent and taste caused by the diffusion of music on records. Scholars have debated the cultural implications of recordings ever since, but few have looked at the culture of recording itself. The recording of music is an activity that combines a very old form of culture, the performance of music, with a variety of technological processes to create a new form of culture. Further, in the United States recording is part of an industry, so commercial concerns also form a part of recording practice. What we are concerned with here is not only music captured on record as an example of mass-produced culture but also recording as a cultural process; not only the meaning of the content of a record but the meaning of the practices which developed around the act of recording. Those practices, applied in the studio, resulted in the cultural artifacts we call records, which are snapshots of their times, which have various meanings to their audiences, and whose meanings change over time and are difficult to predict. The culture of recording is also a product of its time. It too is influenced by musical styles, but also by the needs of the music business and the practice of engineering. It has as much significance for mass-produced music as the music itself.

The field of sound recording is much broader than just the recording of music, but nowhere are the technologies and practices of sound recording as impressively elaborated as in the studios of the companies that record music. Since the invention of recording in the 1870s, American record companies have gradually transformed the act of recording from a simple shout down a horn into a complex and capital-intensive ritual of musicians and machines, solemnly overseen by a priesthood of specialized technicians. The details of the machines and practices of operating them reflect far more than just the cumulation of improvements prompted by purely technical concerns, but are the result of decades of negotiation between musicians, sound engineers, production engineers, and businessmen. Despite the glaring imbalance between the economic power of record companies and the artistic aims of performers, technological development has not been overwhelmingly oriented toward business ends. Instead, engineers and musicians have participated in the development of technologies serving their own interests as much as managers and business owners during the course of sound recording's hundred-year history. Consumers, too, have acted as agents of change through their purchases of recorded music, for ultimately the success or failure of new recording technologies or practices depend heavily on the purchasing decisions of millions of record buyers.

The basis of today's huge record industry is, of course, the making of music recordings for sale, but this particular form of business was not the natural outcome of the introduction of the phonograph. At first, phonograph manufacturers were only interested in selling the machine itself and expected their customers to make their own recordings. Their initial interest in making recordings was merely to demonstrate the device effectively to customers. The limited success of this approach prompted them to cultivate their own sources of "content," to develop practices and techniques of sound recording, and to find ways to duplicate those recordings in large quantities. Later, the rising popularity of the entertainment phonograph spurred more systematic recording activity, and the practice of sound recording became the core of a new business by the turn of the twentieth century, one concerned primarily in making sound recordings rather than making sound recorders.

The record industry in the United States is one of the most thoroughly studied of all businesses, and its products, music records, are the subject of countless books, theses, and articles. Music recordings are the only form of sound recording that has its own secondary industry, which publishes hundreds of fan magazines, catalogs, and discographies, and justifies the careers of the academics who study recordings for a living. However, few historians of technology have contributed to this effort. Instead, this is a field that has drawn scholars of communications, popular culture, music history, business history, and other specialties. Music historians have explored how recording has affected music, or have written the biographies of particular artists or bands partly through the exegesis of their records.[1] Business historians have written about the exploitation of artists or the monopolistic tendencies of the record companies. Communications scholars have described sound recordings as a form of mass communication. These scholars rightly believe that the products of a relatively small number of recording studios have a wide-ranging economic, social, and cultural significance. Few, however, have looked closely at the process of recording and the relationships between recording technology and recording practice.[2]

It is important to distinguish between the culture of recording, which refers to the practices surrounding sound recording technology, and music as culture. The sound recorder plays an important role in transmitting musical culture. Its limitations (and possibilities) have shaped musical expression in various ways. The mass production and broad distribution of musical records is also an agent of cultural change. Music historians have noted the extent to which the phonograph broke down social barriers and disseminated culture in a stratified society, bringing black music to white audiences, for example. They have been less successful in showing how culture, including musical culture, influenced technological change in recording, or how the making of phonograph records itself constituted a new form of culture. Another major stumbling block has been the concept of "high fidelity," or truth to the original source of the sound. Steven Jones and others have demonstrated how little real meaning the concept of fidelity holds in terms of today's popular music, which is largely electronically generated. They have also pointed out that "fidelity," or accuracy remains central in the technical vocabulary of music recording and reproduction, though practice has strayed ever further from the ideal. One important question that remains is how this situation came to be, and where it is likely to lead.

The problem of high fidelity is further confused by the assumptions that engineers, equipment manufacturers, and marketers make about fidelity, making the concept dependent on references to the performance of "highbrow" forms of music.[3] In its original form, the cult of high-fidelity recording and listening in America was completely devoted to classical, orchestral, or operatic forms of music, pieces that could be performed live in a concert hall and which were generally agreed to represent the best possible sound. Much of the scientific understanding of recording also depended upon these same high culture references. Further, to this fertile mix of musical traditions, engineering knowledge, and consumerism we must add corporate culture. Technical changes in recording technology sponsored by the record industry often made little business sense, unless one factors in the unique corporate attachment to high culture in the United States. Although the American

FIGURE 3. Edison poses with the phonograph, 1878. U.S. Department of the Interior, National Park Service, Edison National Historic Site.

public gave its money to the manufacturers of low culture music, even the musically "unsophisticated" often admitted the cultural superiority of the high-brow. Recording company executives sometimes revealed that their catalog of classical recordings was mainly for prestige, not money. The influence of high culture music in the development of recording technology greatly exceeded the economic importance of classical record sales or the size of the audience for such music. Indeed, high fidelity and high culture played the most important roles in establishing the engineering basis of sound recording, and continue to exercise an influence today.

Records and Early Record Production

The tinfoil recording process that Thomas Edison invented in 1877–78 was crude indeed. Many critics charged that a voice recorded on the machine sounded more like a squawking bird or shrill screech, so Edison and other inventors sought ways to improve the playback quality. The "improved phonograph" of the 1880s and its competitor, the graphophone, abandoned tinfoil in favor of a more reliable medium, the wax cylinder, and included an electric or clockwork motor and various controls. The purchasers of the patent rights to these inventions then set out to find agents to market the phonograph as a business dictation machine, and by 1890 over a dozen companies across the country were doing just that. The business phonograph had some commercial success, but later the local sales companies discovered an important new market after experimentally installing coin-operated phonographs for public amusement. The number of these proto-jukeboxes in use in the mid-1890s was still smaller than the number of dictation machines, but the revenues they generated were sometimes staggering. Hoping to interest individuals in the phonograph, Edison also designed a less expensive type for use at home, and he simultaneously went into the business of selling recorded cylinders.[4]

In retrospect, Edison might have been better off promoting the phonograph for entertainment right from the start. Business dictation required clear, intelligible records that the early phonograph simply was not capable of producing, at least not without careful attention from the machine's operator. Music, ironically, was in some ways well-suited to the phonograph's limited sonic range and high levels of noise and distortion. Listeners often knew the words to popular songs already, or could recognize the melody of even a badly recorded song. Then as now, it was not usually necessary for the recording of a song to be perfectly free of scratches, hissing, or distortion for it to be thoroughly enjoyable. Further, the recordings that Edison's experts made under ideal conditions were more likely to be satisfactory than the home made kind, and hence consumers might be willing to pay for a good recording rather than struggle to make their own. Belatedly, Edison and his competitors shifted their attention to the entertainment market, and by the turn of the century, office recorders and the entertainment phonograph had diverged technically and commercially.

After the introduction of coin-operated phonographs, and particularly after the home phonograph began to garner sales, the phonograph companies began to ponder the problems of the high-volume production of records. The making and duplication of records for sale posed a new set of technical problems to which the original phonograph technology was poorly suited. Recordings for the business phonograph were unique, ephemeral products to be consumed within offices, not a commodity for sale to the public. Making permanent records for duplication and sale would require technologies that Edison had yet invented.[5]

Edison's work on the cylinder recording process in the 1870s and 1880s focused on producing a record that would duplicate the timbre and volume of the original sound. The life span of wax-cylinder records was short, and many inventors experimented with recording media that would harden after the record was made. One of Edison's approaches was to reproduce the cylinders in a mold, but others gained key patents for this technology. For the next ten years, Edison's workers had to rely on reproducing cylinders by a pantograph process, which mechanically coupled a reproducing stylus traveling in the groove of a recorded cylinder to a recording stylus cutting a new groove in a blank cylinder made of a soap-like compound (stearate of soda). Columbia, Edison's first major competitor, also used the pantograph method. This mechanical method made acceptable records, but sound volume was always lost in the process and distortion added.[6]

Within a few years, Edison found a patentable way to make a mold of a cylinder, which could then be the basis of numerous exact copies. This "gold molding" process involved electroplating the original cylinder and using the resulting negative copy to make a metal mold. Formed in celluloid, a plastic material, molded copies lasted longer and could be turned out in rapid succession. However, some of the sound information in the grooves was lost during the molding process, affecting the volume, and Edison struggled to overcome this problem. By 1912, Edison had a commercially viable cylinder molding process in hand, which became the basis of his "Blue Amberol" celluloid cylinders.[7]

The success of the phonograph, the expiration of some of Edison's patents, and other factors encouraged new phonograph manufacturers to become active in the United States in making records and players, sometimes using new technologies. The most important of these was the gramophone of Emile Berliner, a disc recording system developed in the late 1880s and 1890s. Berliner's disc recording technology differed from the Edison system in a number of ways. The disc used a lateral recording method, in which the stylus moved from side to side in a groove of constant depth, rather than the Edison "hill and dale" method. Although many thought that the hill-and-dale recordings resulted in a better sound, Berliner chose lateral recording to avoid infringing on the Edison patents. The method that Berliner had worked out for reproducing the records was the primary reason for employing a disc rather than a cylinder. By a multi-stage electroplating process not unlike the one Edison used, an original recording in soft wax could be transformed into a metal stamper, which could press copies more rapidly and efficiently than was possible with cylinders. Perhaps more important was the fact the discs could be stamped out of a harder material than Edison's cylinders, allowing the stylus of a gramophone player to press harder into the groove to produce more volume. As Edison worked to perfect his cylinder molding process, Berliner's inexpensive gramophone took a growing share of the marketplace, and he foresaw what he imagined to be an immense untapped market for factory-produced records for home entertainment.[8]

The First Studios

Berliner opened his first music recording studio in 1897 in Philadelphia, and began selling recorded discs and players. The playback machine was simple, relatively inexpensive, and marketed to consumers only as a form of home entertainment—it did not appear in the form of a business machine. Because of the disc manufacturing process, the gramophone was only suitable for playback and did not include a recording attachment.[9] Other companies appreciated the Berliner system's advantages for the entertainment market and began producing imitations. The American Graphophone Company, the prominent maker of cylinder machines, by 1899 already had a competing disc player out on the market. Eldridge Johnson, a former contractor to Berliner, also began producing discs and players in the 1890s. He formed several new ventures before establishing the famous Victor Talking Machine Company in 1901.[10]

The adaptation of the phonograph dictating machine to the recording of groups of musicians or performers posed daunting technical problems.[11] Edison, Victor, and Columbia all made early attempts to record large orchestras, but there was simply no way to crowd even a small fraction of the musicians in an orchestra close enough to the recording horn to pick up all the instruments. Further, the dynamic range, meaning the difference between the loudest and softest sounds, of many performances was simply too great for the phonograph to bear. A recorder equipped with a sensitive diaphragm could

FIGURE 4. An early recording session with the Edison phonograph. U.S. Department of the Interior, National Park Service, Edison National Historic Site.

catch even a whisper, but the same diaphragm would break into unintelligible distortion when it was confronted by louder sounds. The compromise design could handle neither very loud nor very soft passages. The use of larger recording horns was a second tactic for trapping more of the sound in a room, but there were physical and practical limits to this technique. Edison, ever the experimenter, built a 200-foot long recording horn for orchestral recording, but it failed to work well.[12]

The most successful recordings of the "acoustic" recording era were of individuals or small groups of singers and musicians. In the early years, studios made multiple recordings simultaneously by clustering recording horns in groups of up to twenty. This meant that all the performers had to be crowded close to the horns, so studios had platforms to raise those at the back of the group up. Early recordings were made outdoors, in tents, or in Edison's laboratory, but soon record companies built special rooms for this purpose. Even in the early days, the recording companies sometimes had contradictory ideas about how to build a studio to suit phonograph recording. Edison's studio had thick, soundproof walls insulated with seaweed or cow hair, but Victor's recorders preferred a "livelier" room with more reverberation, which gave Victor records a distinctive sound. In general, however, reverberation

FIGURE 5. Edison's "perfected" phonograph of 1888, shown here without its speaking tube or amplifying horn. U.S. Department of the Interior, National Park Service, Edison National Historic Site.

was the bane of early recording sessions, and most studio surfaces were well-padded.[13]

The recording process itself reflected the severe limitations of phonograph technology. During a recording session, a recording director (who might also be a conductor or serve other functions) physically arranged the musicians and managed the details of the session. During the session, the director motioned to vocalists to indicate when to lean in close and when to duck or step away from the horn during instrumental solos, allowing the musicians to come forward. More than a few stage performers, used to gesticulating or moving about on stage, found singing for the phonograph constraining. Further, inexperienced phonograph singers who had not yet learned how to control their voices or step back during loud passages had to be physically jerked to and fro during recording sessions to ensure a good product.[14]

The phonograph's limited capabilities also encouraged the culling of repertoire, the careful arrangement of songs, and the selection of musicians based on their recorded sound. Since the process could not capture the highest or lowest musical registers, record companies chose musicians who could make the most of what the phonograph could do. Enrico Caruso and many others owed much of their success to the limitations of the acoustic recording process and the way it made them sound better than performers with different singing styles. Record companies eliminated many instruments, although at least one new one appeared, the Stroh violin, designed especially for the phonograph. Additionally, the fact that a cylinder or disc could only hold a couple of minutes of music (later increased to about four) meant that songs had to be abridged to fit the medium.

The inconsistency of recording diaphragms and cylinders or discs meant that multiple recordings had to be made simultaneously at a session, from which a few would be selected to become masters.[15] A recording session at Berliner's studio was not much different than one for Edison, except that the finished master could not be played back immediately but had to be chemically etched first. In the early years, Berliner's technicians etched the discs in the studio immediately following a recording session, a process that never failed to amaze the artists. However, the record companies did not stay with this direct method of etching metal master discs for long, and instead replaced the etching with an electroplating process more like the one Edison used, resulting in a "matrix" that could be employed to make a metal stamper. The delicate, soft wax of the recording disc, on the other hand, remained an excellent way to capture sound, and it soon became the industry standard.

Both cylinder and disc methods produced acceptable records, but the disk's eventual triumph had much to do with the shifting market for records and phonographs. By the early 1920s, the Thomas A. Edison Company was virtually alone in supplying cylinders. Many other companies had sprung up, and almost all chosen to use the disc. The price of Edison cylinders, mass produced by the molding process, actually dropped below the price of competing discs from Columbia and Victor, but it came too late to save the format.

As acoustic recording and disc production technologies gradually improved in the first decade of the twentieth century, the aural characteristics of records began to overcome the phonograph's earlier reputation for tinny, screechy reproduction. It was Thomas Edison, the pioneer in the field, who first articulated the notion that phonograph reproduction should sound exactly like the source in terms of timbre and volume. When the Edison Company finally bowed to pressure and introduced its own disc record, which it called the "Diamond Disc," the firm embarked on a series of public demonstrations called tone tests. These tests challenged the audience to detect the difference between the sound of new Diamond Disc records and the sound of the performers who made them. According to one account, millions of Americans took the test between 1915 and 1925.[16]

The claims that Edison made for the Diamond Disc revealed how the company had both technical and social goals for home recording and reproduction. In the first place, Edison wanted consumers to think of the phonograph as a new form of musical instrument, capable of reproducing not just popular tunes but also "serious" music. To do so, he claimed that the phonograph, unlike a real instrument, had no "tone." Instead, it faithfully reproduced the original sound without adding or subtracting anything. As one phonograph customer (or perhaps the magazine's staff) wrote to the *Phonogram*, "The phonograph never imitates, it reproduces the actual music as played by the performer." This was the root of a powerful idea that has persisted throughout the history of the record: that a sound recording should not simply sound pleasing, but should sound just like the original.[17]

The tone tests invariably proved the validity of Edison's claims. However, Edison carefully chose singers, usually women, who could imitate the sound of their recordings, and only allowed musicians to use the limited group of instruments that recorded best for demonstrations, such as strings or the flute. Nonetheless, it was also true that the Edison recording technology, using hill-and-dale acoustic recording, could provide remarkably realistic sounding records. The accounts of "reporters, reviewers, and music critics show that they took the challenge seriously, listened critically, and usually concluded that the Diamond Disc did indeed at least come very close to 're-creating' live music."[18]

Recordings, the Consumer, and the Status of Music

The tone tests, Thomas Edison's own musical tastes, and the numerous published histories and reminiscences of the early years of the phonograph share a striking feature: the special status of classical, opera, and related types of "highbrow" music. These sources give the impression that high culture records were the most significant of the pre-1945 period, and that the desire to reproduce high culture music faithfully has driven technological change in the record and record player industries. Against this is the reality of the record market in the United States, which seems to indicate the overwhelming economic importance of popular music, presumably not artistic in nature and therefore not necessarily as demanding of technical excellence. These two very different types of music must have favored different technologies of recording, mass production, and home reproduction, and yet the evidence suggests that popular music and its makers had only a minor influence. How could this be?

Fred Gaisberg, a pioneering "artist and repertoire" man who located and recorded talent for Berliner's company around the turn of the century, admitted that in the early years "the main record sales were from such popular titles as 'Down Went McGinty to the Bottom of the Sea,' and 'Daddy Won't Buy Me a Bow Wow.' "[19] Yet he devotes most of the rest of his autobiography to descriptions of recording activities in connection with high culture singers and musicians, suggesting that these were the most important and fulfilling activities of his career. Similarly, Roland Gellatt, whose 1955 *The Fabulous Phonograph* became one of the standard histories of recorded sound, focused almost exclusively on high culture recordings, decrying the lack of "serious" music in the early catalogs of record companies and making broad claims about the "rebirth" of interest in good music after the introduction of the LP record. His subsequent description of technological development presents most of it as if it were explicitly linked to the desire to make better-sounding recordings of highbrow music. The task, then, is to reconcile the limited economic importance of high culture music during most of the history of recorded sound against its apparent influence in driving technological change in the industry.[20]

High culture music has had an influence in the record industry that exceeds its economic importance. The reason for this reversal of economic logic is related to the fluctuations of the popular music market, the prejudices of engineers and musicians, and the social agenda of the record companies. Within record company studios, engineers and musicians constantly sought ways to improve the recording process (although sometimes for different reasons), and considered orchestral and operatic recordings the highest form of their art. The bad times the industry periodically suffered convinced some in the record companies that their only faithful customers were buyers of classical music, and these companies repeatedly fell back on the consistent buying habits of these "cultured" consumers by introducing technical improvements intended to appeal to them. The special status of highbrow culture within the record industry even today rather dramatically bucks expectations based on economics. One record producer for Columbia noted that as recently as the 1980s, the company's classical releases accounted for 20 percent of the catalog but only 5 percent of its sales. Even more surprising is the fact that despite minuscule sales, classical recordings were often very expensive to produce; $6,000 for a soloist, $8,000 for a chamber group, $50,000 for an orchestra, and $100,000 for a full-length opera at 1970 prices. The costs had doubled by the late 1980s.[21]

FIGURE 6. Early disk recorders in use at Western Electric, circa mid-1920s. Property of AT&T Archives. Reprinted with permission of AT&T.

Electrical Recording

Music, and particularly classical music, attained a special status as an artistic endeavor before the introduction of the phonograph, and this fact had important implications in the record industry. When musicians and engineers considered the problems of the recording and mass production of high culture, they looked for ways to shape the development of the technology in ways that sometimes ran counter to the demands of capitalist production. The recording of music gave rise to a unique culture of production in the record industry and spurred a particular brand of technological change. Technology has steadily grown more complex in the recording studio, but unlike so many other twentieth-century production processes, the development of recording technology has not moved consistently toward greater mechanization or automation. Instead, musicians and engineers worked together to develop new technologies without particular concern for the costs of production, and sometimes without much concern for the other steps necessary to transform a master recording into the final consumer product.

One of the most important shifts in studio recording after 1920 was the adoption of electrical technology. The record industry after the turn of the century fell under the sway of this new and exciting technology as engineers discovered ways to electrify a previously mechanical process. Most of the new technologies came from the large research and development laboratories at General Electric and AT&T, which also gave rise to new systems of wireless communication and motion pictures. With these developments, the relatively new profession of electrical engineering was immediately thrust into the unfamiliar, unscientific realm of aesthetics, as engineers faced the task of improving the "quality" of the crude audio and visual media they had invented. Already steeped in the methods of science, electrical engineers responded by creating instruments to measure audio "signals," and borrowed heavily from the methods and vocabulary of acoustics. From the entry of Western Electric into investigations of the nature of sound until well after World War II, the electrical engineer was virtually unrivaled as master of sound recording in the radio and motion picture industries. Yet at the time radio broadcasting took off in the mid-1920s, the phonograph industry was still engaged only in acoustic recording, employing no microphones or amplifiers. Other than the electric motors that drove some home phonographs, there was little electrical engineering in the phonograph at all.[22]

Record companies welcomed the subsequent transfer of electrical technology from radio and motion pictures to the phonograph industry, but hated the effect these two new forms of entertainment had on the record business. Radio was the biggest threat. On the eve of broadcasting's debut, between 1914 and 1921, record sales had doubled, largely because of sales of popular music. With the inauguration of network radio in the middle 1920s, the market for popular recordings collapsed, resulting in a number of companies leaving the field or changing ownership. Classical music fans, however, continued to buy recordings, and record companies recognized their importance in bad times as loyal customers. In an effort to build up sales from the base of their remaining customers, record companies turned to technical innovations that would, they hoped, appeal to classical music lovers.[23]

Edison in 1877 had first proposed to use the electrical output of the telephone, driving an electromagnetic recording stylus, to make phonograph records, but he could not make this technology work as well as the acoustic recording process. By 1924, engineers at Western Electric took up this line of development, combining it with the new technology of electronic amplification to produce the "electrical" recording technique. AT&T's leaders at first thought to use the new technology within the Bell System, but later decided to market it to outsiders such as the motion picture, radio, and phonograph industries.

What Western Electric engineers proposed was a new disk for home reproduction compatible with the existing phonographs and disk manufacturing technology. The recording process would replace virtually every aspect of the previous acoustic technology. Instead of having performers shout into a recording horn and using sound energy to record directly, the electrical recording process converted sound into electricity in a microphone. The signal from the microphone was amplified electronically and then fed to an electromagnetic record "cutter" to produce a recording on a wax-coated disk. The disks could be manufactured in the usual way, and even played on existing equipment (though with reduced effectiveness). Western Electric's engineers believed that electronics was still too expensive and balky for the home, so they designed a new acoustic phonograph to reproduce the disks. This acoustic, but scientifically designed record player did represent a noticeable improvement over earlier models. It was apparently easy to sell the American record companies on the new technology, with its distinct and more detailed sound. Some consumers also seemed to see them as an improvement, and in fact, the new disks and players sounded a great deal like the radios that were by then taking so much business away from the record companies. However, the shift to electrical recording had little effect on sales outside the field of good music. Some consumers, used to the more mellow sound of acoustic recordings, rejected the bright-sounding disks as too shrill.[24]

The transition to electrical recording offered few benefits to artists, who had to work harder than ever. Although they could now put a little space between themselves, they were no more free to move or turn their heads than they were in the days of the recording horn. The sensitivity of the new microphones was such that the rustling of sheet music, the shuffling of feet, and even noisy breathing had to be curtailed. "[The musician] can't move six inches from where he is standing for fear of upsetting the tonal balance; if he hums while he plays, he must stop it; and if he breathes through his nose, he must open his mouth a little so that he may avoid what can sound like a consumptive intrusion on the finished product."[25]

The introduction of the radio initially cut deeply into the sales of home phonographs. Soon, the cost-cutting measure of sharing one electronic amplifier between a radio and a phonograph cemented the link between the two devices. Although the original Victor Orthophonic reproducer was acoustic, manufacturers soon offered electromagnetic pickups suitable for use with electronic amplifiers. With such a pickup, a very inexpensive record player could be easily wired into a radio, and the sound reproduced through the radio's amplifier and loudspeaker. Radio-phonograph combinations and inexpensive, add-on phonograph players probably contributed more to a revival of record sales between 1926 and 1929 than the introduction of the electrically recorded disks.

However, the onset of the Great Depression immediately halted grow-ing record sales. Edison dropped out of the business completely in 1929, before the stock market crash. The situation was so dire that Columbia and Victor both went into receivership and were sold to new owners. Sales that had hov-ered between $70 and $75 million from 1926 to 1929 fell almost 39 percent the next year, then plummeted to only $6 million in 1933.[26]

The record's comeback in the late 1930s (which continued until the musi-cians' strikes of 1942) was stimulated by price cuts, increased advertising, and jukebox sales. Decca,[27] Columbia, and a number of newer companies began to offer disks for as little as $0.35, which was about half the normal price, and Columbia in 1940 spent $1 million advertising them.[28] The nation's hundreds of thousands of jukeboxes were the outlet for as much as half of record sales in the late 1930s. Popular music, alternately known as "light," "swing," or sometimes "jazz," accounted for 85 percent of record sales by 1941. Ironically, music historians look to this period as one of the most impor-tant eras in jazz history, partly because of the spate of "field" recordings under-taken by the record companies in these years. While those recordings have had a persistent influence on musicians, at the time they reached a relatively small audience. In fact, much of the "jazz" that reached America's ears was jazz-influenced popular music of the watered-down, cleaned-up variety, per-formed by white, mainstream musicians.[29]

Despite the evidence against it, scholars, journalists, and musicians alike have also repeatedly emphasized the role of "good" music in the periodic revivals of the record industry. The essential thrust of this argument is that the increased availability of serious music and better technology with which to record and reproduce it meant that it was having a significant influence on the general public. "Although the biggest business is still in jazz," an author for the *New York Times* wrote, "the most important, manufacturers agree, is in the classics."[30] This way of describing the record market undoubtedly grew out of the chauvinism of music critics and journalists, many working in the urban cultural centers of the nation, who acted as cultural gatekeep-ers during these years, trying to encourage the "development" of musical taste.[31]

Market downturns of the late 1920s and 1930s encouraged the record companies to emphasize their classical offerings and offer innovative new technologies suited to classical music, but neither the number of classical titles nor the appearance of new technology can be counted as a true indication of the significance of these developments. The radio networks, under constant scrutiny from government regulators, became self-styled social reformers and educators, pushing their highbrow predilections on the American public at the same time they promulgated popular culture. Thus while serious music was well represented in the programming of American radio, there was little indication that it was universally appreciated by listeners. What corporations, writers, and critics said must be balanced by an appreciation of just how tiny the classical music market was in these years. Further, this economic data regarding classical music sales has to be couched in disclaimers. The higher price of classical music meant that it accounted for a larger proportion of record company income than its sales would otherwise have suggested—15 percent of sales in 1940 but 30 percent of income. At $0.35 per disk in the late 1930s, a top selling record could have less economic impact than, for instance, the recording of Leopold Stokowski conducting the Philadelphia Symphony in the Blue Danube Waltz, which brought in about $500,000 for Victor between 1926 and 1939 but sold only 225,000 copies.[32]

Nevertheless, there is strong causal link between high culture and changes in recording technology. Within the record companies, influential people involved in sound recording often had highbrow tastes, and developed or encouraged technologies and practices that favored these types of recordings. Further, record companies and equipment manufacturers shaped many of the new consumer phonograph technologies to suit classical music customers.[33] The overall depression of the record industry in the 1920s and 1930s slowed consumer sales of new technologies, but not their adoption in the studio.

Diminished record sales persisted through most of the 1930s, yet this was a decade of great technical change in audio technology. While the record industry languished, most innovations in sound recording came out of the fattening movie and radio industries. These industries were already interwoven through corporate ownership or, indirectly, through their common connections with electrical equipment manufacturers such as Western Electric. The links that record companies made to radio and the movies when they adopted electrical recording in 1925 were only the beginning, and after that time motion picture and radio practices began to have a more noticeable influence on record making. Western Electric, in fact, sold many of its electrical disk recorders to motion picture producers in the 1920s, and provided considerable technical assistance to movie studios. Electrical Research Products,

Inc., the Western Electric subsidiary which handled sales, installation, and maintenance of electrical recording equipment, provided trained personnel to run the equipment, or trained technicians for clients. In radio, where less actual recording took place, engineers contributed to the development of new techniques using microphones and electronics, many of which were directly applicable in the record industry. Sometimes the link between movies or radio networks and the record industry was even more direct, as when the radio networks and motion picture producers worked in conjunction with record companies to make recordings or operated recording companies themselves. Often during the 1930s record companies released recordings made at the studios of NBC, CBS, or the larger radio stations.[34]

These associations tended to counteract the technical stagnation that might have set in due to the record industry's hardships and stimulated rapid development in sound recording technology. The 1930s and early 1940s, for example, saw significant changes in the design of recorders and related technologies, including microphones, amplifiers, and sound studios, all reflecting the scientific findings of electrical engineers at Bell Laboratories, RCA, and other companies, and the increased use of sound measuring instruments and procedures in the design process. The science of acoustics was already quite old by the 1930s, but never before had record companies had such a variety of instruments available to measure sound. The numerous technical articles on sound measurement, many written by scientifically trained engineers, gave the strong impression that what was measurable in sound was what was most important. Sound recording personnel in the record studios took on the mantle of science and engineering by adopting its terminology, instruments, and values. As sound recording activities became more professionalized, and as the position of "recordist" of the 1920s gave way to the "recording engineer" of the 1930s, the role of formal knowledge grew in importance, and the recording of sound took on a new, measurement-based aesthetic.[35]

What mattered most to engineers of the 1930s was not the subjective quality of sound but its measurement. Consumers, on the other hand, had little recourse but to evaluate a recording subjectively, "by ear." This disparity may account for the fact that many early reviewers admitted the technical superiority of electrically produced commercial recordings, yet they still objected to the way they sounded. But the growing divide between engineer and listener did not necessarily imply different values, since the electrical sound recorder and its corresponding home phonograph player were intended to reproduce, as closely as possible, the original sound.

The growing engineering orientation of recording in the studio did not

FIGURE 7.   A bank of disk record cutters in use in 1949. *Audio Engineering,* June 1949. Reprinted by permission.

always suit artists or music critics. Too heavy a reliance on instruments and measurements could ruin a recording for listeners. Having the equipment work "right" did not always result in a record that was pleasing to hear. The problem, some critics charged, was that the technically proficient but musically inept engineer had taken control of the recording process. "He is all technician when he should be part technician and part artist," one author wrote in reference to the making of motion picture sound tracks in the early 1930s. "He is interested largely in microamperes and the response curves of audio-frequency transformers when esthetic effects and realism should be uppermost in his mind."[36]

Yet the recording engineers themselves were not all of a mind when it came to the question of how to preserve the original sound. Some of them took advantage of the enormous potential of the new electronic equipment to "enhance" the sound rather than be satisfied with preserving the original. The technology of sound manipulation was part of an electrical recording process that ideally was to be used only to bring degraded signals back to their original state or compensate for the differences between the way the human ear and the microphone responded to sound.

One example from the late 1930s, which originated in the motion picture industry, was the replacement of a single microphone with several, which fed into a common recording channel. A new sound craftsman, the balance engineer, took on the task of listening to the rehearsal to determine just where the microphones should be placed. He also operated the mixing board to raise or lower the output level of each microphone channel before all the music was mixed together and recorded. In theory, multiple microphones overcame the fact that a single microphone could not "hear" sound just like the ear. Particularly when recording large ensembles, placing several microphones in and around the group allowed the engineer to record all the instruments more faithfully.

A related technology was equalization. An electronic equalizer emphasized or de-emphasized certain bands of frequencies in a fashion analogous to the "tone" controls on a home audio system. Recording engineers equalized recordings in order to compensate for the uneven response of microphones, recorders, and the disks themselves. Boosting certain frequencies during recording would be counteracted by their partial suppression upon playback due to the deficiencies of the medium, with the end result being sound more like the original.[37]

All these devices had in them the potential to reshape sound, creating something new. Yet through the middle 1940s, most recording engineers adhered to the ideals of accuracy in recording, even if consumers and critics questioned their success in doing so. Changes in electrical recording technologies and practices all moved toward improving the "realism" of the master recording. Improvements in the record manufacturing process or the final product, however, were not forthcoming.[38]

The Birth of Consumer High Fidelity

By the early 1930s, with both the radio receiver and home phonograph markets hitting rock bottom, the influence of high culture music in technological design was becoming especially apparent in the offerings of desperate equipment manufacturers and record manufacturers. In the midst of depressed sales, manufacturers introduced new lines of improved home equipment designed to reproduce a wider range of frequencies. One of the new consumer products from Victor during the 1930s was a twelve-inch, fine groove, extended play, $33\frac{1}{3}$ disk. Victor's claims for better sound were specifically targeted to classical listeners, as was the disk's ability to hold more than the usual four minutes of music. Unfortunately, the experiment was a commercial failure. The grooves were too fine for the home phonograph pickups then available, and the disk manufacturing process could not accommodate the higher-quality recordings.[39]

Radio receivers and improved radio-phonograph combinations designed to play ordinary disks but reproducing a wider frequency range were more successful, and electronics manufacturers in 1934 gave these new products a name: high fidelity.[40] The phrase captured perfectly what Edison had tried to achieve in sound recording and reproducing, and what studio engineers were striving to perfect in the recording of classical music. High fidelity was a powerful and lasting marketing concept, though access to high-fidelity equipment remained very limited in the 1930s and 1940s. High-fidelity music did not emanate from the paper cones of the loudspeakers in the cheap radio sets and phonographs that utterly dominated the market; nor did it reach the ears of many movie patrons, since few movie houses invested in top-quality sound systems. The enhanced sound of the new FM radio system available in New York and some other cities after 1939 reached almost no one because so few people bought the necessary receivers. In sum, high fidelity's time had not yet come.

The high-fidelity hobby of the 1930s was the province of an elite group of relatively wealthy record buyers. These consumers invariably used high culture as a point of reference, ensuring the continued association of high-fidelity technology with high culture music. Classical music, opera, and other forms of highbrow entertainment had temporarily risen in commercial importance relative to popular music, but would soon fall back to their normal place. The high-fidelity concept as a selling tool for consumer equipment was destined to persist and even expand, to be transferred out of the context of high culture when the market for popular music returned.

When the later 1930s saw the gradual resuscitation of the U.S. phonograph record industry, music aficionados once again credited it to the growth of interest in high culture. "With the reappearance of Toscanini before Victor recording microphones in 1936," one historian has written, "the evidence became unmistakable that the phonograph was on its way back."[41] In fact, the real reason for the industry's rebound was the growth in jukebox sales, a new outlet for popular records that sustained the industry through the end of World War II. Only the major record labels, such as RCA-Victor and Columbia, engaged in much highbrow recording at all during these years; other labels re-pressed imported matrices or simply served the more lucrative popular music markets. Victor's sales of expensive, high-quality "Red Seal" records, the brand reserved for high culture music, were but a quarter of total sales. This, combined with the fact that each popular music record that went into jukeboxes was broadcast to a wider audience, argues strongly against the cultural centrality of "serious" music, at least outside the musicians' journals, New York highbrow magazines, and record studios themselves.[42] The 225,000 jukeboxes in operation in the United States in 1930 consumed 13 million disks, each of which reached perhaps hundreds of individuals. Classical records played at home rarely reached beyond the ears of their buyers, who numbered not in the millions but in the hundreds of thousands.[43]

Even so, many of the important technical innovations in the studio were oriented toward these classical music buyers. Edward Wallerstein, in charge of rebuilding Columbia's catalog after CBS bought the ailing record company in 1938, recognized that they were the backbone of the industry and made sure they were well provided for. As part of the ongoing drive to improve studio recording, most of the record companies around 1938 adopted a new disk for making master recordings. This acetate-coated aluminum disk offered less surface noise than its wax predecessor, resulting in low-noise stampers. But technical change in the studio had little effect on the final product. Audiophile engineers in the studio ran up against the same wall with the acetate master that they had encountered with the $33\frac{1}{3}$ disk years earlier, in that an improvement in the studio meant nothing without improvements all the way down the line from master record to final product.[44] Although consumers did not know it, Columbia in the early 1940s was preparing to offer a new long-playing disk, especially suited to classical music, and began using acetate masters in anticipation of the changeover. However, the expansion of the record industry was once again making sales of individual classical titles less significant than popular record sales; one top-selling symphonic staple of the Victor catalog sold a mere 62,000 copies in 1946, compared to Victor's total sales of over 55 million disks.

In the midst of these changes, the record industry's consumer offerings were artificially restricted in the early 1940s, first by a major musicians' strike, and then by wartime restrictions. With the resolution of these problems in 1945, record companies prepared to dazzle consumers with exciting new technologies for the reproduction of music.

Tape Recording and Other New Studio Techniques

The postwar period saw the erosion of the ideals of high fidelity in the recording studio, ironically just as it was taking hold as part of a new consumer movement. The single most important factor in decline of the high-fidelity ideal in the studio was the use of the tape recorder. The studio tape recorder was a German invention that American companies copied and improved upon after 1945. Tape recorders could not always outperform the disk recorders that record companies used in their studios, but they could do several things that disk recorders could not. One was to go "on location" with great ease. A tape recorder needed little set-up. It could be operated in a wide range of temperatures and humidity levels, and didn't require a separate recording room or even a level surface to sit on.[45]

Tape recorders were less prone to mechanical failures than a disk recorder. A tiny bit of the "thread" that a record cutter carved out of the groove during recording could fall under the cutter and ruin an otherwise perfect recording. The reliability of the studio tape recorder convinced engineers to insert it into the process of disk record-making. By recording onto tape and then copying to disk, if a master recording on disk failed, a new disk could be cut immediately at little additional cost. A tape could break, but record companies learned not to depend on reused or spliced tapes for master recordings. While disk masters had to be stored in a temperature-controlled environment and required surgically clean conditions, tape was robust and virtually immune to dust, cigarette ashes, or anything else that might be floating around a studio. A disk recorder was often isolated in a separate recording room, but the tape recorder could be placed in the control room, allowing an engineer to operate both the mixing board and the recorder.

Tape posed no serious threat to the disk recorder, but rather enhanced its value. After all, the making of a disk recording was still the final step before making a master for conversion into a stamper. The first hint that the tape recorder might change anything in the studio was the importation of editing techniques in the early 1950s. Motion picture sound men had used editing since the early 1930s, when film sound recorders came into widespread use. These devices recorded sound optically on motion picture film (though not the same film used to record the video portion of the movie). Once processed, editors could easily cut and paste bits of the sound track to fit the action on the screen, which was also heavily edited. Then the audio and video portions would be rerecorded together on the final master copy. Sound-on-film, as it was called, was a powerful technology for making edits, since an engineer could look at the film to see exactly where to make a cut.[46]

A magnetic recording on tape was, unfortunately, invisible, yet it offered many of the other advantages as sound-on-film editing. Engineers almost immediately discovered that with practice they could edit tape as accurately as they could edit a motion picture film. Until the introduction of tape, editing was very rare in the record industry, but not for any lack of desire to edit. A disk recording dubbed from an existing disk in order to edit was sometimes noisy and muddled, and it took great skill to blend seamlessly two segments of the recording.[47] By contrast, engineers could create a high-quality disk master recording even from a heavily edited tape. Engineers began using their tape recorders to improve imperfect recordings, replacing missed notes or other flaws by cutting out the offending portion and replacing it with what they wanted.[48]

When music critics discovered this practice, many of them were horrified. "I discovered to my astonishment recently that many a popular song-with-accompaniment is recorded in two separate pieces," wrote Edward Tatnall Canby in 1950. "First, the instrumentalists record their parts on tape. Then, perhaps weeks later, the vocalist comes along, listens to the recorded accompaniment (via earphones, I suppose) and records a separate vocal sound track. Finally the engineers re-record both into a blend. . . . there is never an 'original.' . . . How far ought we to go?"[49] Musicians saw it differently, since it was their flaws and imperfections that a "one take" recording session captured for public inspection. In the past, some musicians had insisted on rerecording an imperfect performance until they were satisfied that they had done their best, but this was a luxury available only to well-established performers. With tape, it was easier to construct something better than any single performance from portions of several performances, and it was usually less expensive than rerecording.

The use of technology for manipulating sound and creating new effects, rather than maintaining high fidelity, drew similar criticism. Recording engineers in the 1950s more regularly employed the practice of using multiple microphones and more obvious sound "enhancements," including techniques such as artificial reverberation. Acerbic music critic B. H. Haggin decried the "possibility [magnetic tape] had offered of altering the original sound, and

the most notorious examples of such electronic manipulation—RCA's mon-
strously falsifying 'enhancements' of Toscanini's recordings."[50] After the
LP record made it easier for consumers to hear the details of a recording, some
began to notice that high-fidelity recording techniques seemed themselves
to be a source of distortion. "Listen to some recent opera recordings and ask
yourself whether in any seat in any known opera house you ever heard comparable tonal balances between soloists and orchestra," E. T. Canby charged
in 1954.[51] The practices of using multiple microphones and synthetic reverberation, (which had taken hold in the record industry only after World War
II) was by 1954 already creating a backlash among purists, who reverted to
using a single microphone and the reverberation provided by the concert hall
itself. John Hammond of Vanguard Records sought a "natural sound," using
a single microphone, and he denounced popular record producer Mitch
Miller's use of artificial reverberation as "horrible" and "phony." "What's the
good of having every instrument in a band sound as if it were being played
in the Holland Tunnel?" The use of tape-based special effects became completely obvious to the public in 1958 and 1959 with the release of a series
of popular songs by "The Chipmunks," allegedly a group of singing rodents
(all the voices were composer Ross Bagdasarian) created through the machi-
nation of tape recordings.[52]

E. T. Canby assured his readers that these practices would find a permanent place only in the popular music foisted on the enormous but "esthet-
ically infantile" general public. He was wrong. More significantly, it was not
the creators of popular music recordings who were solely to blame for this
turning away from high fidelity. Rather, musicians themselves, and especially
prominent composers and conductors, would begin to enter the control room
to manage the details of the recording process. Even in the 1930s, more priv-
ileged conductors like Leopold Stokowski were taking a more active role in
the recording process, placing microphones, setting the balance, equalization,
and mixing, and specifying the details of editing.[53] Some later insisted on creating an annotated score, marked with instructions which the engineer was
to follow. By the early 1950s, the recording engineer's technical control was
often challenged by the recording director (or later the record producer), who
did not replace the work of the engineer so much as supply an additional layer
of creative input. Postwar recording directors often emerged from the ranks
of artist and repertoire men, the agents of record companies who put together
new talent and songs. Mitch Miller, a former oboist for the NBC Orchestra,
was by 1950 an A&R man for Columbia. Pop musicians auditioning for Miller
always made a test record, which he then played back on an inexpensive

phonograph that he kept on his desk. If the artist sounded good on a cheap phonograph, he or she passed the audition.[54] Miller, like many other recording directors, was not as committed to the old style of high fidelity, with its emphasis on capturing and reproducing a real performance, as he was to creating a perfect recording or simply a pleasing sound.

By the early 1960s, some of the most successful record producers were using the possibilities of electronic sound manipulation and tape recording to create their own unique sound or sonic "stamp."[55] The engineer's role in the 1950s retained most of the old principles of high fidelity, for as one wrote, "when an engineer takes part in a recording session he almost never tries to improve on the resulting music, except for routine splicing of takes."[56]

The Consumer High-Fidelity Movement in the 1950s

As the goals and ideals of high fidelity were being subsumed under the new techniques in recording studios of the late 1940s and early 1950s, consumers were discovering hi-fi in greater numbers. The hi-fi hobby was underway as soon as the war ended, with customers creating a demand for the audio components manufactured mainly by a group of smaller, specialized companies. Victor tried to appeal to them by offering some of its classical recordings on 78-rpm disks made of a new, low-noise material called vinylite. Decca records in Britain similarly began selling its new hi-fi disks in the summer of 1946, calling them Full Frequency Range Recordings.[57] The high-fidelity movement and the vinyl disk passed a landmark a few years later in 1948–49 with the introduction of the 45-rpm and long-playing microgroove records.[58] Peter Goldmark and Edward Wallerstein, the CBS employees who publicly promoted the LP, were models of the record industry's high-fidelity culture. Well-educated, musically talented or at least good-music enthusiasts, and in positions of great power within a leading record manufacturing firm, the two envisioned the LP with classical music in mind. Even after the microgroove recording process and low-noise medium were available, Wallerstein sent engineers back to the drawing board to increase the playing time from its original duration of just over twelve minutes. "I timed I don't know how many works in the classical repertory and came up with a figure of seventeen minutes to a side. This would enable about 90 percent of all classical music to be put on two sides of a record. The engineers went back to their laboratories."[59] The final form of the LP, which held up to about twenty minutes of sound per side, made sense only in the context of the long passages typical in classical music. It was also considerably more expensive than a single disk, although it was less expensive than the "albums" of 78-rpm disks on which classical music had previously been offered. Columbia did not plan to replace the 78-rpm single, which was the mainstay of its business, but hoped to expand its market for classical music and certain other niche products such as Broadway-musical recordings.[60]

The very next year, RCA introduced a product that incorporated significant technical improvements in a package suited for the mass market: the seven-inch 45-rpm single. The 45-rpm disk combined many of the technical improvements of the LP with the inexpensive package of the 78-rpm single. For the tiny classical market, RCA proposed albums of several disks, to be used on the new RCA fast-drop record changer. At first, the RCA approach seemed to be on the mark. The LP was not the instant success that Goldmark had hoped. It did not begin to outstrip the combined sales of 78- and 45-rpm singles until the late 1950s.[61]

Sales of phonographs and high-fidelity equipment gained momentum in the early 1950s, particularly in the traditionally strong urban markets for music, such as New York and Chicago. There, high-fidelity promoters staged elaborate audio equipment "fairs" beginning in 1949. The focus of numerous magazine and television features on audio, high fidelity became a mass-market phenomenon after 1952. The essence of high fidelity, the notion of "realism" and the uncolored reproduction of music, dominated almost every discussion of home audio equipment. However, commercial recordings themselves betrayed the growing divide between the ideals of high fidelity and the reality of what happened in the recording studio.[62]

Multitrack Recording: Beyond Hi-Fi

One common characteristic of the constantly changing technologies of home music listening is that manufacturers and record companies have sold every new innovation as an improvement in fidelity. Even today, companies seem unable to invent a new vocabulary to describe their products, and instead revert to the obsolete notion of high fidelity, usually accompanied by references to high culture music. A particularly important example of this was the introduction of the multitrack tape recorder.

The tape recorder diluted the pure version of high-fidelity culture through practices such as editing, but an even more important technique came later, beginning with the development of stereophonic recording. Stereophonic sound has been in existence since 1881, when Alexander Graham Bell demonstrated a stereo telephone transmission in Paris.[63] The Columbia Phonograph Company as early as 1899 offered for sale its "Multiplex Graphophone Grand," a three-horned cylinder phonograph employing three separate sound tracks interleaved on a single cylinder. The machine's $1,000 price tag undoubtedly discouraged sales. Western Electric engineers made multi-channel disk recordings in the 1930s, though they were not available for sale until decades later. The public's only exposure to stereo, if they were lucky enough to have access to one of the handful of theaters equipped to reproduce multi-channel recordings, was in 1930s films such as Walt Disney's *Fantasia*. Demonstrations of two- or three-channel magnetic tape systems for the studio began in the late 1940s, but these did not become commercially available for a few more years.[64]

In the early 1950s, however, manufacturers offered more affordable "binaural" reproducing equipment. The early binaural recordings were for headphones only, so that each ear received the sound of separate channel. This way, the listener could use the mind's eye to "see" the spot where a sound originated. With recordings of Ping-Pong games, a listener could follow the ball. With musical recordings, the listener could place each performer on an imaginary stage. One important but short-lived binaural medium was the Cook disk system of 1952, an ordinary phonograph disk with two separate, concentric grooves, each containing a distinct recording. The Cook phonograph required a dual tonearm with two separate pickups.

Stereophonic recording was a distinctly different approach intended to be heard through ordinary loudspeakers, not through earphones. Since each ear heard the output of both channels, recording engineers had to mix the recording just so to achieve the desired "sound stage" effect. Stereo tape recordings appeared around 1952, the products of home tape recorder manufacturers or independent record companies. Consumers could modify their existing tape recorders to play stereo tapes, adding a second playback head and an external amplifier. Radio stations also helped to popularize the technique, broadcasting the two programs simultaneously on two separate channels. Listeners had to tune in both stations on two different radios, and often one channel was on AM and the other on FM.

By 1953, the recorder manufacturers devised a way to squeeze two playback heads into one, rendering obsolete the earlier form of stereo tape. Finally, in 1958, RCA introduced a new stereo tape recording system for the home and a stereo LP record. It was the disc technology that found widespread acceptance in the marketplace. Manufacturers promised consumers that stereophonic recordings offered high-fidelity reproduction never before possible. However, many engineers and acousticians recognized that stereo reproduction, while pleasing, was not necessarily more accurate than monophonic reproduction. The stereo illusion was just that. As one 1967 recording manual put it, "In stereophonic recording, duplication of reality is only one of the objectives."[65] Achieving a subjectively pleasing final product was more important. Further, the introduction of stereo recording came just a few years after rock and roll music became popular, and rock producers would soon take advantage of stereo's possibilities. Many rock and roll recordings continued to be monophonic well into the 1960s, but when rock record producers took up stereo, they rarely claimed to use it to preserve the original instrument placement. Instead they used it to achieve psychedelic effects or simply to create a powerful and satisfying "sound."

Multiple track recorders also played a major part in the ongoing development of editing techniques in the 1960s, pushing the practice of recording farther from the ideals of high fidelity. Multitrack recording for motion pictures was familiar to studio engineers by the time the first two-channel tape recorders appeared. RCA's Camden, New Jersey studios had been recording movie sound tracks this way since the early 1930s. By making separate recordings of groups of instruments, or perhaps putting vocals and instruments on different tracks, studio staff could have greater flexibility in creating the final recording. If the mixing process or the final record did not sound right, the source material was there to allow another try.[66]

While early stereo recordings were a break with the high-fidelity ideal, making them did not fundamentally alter the recording or editing process. Recording engineers still faced the problem of setting the recording levels of a multitude of microphones and mixing a number of inputs, although now there were two output channels instead of just one. In fact, since it was impossible to edit just one track of a two-channel tape by the old cut-and-paste method, making a stereo record could be a challenge. "[In] the days of two-track stereo recording . . . it was essential to get the right sound on the sessions; there was no possibility of subsequently fiddling with the balance . . . you can never really correct faulty balance of either performance or recording—you can only alter it to make it sound less objectionable."[67]

The commercial success of stereophonic recordings on LP records came late, but was impressive; sales rose on average about 25 percent per year between 1959 and 1961. Yet even though "the cry no longer was for hi-fi but stereo," stereophonic sound remained linked to notions of "realism" in musical reproduction. All the while, practices in the studio continued to carry sound recordings further from realism in the quest of a more pleasing stereo illusion.[68] With the advent of three-, four-, and eight-track studio recorders in the 1950s, record producers and recording engineers found it easier to record instruments or vocalists (or portions of songs) separately for combination later. Once again, the pioneers experimented with the recording of symphonic music, where the large number of musicians multiplied the opportunities for bad balances or flubbed notes. Where in the early 1950s recording engineers had started to mix the output of several microphones together into a single channel, after 1966 and the introduction of three-track recorders, they began to use more microphones. The ratio of microphones to tape tracks tended to converge after 1968, when four- and then eight-track tape recorders appeared. The practice in symphonic recordings by the early 1970s was to use two dozen or more microphones for a full orchestra, some of which were mixed to get the full recording on an eight-track recorder. More affluent studios used tape recorders with twenty-four or thirty-two tracks, a feature that carried over into the digital recorders of the 1980s.[69]

The establishment of tape recording in the studio clearly owed a great deal to three somewhat contradictory factors: the drive to improve fidelity, the desire to record perfect performances, and the effort by engineers to enhance their control over the recording process. What linked these together was the recording of high culture music. However, in more recent years the recording of popular music has taken a role in relation to technical change that is more consistent with its economic importance. The use of recorders with multiple channels, for example, contributed significantly to the recording of rock and roll music, but not until the late 1960s. Rock and roll as a recorded product was not pioneered by the large, established record companies with the latest equipment but by independents, and the lesser financial stature of these firms was reflected in their studio equipment. Tape recording did not penetrate all of these studios in the 1950s, and when it did it was rarely the best grade of equipment. These studios did not have the facilities or equipment to make strides in high-fidelity recording, but they could use what they had to achieve something more important for rock and roll: a new sound. The way most Americans experienced the new music was through recordings rather than live performance, so recording techniques were essential, even if high fidelity was not. The use of electric guitars, amplification, and an emphasis on percussion in rock and roll, while well-suited to live performance and large venues, also provided new opportunities for the creative manipulation of sound in the studio. Musicians and engineers found that rock could often be successfully captured and canned in the crudest of studios.

Some of the same features that made the new recording technologies appealing to high-fidelity enthusiasts were also suited to the production of rock music. The relationship between rock music and the recording medium is extremely important. While "records" (either the original recordings made in the studio or the mass-produced kind heard by the audience) had in past years been "byproducts of performances," with the advent of rock music, records themselves became the performance for the majority of the audience. Through rock music, recording devices and specifically editing and overdubbing techniques became part of the performance rather than simply an intermediate stage intended to be inaudible. Clearly, though, these artistic techniques were developed before rock emerged.[70]

Just how this came about is not well-documented. At this time, it is clear that the role of the engineer was changing, and musicians were taking a greater role in the recording process. Just as conductors, arrangers, A&R men, or sometimes musicians (if they had considerable clout) had sometimes appropriated an active role in classical music recording, so too did rock producers and musicians become more prominent in studios by the 1960s. This trend was magnified in the smaller, independent studios that sprang up in the post-1945 period, where recording engineers were less often unionized, making it easier for other to appropriate the use of recording equipment. The first expressions of this came from producers such as Phil Spector. Working with engineers or sound mixers, Spector set out to use the capabilities of tape, equalization, compression, and other electronic technologies to invent sonic "signatures" that identified the recordings he produced. By the later 1960s, rock artists also discovered more inventive ways to use studio equipment to record music in ways that sounded good to them but might bear little resemblance to the original performance. The perfect example of this is the Beatles' use of multitrack recording and special effects ideas borrowed from avant-garde music to create the *Sergeant Pepper* album in 1967.[71]

Copying and recopying of bits and pieces of recordings in the studio before finally committing them to a two-track stereo tape and then a stereo master disk required other incremental but significant improvements in studio tape recorders. Part of the reason that the Beatles and other groups were able to do so much manipulation was that low-noise tapes, Dolby noise reduction and other ancillary technologies had arrived in the mid-1960s. These allowed the record producer or engineer to rerecord several generations before the inherent signal degradation became noticeable.[72]

The 1970s: The Triumph and Failure of High Fidelity

By the 1970s, technological innovations put home high fidelity within reach of many more Americans. The transistorization of tape recorders, radio tuners, and preamplifiers began in the late 1950s; along with car radios, home audio products were among the first consumer products to use transistors. The high power requirements of amplifiers, however, remained out of reach for several years. Long after vacuum tubes were replaced in computers and military electronics, they remained the standard for most consumer audio amplifiers. Only in the mid-1960s did high-current bipolar transistors appear that could handle more than a few watts of power. By the mid-1970s, transistors themselves were being replaced in many applications by integrated circuits. The overall effect of the use of semiconductors was to reduce significantly the price of hi-fi home equipment.

Yet it would be many more years before equipment manufacturers acknowledged the fact that the technical capabilities of high-fidelity equipment were also well suited for the sound of rock music, and that their continued efforts to market hi-fi as a medium of high culture were misplaced. Though the approach has diminished in the last two decades, it is still not unusual to encounter advertisements promising to recreate the concert hall in the living room. Yet the continued changes in audio technology have not increased the sales of serious music relative to the popular kinds. Further, even today the vocabulary of high fidelity is still infused with the language of science and quantitative measurement. Only recently have manufacturers acknowledged that the same technologies that allow an amplifier or a set of stereo loudspeakers to handle the crescendo of a full symphony orchestra can also handle the sustained loudness of a "cranked up" rock and roll recording. Consumers, even those who recite the technical specifications of their equipment, are understandably concerned more with the subjective experience of listening.

Studio recording, on the other hand, reflects popular taste more and more. The digital recording and synthesis technologies that began to proliferate in the 1980s make it easier than ever to create and manipulate new sounds and have little relevance to the concept of high fidelity. Much of the popular music available today is composed on a keyboard instrument and is generated electronically by synthesizers or digitally sampled from existing recordings. These techniques make the concept of fidelity irrelevant, and even where the source is actually sung or performed with traditional acoustic instruments in the studio, the ultimate criteria for judging the resulting recording is whether it sounds good, not whether it mirrors the truth.

Conclusions

Technological change in the making of records for the recording industry has followed a unique path. For example, where many industries de-skilled, mechanized, or automated, the record industry continuously elaborated the recording process, demanding of its "production workers" greater and greater responsibility and skill. The motivations for technical changes in recording also run counter to the accepted wisdom about the way production evolves. Between the 1880s and the 1920s, recording directors, inventors, and record company engineers strove simply to produce cylinders or disks that were audible and intelligible. Yet once the technology of recording reached a certain level of refinement, other factors became more important as agents of change. One of them was the desire to duplicate an original performance. Edison, though fighting a rearguard action to save the defeated acoustic recording process, did succeed in popularizing the concept of faithfulness or fidelity to the original performance. The concept would have real meaning only as long as he kept alive the acoustic process and his "tone tests." A second driving force was the desire to promote high culture music, which critics, inventors, and record companies hoped would change the tastes of the public.

It is not too surprising that the leaders of the record industry presented themselves as the bearers of positive cultural influence through the release and promotion of highbrow music. High culture music represented an unassailable social good that record companies could hold up to counter accusations that their products undermined good taste. There was a significant market for serious music which during some years grew in importance. In fact, sales of highbrow music were, during the dark years of the interwar period, the core of the record business. The influence of high culture in the record companies also had important implications for recording technology. Many in the record companies were high culture aficionados who used their positions to further the cause of technological development geared toward "good" music listening and sincerely hoped that the public would respond. Similarly, when inventors and engineers proposed changes to recording technology and practice, they explained the potential benefits not only in terms of greater sales but in terms of the good they would be doing for highbrow music listening. The enthusiasm for high fidelity that drove technical change was also an enthusiasm for high culture that record companies nurtured quite independently of their commercial aims.

Many of the technologies that grew out of the high-fidelity movement in engineering contributed to unexpected outcomes in the recording of music. The introduction of electronics and electrically recorded disks simultaneously promoted the concept of fidelity and made it less meaningful. In terms of measurable sound, electrical recordings bested the acoustic record. Yet the possibility of remaining faithful to a live performance as heard by a real person was gone forever. What remained constant in this radical transition was the high culture orientation of the most important agents of change in the 1920s; the engineers who invented electrical recording, the record producers who used it, and the consumers who were still willing to buy it.

The improved technologies of studio disk recording that came in the 1930s, the new technology of tape recording that arrived in the studio in 1947, and the introduction of the LP in 1948 all demonstrated how high culture remained important in pushing forward technological change, even though the new technologies reflected the interests of only a minority of consumers. In the postwar period, as high fidelity was finally becoming a popular fashion, the recording studio was also becoming a contested terrain. Performers, composers, managers, and engineers all had their own ideas about how to make a good recording, and increasingly these ideas strayed from the notion of high fidelity.

The decline of the engineer's dominion in the studio can be linked, albeit imperfectly, to some of the very technologies that engineers championed. Where electrical recording briefly gave technical personnel control over the process, the coming of the tape recorder after 1945 undid all that. Tape destroyed the already tenuous concept of an "original" performance and made the performance a source of content to be refined rather than something to be preserved. Some of the same technical features that made the tape recorder so desirable for high-fidelity recording contributed to the movement toward recordings that bore almost no resemblance to the studio "performances" from which they were derived.

"As popular music has evolved from the early twentieth century and Tin Pan Alley days to rock music," writes Steve Jones, "it has become sound—and not music—that is of prime importance in popular music production and consumption."[73] The search for better sound has indeed been a factor driving technological change in the recording studio, but until recently it was the sound of highbrow and not popular music that set the standard. However, highbrow culture and the cult of high fidelity seem to have a permanent place in the recording studio. Today, the technologies originally developed to serve high culture are embedded in more recent inventions used to produce popular culture, and seem destined to stay there. It is difficult, for example, to imagine a new recording system that would restrict recording to a more limited range of frequencies, or inject a higher level of noise or distortion. Such changes would be seen as degradation, not improvement. A new form of recording that would not provide stereophonic sound also seems out of the question. The developers of new technologies consider these features the basis upon which new innovations can be added. The machines and practices that comprise recording culture in the studio have absorbed the older values and moved on. This redefinition of aesthetic quality and authenticity occurred within the contexts of science, business, and elite and popular culture. The outcome demonstrates the interactions between different kinds of culture in the history of recording technology. The ideal of authenticity also intersected with business needs, mass-produced entertainment, and recording technology in the history of radio broadcasting, the subject of the following chapter.

CHAPTER 2

The End of the "Canned Music" Debate in American Broadcasting

$\mathcal{U}$nlike the record industry, where a recording is the ultimate product, in American broadcasting, recording is an intermediate process leading to radio's ultimate "product," the sound emanating from a loudspeaker. During the first decades of broadcasting in the United States, commercial networks utterly dominated the business of radio, grabbing up the most profitable stations (through direct ownership or affiliation) and the fattest advertising clients, and reaching the most important segments of the audience. Because radio networks had nothing to sell beyond the sounds they transmitted, the processes involved in making those sounds were at the center of their business strategy. The dominant networks labored feverishly to line up what they thought would be the most popular array of talent, to maintain the loyalty of key affiliates, and to perfect the technology of long-distance program distribution to local stations. Maintaining control over program distribution became problematic by the early 1930s, when improved, low-cost recording techniques threatened to undermine the more capital-intensive system of live distribution that helped maintain the dominance of the largest firms. Through the late 1940s, the networks were able to contain the threat posed by record-using upstarts, and in the process created the lasting impression that recorded sound represented a second-rate form of entertainment.

The resulting bias against recorded sound kept it marginalized in American radio until the late 1940s, when NBC, CBS, and ABC virtually abandoned the medium for the greener pastures of television. After 1950, the new technology of tape recording emerged to fill the void. This fundamental shift in the making of radio programs nonetheless retained much of what live radio had represented. Even though the use of recordings in radio nibbled away at the last vestiges of live talent, listeners hardly noticed. Today recordings, not live performances, constitute most of radio's content. From one point of view recording technology is the real heart of broadcasting, with transmitters and receivers acting simply as a delivery system. Considering sound recording as a mass-communication medium, the task is not simply to explain how recording came to be so central in American radio, but also to explain why it had to remain so undetectable to listeners.

The American System of Broadcasting

During the "Golden Age" of radio in the United States, the period from the late 1920s to the late 1940s, a typical day's fare of programs resembled today's television—a line-up of comedies, dramas, and soap operas, punctuated at regular intervals by commercials and the announcements of anonymous but recognizable voices. Most programming emanated from a small number of "networks," organizations that were rather nebulous forms of business enterprise, but which everyone recognized and associated with radio. The nearly monopolistic structure of the radio business in the United States was a major determinant in the uniformity of technologies used in radio broadcasting, which in turn had important implications for the programs that listeners heard.

One of the persistent myths about the Golden Age of network radio is that all radio programming was live in those days. The truth is, of course, more complex. It is true that the bulk of network programming was performed live, but there were a few network shows based on the broadcast of phonograph records, and network engineers regularly used recordings of various types for secondary purposes such as short announcements or background sound effects. Smaller networks often operated in ways that actually encouraged the use of recorded programs, and local stations made extensive use of records.[1]

Commercial radio in the U.S. changed rapidly between the late 1910s, when it was primarily a message service like telegraphy, and the early 1920s, when businessmen redefined the medium to serve as a form of entertainment. While phonograph records were a potential source of program material for broadcasting, early live transmissions of sports events and similar spectacles seemed to capture listeners' imaginations. Even more intriguing to listeners was the possibility of hearing something that was happening in a far-off city. NBC, already the most important commercial broadcaster in the 1920s, committed itself to building a geographically dispersed network of electrically linked stations broadcasting live entertainment. The success of this system was impossible to deny. By 1927 there were twenty-eight stations in the NBC network and sixteen affiliates of a second network, the Columbia Broadcasting System [CBS]; ten years later the numbers were 111 and 105, respectively, and a third network with eighty affiliates, Mutual, had also appeared. By 1945, 95 percent of all stations on the air were network affiliates.[2]

The business relationships involved in network operation grew much more complex as commercial radio took off in the later 1920s and 1930s, but the essence of the original network form remained. In a few central studios located in New York, Chicago, and later Los Angeles, employees of NBC and CBS (the two largest networks) supervised the performance of music and entertainment, which traveled out across telephone lines to local stations across the country.

Policies on the Use of Recordings in Radio

Recorded sound had an important but controversial place in the radio industry before 1945. Early in its history, the commercial radio industry had rejected sound recordings as inferior. The Department of Commerce, which regulated the practices of the industry, also saw things this way, and imposed policies intended to restrict the playing of commercial phonograph records on the air. Observing that in almost every part of the country phonograph records were readily available for purchase, the Commerce Department decided that radio should give listeners something that they would not have access to otherwise.

NBC and CBS by the 1930s had resources that upstarts and outsiders simply could not match. Their studios were impressively large and their artistic staff talented. The productions they were capable of staging might involve scores of actors, singers, and musicians. Competing with the networks on their own terms soon became almost prohibitively expensive. Nonetheless, local stations had many reasons for wanting to create their own programming, not the least of which was the fact that they had a mandate to serve the local population, and most stations interpreted that to mean that they should allow local artists to perform, or broadcast sports events from the neighborhood high school or college. If the talent could not come to the station, the station often had to go to the talent. Live "land line" connections via the telephone were expensive, so most stations purchased the disk recording equipment that became commercially available in the late 1920s from companies such as Western Electric.

Some stations in large cities did have the resources to produce shows comparable to the network fare, and wanted to become mini-networks themselves. But one of the other major expenses involved in network operation was the cost of leasing telephone lines. An obvious way to avoid this cost was to record the material and distribute it in the form of disks. By about 1928, several stations had begun using special long-playing phonograph recorders to distribute programming on disks. The technology was a somewhat refined version of the ordinary phonograph, developed at AT&T's Bell Telephone Laboratories.

Part of the new disk's appeal was its "instantaneous" recording process. Unlike a regular phonograph record, where the soft master disk had to be duplicated in a more durable material before it could be played, original transcription recordings could be put directly into use. They also had a relatively long recording and playing time of up to fifteen minutes. They could seamlessly handle programs of the same length as the live radio shows originating from NBC and CBS, which were already broken up into segments of about the fifteen minutes. If it were necessary to disguise the fact that a program was recorded, a station could easily insert advertising messages while disks were being changed, and the final product emulated a live network transmission.

But making a transcription recording was a tricky process and something of an art. Often recordings had pops or other background noises that made a recording instantly recognizable to listeners. Additionally, making a recording was difficult and had to be undertaken under carefully controlled conditions by a skilled engineer. Disks were not able to stand up to repeated playings—they could be used only a few times before becoming scratchy sounding.

Transcription disks had one special feature that endeared them to small networks. The disks could be sent to a record manufacturing plant and reproduced in quantity, just like ordinary consumer phonograph records. That meant that a radio station could manufacture recordings for sale to other stations. The reproduction process was capital intensive, having been developed for high-volume consumer phonograph disks, but not so expensive that the price of duplicated transcription disks was exorbitant.

A pioneering example of a transcription program was the *Amos 'n' Andy* show, which got its start in the late 1920s at Chicago radio station WGN. The station formed a network-like arrangement based on the distribution of recordings, which appealed especially to non-network stations, since it was generally less expensive to buy the disks than to try to produce a high quality show locally or purchase network offerings. Further, advertising agencies saw recorded programs as a low-cost way to sponsor radio shows, one that circumvented the expensive rates charged by NBC and CBS for national exposure. The networks rightly saw such syndicated programs as competition, but they could in some instances control competition by purchasing it. Indeed, this was the fate of *Amos 'n' Andy,* which was sold to Mutual and went "live" shortly afterward.

FCC hearings in 1935 revealed some of the reasons why the use of program recordings would become increasingly controversial. Participants like the World Broadcasting System represented the interests of transcription-based networks, who argued that the live networks tended toward monopoly. CBS countered that transcriptions were technically inferior to live broadcasts and that their use would offend the public, undermining the whole radio industry. The American Federation of Musicians opposed the use of any recording for any purpose, arguing that records took away jobs from musicians. Yet NBC by this time was quietly entering the transcription service itself and had to straddle the fence by stating that the service was compatible with the live networks.[3]

Even though NBC and CBS were both involved in manufacturing transcriptions by 1940, recording was decidedly a second-class medium. The typical content of the transcription disks broadcast on the networks consisted only of such things as station identifications, background music, and other "incidental" sounds, not programs themselves. The main products offered by the major networks' transcription divisions were libraries of music, not the more threatening feature programs. Even the ownership of transcription records was restricted. Most of the companies involved in manufacturing and distributing transcription disks adopted strict policies regarding their use and disposal. The disks were rented rather than sold, could be legally played only a few times, and then had to be returned or destroyed.[4]

These restrictions and the prevailing tendency to treat recordings as a lesser form of programming quelled experiments with alternative recording technologies through the end of the 1930s. Though many engineers sought ways to improve the sound of recordings, and the growing use of transcriptions by the late 1930s provided some economic justification for further development, there was not yet an alternative sound recording technology that could easily be substituted for the disk. No other sound recording method available in the United States combined instantaneous recording, a fifteen-minute (or longer) playing time, adequate sound quality, comparable cost of operation, and economical duplication of recordings in quantity.

The commercial history of an invention called the Philips-Miller

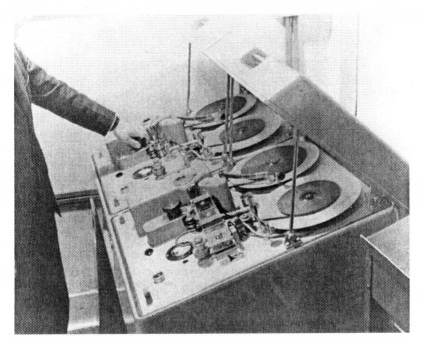

FIGURE 8. The Philips-Miller recorder, used in the 1930s in Europe, recorded sound optically on plastic tape. Courtesy Department of Special Collections, Stanford University Libraries.

recording system is a revealing example of why experimentation with new recording technologies was so limited. Its inventor, James Miller, was an American who had done pioneering work in recording sound on motion picture film in the early 1920s. The Philips-Miller machine recorded sound as a wavering line on a plastic strip but did so by a mechanical rather than the photographic process used to make Hollywood sound tracks. The recording was thus instantaneous, requiring no further processing before it could be played. The machine could record up to sixty minutes of audio material with a sound quality that exceeded the best transcription disk recorders, and the strip could be easily cut and spliced to add or remove material. Miller licensed his invention to the Philips Company of Eindhoven, and by the mid-1930s it was in use in radio stations in Norway, Luxembourg, and England.

It was first used in the United States by New York's WQXR, a station that catered to classical music fans. The station was at the forefront of the nascent high-fidelity movement, and even designed and marketed a special radio receiver in the 1930s that was intended to improve the listening experience. Station managers were open to the idea of any new recording technology that offered better sound than disks, so WQXR agreed to test the Philips-Miller recorder in 1938. The station often recorded local musical performances for later broadcast, and the Philips-Miller recorder was briefly used for this purpose. It offered some advantages over disk recorders in terms of the durability of the recordings, which could be played many times without degradation. Its technical weak point was the lack of a corresponding method to duplicate the tape for distribution to other stations in a network. Unlike a transcription record, which might be sent to a pressing plant and reproduced in quantity, no such high-volume duplication method existed for the Philips-Miller invention. As such, it really had only a limited appeal for American commercial radio stations and companies in the business of program distribution. It was used briefly in 1939 for the unusual purpose of recording and rebroadcasting an NBC series called "College of Musical Knowledge" over the Mutual network, where its easy editing capability allowed engineers to cut out unwanted advertisements. Then it faded into obscurity, at least in the United States. The Philips-Miller system may have been a better sound recorder, but it was not a better business machine for the radio industry.[5]

By Contrast: The Tape Recorder in European Broadcasting

The structure and policies of the broadcast networks of Europe reinforced rather than discouraged experiments with other types of sound recording technologies. By the mid-1920s, most European nations had central broadcasting authorities, national networks of stations and central studios. The integration of these systems was often greater than in the U.S. Most of them also used transcription disk recorders. However, several European nations also inaugurated shortwave services to colonial possessions beginning in the late 1920s. It was this shortwave service that would provide new opportunities for the promoters of sound recording technologies. The Netherlands was the first in 1927, followed by Germany (1929), France (1931), and Great Britain (1932).[6] Shortwave service encouraged different operational procedures, since audiences were typically located in other time zones. Thus the need for a reliable, economical sound recorder for shortwave service stimulated considerable experimentation. The two European systems in which magnetic tape recording was used most extensively in the 1930s were the BBC in Great Britain and the RRG in Germany.

The BBC's "Empire Service," inaugurated in 1932, initially served British nationals living abroad with news and speeches, and was supplemented in 1938 with broadcasts intended for non-British audiences. Practical considerations soon created a need for new recording and reproducing technologies to supplement the live broadcasts and disk recordings used extensively for in-country programs. Because of the time differences between England and some of the British possessions, it made sense to record programs, such as the speeches of political leaders, for later rebroadcast. The BBC and its equipment suppliers began looking around for suitable recording equipment.

One option was magnetic recording. Valdemar Poulsen's efforts to commercialize magnetic recording in Europe had resulted in the sale of his patent rights to two groups of German investors in 1901 and 1902.[7] These ventures soon failed, and apparently there was little commercial interest in the telegraphone until the early 1920s, after Poulsen's patents had expired. Activity revived when an independent inventor named Curt Stille organized the Vox Machinen A.G. in Germany to manufacture a wire recorder of his own design. The recorder, intended to be used as dictating machine, used the new technology of electronic amplification, which offered significant improvements in intelligibility and volume over the telegraphone system.

The Vox recorder came to England via a licensee, the Ludwig Blattner Picture Corporation, a producer of motion picture films. Switching to steel tape instead of wire, Blattner demonstrated his "Blattnerphone" in 1929, but had no success in interesting other studios or theaters to adopt the system.[8] However, the BBC began negotiating with Blattner beginning in 1929 to purchase tape recorders specifically for use in conjunction with the planned Empire Service. During 1930 and 1931 the BBC experimented with a slightly modified Blattnerphone, finally ordering two of them and putting them into regular service for shortwave broadcasts. The significance of this decision was highlighted in the BBC's 1932 yearbook which announced that "in some ways the most important event of the year has been the adoption by the BBC of the Blattnerphone recording apparatus."[9] The use of the Blattnerphone, later renamed the "Marconi-Stille" recorder, enabled the BBC to make instantaneous recordings of high quality and long duration, broadcast them at a convenient hour, and even reuse the steel tape any number of times.

The BBC's use of tape recording in the 1930s demonstrated that magnetic tape recording was not only a viable competitor to the transcription disk, but offered operational advantages for shortwave services. It also showed how technical choice can be determined by nontechnical factors such as the desire to broadcast information to colonial possessions. However, the Marconi-Stille system had its own set of drawbacks. These machines weighed

FIGURE 9. The "Blattnerphone" steel tape recorder in use at the BBC in 1932. *BBC Yearbook 1932.*

over a ton and used an expensive, bulky, and heavy medium. Because of the use of the heavy steel tape, the recorders were neither portable nor likely to be redesigned as portable devices (although "portable" is relative—they could be and were mounted in trucks). The mass of the full reels of steel tape was so great that rapid starts and stops were not possible, making the machine suitable only for uninterrupted recordings of relatively long programs. The ability to handle such long programs was tape's main virtue, but it also made the system less flexible. By contrast, disks were relatively inexpensive, could be used for anything from ten-second station identifications to fifteen-minute program segments, and any portion of a disk could easily be accessed. While the BBC continued to use its Marconi-Stille tape recorders until 1945, for the bulk of their recording needs they relied more heavily on conventional transcription disk equipment.

The situation was very different in Germany. The German national broadcasting system was established in 1926, when a new organization took over all existing radio stations in the Republic. In 1933, the Nazi party seized control of the system, forming the Reichs Rundfunk Gesselschaft (RRG), and purged political enemies from important posts at all the transmitting stations. The Nazis took a special interest in the radio system, preferring to supervise and direct its programming, especially the news.[10]

Like the BBC, the RRG had an immediate operational need for high-quality sound recording and reproducing equipment capable of handling long programs for radio broadcasts. German magnetic recording equipment was sold throughout Europe, especially telephone recorders for message taking. Magnetic wire recorders such as the "Textophone" and "Dailygraph" were used all over Europe to provide a central station telephone answering service or to provide centralized office dictation systems. While there are no reliable overall sales figures available, about 400 wire recorders made by one company, International Telephone and Telegraph, had been sold by early 1935, and one expert estimated that hundreds of magnetic wire recorders were in use in the 1930s in Switzerland alone.[11]

The manufacturing rights to one of these recorders, the Dailygraph, were purchased by ITT and transferred to a subsidiary, Carl Lorenz. At Lorenz, an engineer named Semi J. Begun began working on the problems of magnetic recording, and switched (like Blattner) from wire to a tape medium. In 1936 the company was manufacturing a new steel tape recorder called the Stahltonbandmaschine. Carl Lorenz found success in expanding the market for magnetic recorders by courting the RRG. By the end of the decade,

FIGURE 10.   A steel tape recorder made by the Carl Lorenz Company in Germany. These were used extensively by the RRG. *Wireless Engineer,* April 1936.

some of these tape recorders were also in service in broadcasting elsewhere in Europe, particularly in France.[12]

These expanding markets for magnetic sound recording stimulated the development of a new design by the large German electrical equipment manufacturer, AEG. This firm entered the field through the purchase of several of the patents of an independent inventor, Fritz Pfleumer, which described a new process for making recording tape. Instead of using a solid steel band, Pfleumer's method involved coating a mixture of pulverized iron and lacquer onto a lightweight, inexpensive strip such as paper or plastic. The new tape promised to be lighter, less expensive, and easier to manufacture than steel wires or tapes. Pfleumer's idea for a "coated" medium is still used in today's audio and video tapes, floppy disks, credit card stripes, and other magnetic media.

While AEG worked on the recorder itself, it turned over development of the new medium to the giant chemical firm I. G. Farben. Farben had expertise in the manufacture of iron oxide powders for pigments (in fact, a form of paint pigment already in production proved to be the basis of a suitable recording medium), and the company manufactured a line of acetate plastic films that would be used for the tape base. Production of the tape officially began in August 1934, when the company shipped 10,000 meters of it to AEG.[13]

The first of the new AEG "magnetophon" tape recorders proved to be a disappointment. Because the magnetophon was unreliable and barely able to record the relatively narrow band of frequencies present in the human voice, AEG canceled its public debut and turned engineers back to the laboratory. During 1935, AEG engineers worked on the recorder design while I. G. Farben developed a new oxide coating that was smoother and seemed to result in better recordings.[14]

AEG reintroduced the magnetophon in 1935 with a spectacular demonstration, recording a performance of the London Philharmonic Orchestra in Berlin and replaying it at I. G. Farben's Ludwigshafen plant.[15] The RRG immediately bought one, and the magnetophon had displaced the Stahltonbandmaschine by about 1940. After 1940, tape replaced disk recording as well "in a remarkably short space of time," according to one engineer, "in spite of the obstacles of conversion resulting from wartime conditions." Like the BBC's recorder, the magnetophon combined the high quality and long recording time of a disk recorder, but added certain features that appealed to radio men. Though hardly light in weight, the magnetophons were suitable for making recordings outside the studio because they were not affected by shock or vibration. Further, recordings of speeches or similar material could be easily excerpted by cutting the desired portion of the tape and splicing it.[16]

The twenty-six linked stations of the German system, once controlled by the Nazis, also used the magnetophon to broadcast lengthy classical music programs intended to inspire the public. Tape recording was well-suited to such long recordings, and the magnetophon's high-fidelity sound made it appealing for "serious" music. Though limited to radio stations, telephone offices, and the military market, AEG sold 379 magnetophons in 1939–40, and sales rose to over 900 units in 1943–44.[17]

The Armed Forces Radio Service as Agent of Change

In 1942, as America mobilized for war, the Federal Communications Commission organized a new Office of War Information.[18] The OWI soon became involved in the operation of dozens of small stations located in American military training camps and overseas bases. Some of these stations had originally been set up by the soldiers themselves and operated independently. But soon the servicemen began to request that the civilian networks supply them with some of the popular commercial programs. The OWI at first responded by rebroadcasting recorded network programs over its shortwave transmitters. Later, officials decided to begin distributing copies of these programs to the distant stations on disks, and the OWI transferred responsibility for the production of the programs to Thomas H. A. Lewis, a former Young and Rubicam employee with years of experience producing entertainment for network radio.[19]

Lewis proposed a new Armed Forces Radio Network to serve the needs of the military. The AFRS was headquartered in Los Angeles, close to a major center of radio talent but far from New York, where NBC and CBS made their homes. Recordings of network programs were "sanitized," or stripped of all commercial announcements, and duplicated on 16-inch disks by companies such as the Allied Record Manufacturing Company of Los Angeles.[20]

AFRS recording activities had two major effects. The first was the stimulation of considerable business for transcription duplicating firms on the West Coast. The volume among Los Angeles-area transcription disk duplicating companies increased from about 500 disks per month in 1942 to over 4,000 in 1945. The new network would consume well over a million disks before the end of the war, and the continued use of transcription equipment in the postwar period sent the figures soaring to 40,000 disks per month by 1951.[21]

More significantly, the AFRS proved to everyone involved that transcription records could be entirely satisfactory for the recording and distribution of commercial radio programs. Furthermore, the transcription disk was the only commercially available system suited for both the high-fidelity recording of long programs and their rapid duplication in quantity.

These activities of the AFRS began to undermine the argument that live radio was somehow special, and made recorded programs seem more acceptable. But the new network also encouraged the use of recording equipment in other important ways. The complete lack of restrictive policies or formal regulations regarding the use of recordings coincided with the appearance of a range of new sound recording technologies that seemed well-suited for use in radio. Among these new recorders were new types of portable equipment that could be used by reporters to gather eyewitness reports and interviews. Local radio stations in the U.S. had sometimes used disk recorders for news reporting, but there was no truly portable sound recording equipment in widespread use in radio before the early 1940s. Small, battery-operated sound recorders were not generally available, so portable recording entailed loading equipment into a specially prepared "sound truck." With the sound truck parked near the scene, recording engineers would operate the equipment inside while a reporter described the events. This was just the situation in which reporter Herb Morrison found himself in 1937, when he recorded the crash of the *Hindenburg*. The cables tethered a frantic Morrison to the sound truck until he finally put the microphone down and ran to help the victims. The resulting disk was one of the rare instances of recorded news to be broadcast by the major networks.

Wartime reporting in Europe and the Pacific posed new problems to journalists and radio technicians. CBS and NBC preferred to report live via short-wave links, even if that meant coordinating events internationally, tying up expensive transoceanic radio channels, and stringing hundreds of yards of microphone wire at the scene. Some network reporters, including Edward R. Murrow, broadcast from the relative comfort of the London rooftops; others, like H. V. Kaltenborn, found themselves dodging bullets as they attempted to drag microphones and long cables into the battlefields. The AFRS, on the other hand, took advantage of new opportunities to test smaller, battery-operated portable equipment just appearing by about 1943. For promoters of these new sound recording inventions, AFRS sponsorship represented a valuable opportunity to introduce new technologies into the resistant structure of American radio.[22]

Though there were several different types of portable recorders used extensively during the war, the one with the most lasting postwar impact was the magnetic wire recorder. While several companies made wire recorders for the military by the end of the war, the leader of the group was the Armour Research Foundation, the research branch of the Illinois Institute of Technology in Chicago. Its chief researcher in this area was a young electrical engineer named Marvin Camras, who had started work on a home wire recorder shortly before the war. After Camras showed his design to military officials, Armour was given contracts to further develop the recorder and supply them to the Army, Navy, and other agencies.

By about 1942, Camras had redesigned his wire recorder to suit the special needs of the military. The new machine was rugged and durable, but relatively small, light in weight, and portable, operating on battery power. Armour supplied several variations of the recorder, such as a model used in airplanes, but it reaped the most publicity from those it put into service for the AFRS. Later, when orders for the wire recorder outstripped Armour's ability to build them, the organization licensed the General Electric Company to make them. AFRS reporters first used them during the North African campaign, and they were widely used in the Pacific theater. The OWI put many reporters into combat situations with Armour wire recorders, and got back news reports that had an element of "being there" not ordinarily possible even with live broadcasting. Edward R. Murrow used one of the Armour machines to narrate a bombing mission over Germany, and another journalist took one

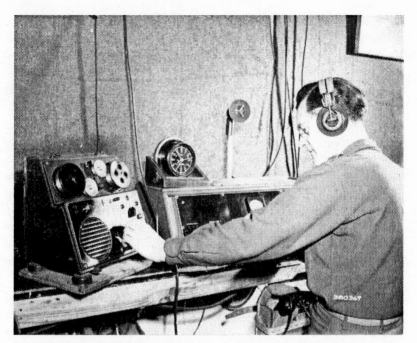

FIGURE 11. An Armour Research Foundation wire recorder in use at a small U.S. army radio station in 1945. National Archives and Records Administration.

with him on a paratrooper mission, describing in midair the experience of parachuting. The use of these portable recorders would soon have a significant impact on news reporting in commercial radio, since so many AFRS-trained technicians and announcers returned to civilian radio after the war.[23]

The FIAT Program

A second recording technology–related activity undertaken by Americans in Europe was part of the transfer of technologies from a defeated Germany to U.S. companies, an activity sponsored by the military and the Department of Commerce. One part of this technology transfer program, known as Project Paperclip, resulted in the wholesale expatriation of German aeronautical technologies and personnel after 1945. The less well-known civilian side of the effort, run by an agency with the acronym FIAT, was more limited and ultimately less successful, but one of its most effective operations

FIGURE 12.   An Armour portable wire recorder in use in the early 1940s. National Archives and Records Administration.

concerned the AEG magnetophon tape recorder. American and British investigators seized documents and interviewed personnel involved in the manufacture of the AEG magnetophon and its recording tape. They brought back examples of the machines and produced an important series of technical reports, which the Commerce Department sold to the public.

The transfer of German technology was crucial to the subsequent development of the American tape recording industry. There were a number

FIGURE 13. The Armed Forces Radio Service employed a number of recording techniques simultaneously. Left to right, an Armour wire recorder, Amertype Recordograph, and a conventional disk cutter. Paul V. Galvin Library, Illinois Institute of Technology.

of FIAT investigators who gained an intimate knowledge of German magnetophon technology while participating in technical intelligence missions and who used that knowledge to great advantage after they returned home. These included Jack Mullin, an electrical engineer whose initial impressions of the magnetophon inspired a career in the magnetic recording field after he returned to the United States. Richard Ranger, an army colonel and electronics entrepreneur, copied the magnetophon after the war and sold it in the U.S. under the name Rangertone. Similarly, the Audio Devices Corporation used captured German knowledge to enter the field of recording tape manufacture in 1948, as did Orradio Industries in 1950.[24]

At the end of the war, Americans marveled at the extent to which the magnetophon had been employed in European radio. They discovered the wide range of models available and to what ends they had been employed. To most investigators, the only magnetophon that truly mattered was the Model K7, the high-fidelity recorder for music. At the end of the war it had not yet been put into regular production, but based on listening tests of a few prototypes, the design was capable of sound quality that all listeners agreed was excellent. Thus the magnetophon's appeal to these men was based not so much on careful market analysis for tape recorders, but simply the awe-inspiring performance of the machine itself.[25]

Establishment of a Magnetic Recording Industry in the U.S.

At the end of the war in 1945, the Armour Research Foundation was already well underway with its plan to commercialize consumer magnetic wire recording. Several firms had taken manufacturing licenses in addition to GE, and foundation representatives now worked to recruit many more. A U.S. firm unaffiliated with Armour that had developed its own version of magnetic recording was the Brush Development Company of Cleveland. Brush in 1939 had hired a German immigrant, S. J. Begun, who had been the chief designer of the Carl Lorenz Company's Stahltonbandmaschine tape recorder a few years before. Brush took an active role during the war in promoting the use of the tape recorder in radio and motion pictures and as a home entertainment device.

At the same time that Armour and Brush were busily orchestrating the development of the consumer wire recorder industry, other firms were attempting to manufacture tape recorders for the "professional," or radio and recording industry markets. The principles of tape recording were essentially the same as wire recording, but the early "professional" tape recorders were built differently than wire recorders or the Brush tape recorder. The professional recorders cut fewer corners and achieved better sound quality, and could be used continuously without suffering breakdowns.

Many of the pioneering magnetic recorder manufacturers had considerable success, though it sometimes came from unexpected sources. An early entrant into the field was the Ampex Corporation of California, formerly a manufacturer of small electric motors for the military. Company president Alexander M. Poniatoff became interested in the possibility of manufacturing professional audio equipment and hired Harold Lindsay, an audio engineer. Lindsay convinced Poniatoff to produce a tape recorder after hearing a 1946 demonstration of the magnetophon given by former Signal Corps engineer and FIAT investigator Jack Mullin, given before the Institute of Radio Engineers.[26] Ampex got technical assistance from Mullin, and the company also became a licensee of the Armour Research Foundation, thereby gaining access to Armour's vast experience with similar magnetic recording technologies. Ampex began to produce its Model 200 recorder in late 1948.[27] The Model 200's early demonstrations attracted considerable attention and even a few orders, but it was still uncertain how tape recording would fit into network operations.

The Rise of Tape

Manufacturers seemed almost surprised by the warmth of the broadcast industry's reception of the new machines. Without much warning to makers of broadcast recorders, the practices of network radio were changing in a way that encouraged the innovative use of recording technologies. The first evidence of this was the widespread adoption in broadcasting of recorders intended for other markets.[28]

In 1945 and 1946, perhaps at the suggestion of Armour Research, some stations began using portable wire recorders for radio news programs.[29] As early as July 1944, for example, Armour representatives convinced Chicago station WGN to begin using a General Electric wire recorder on the air for news. The station recorded the 1944 Republican national convention in its entirety and made portions of the recording available for broadcast. Station WENR, also in Chicago, highlighted the use of wire recording equipment in its show called "Hot off the Wire" in 1945.

In 1946 Brush Development Company began advertising its Soundmirror tape recorder, a device based on some of the same ideas as the magnetophon, though intended for consumers. Ironically, it was engineers at radio stations who began buying them in large numbers. In 1946, for example, CBS recorded the national political conventions on a Brush Soundmirror Model BK-401 tape recorder and aired an edited version later. There were also shows built around the portability of tape and wire recorders. For example, ABC began airing a show in 1947 called "Candid Microphone," in which a concealed microphone captured people unaware. The show innovated the use of "blooping" out foul language, although sometimes the offensive words were simply cut out of the tape.

Professional users complained that the Soundmirror could not be operated for more than a few hours before overheating, that its sound quality was not very good, and that it gave constant mechanical troubles. Still, many stations began experimentally using Soundmirrors for on-the-spot recording, which was much easier to accomplish with a tape recorder than with previous transcription technology. In part, this was because a skilled operator and optimal conditions were not needed to make a good recording. Further, unlike a disk, the tape medium could be easily cut and spliced to suit on-air requirements. This was an especially useful feature for news, where bits of interviews could be spliced between a narrator's announcements.[30]

Antirecording restrictions began to break down after 1945, as networks began to admit that transcription recording technology had "progressed" to the point of commercial acceptability. But their cautious endorsements were not as influential in the spread of sound recording usage as the actions of numerous individual engineers, local stations, and even performers. The entertainer Bing Crosby in 1946 became the unlikely protagonist in an effort to put recorded programs into prime time.[31] Crosby was at the height of his career at the end of the war and had more say in the production of his shows than many lesser performers. After the war he announced that he was tired of the stresses of a live-performance schedule that put him in NBC's New York studios several times a week. He left NBC in 1944 to join ABC partly because the new network promised to let him record his shows three or four at a time for later broadcast. For ABC, recently spun off from NBC and struggling to survive, allowing artists to record emerged as a corporate strategy to lure stars away from competitors.[32]

Former FIAT investigator Jack Mullin was invited to ABC studios in Hollywood in August of 1947 to tape the season premier of Crosby's show using a magnetophon. After Crosby listened to the tape, he hired Mullin and asked him to build copies of the machine so as to become less dependent of the only two working magnetophons Mullin had in his possession. Others at ABC also became interested in the tape recorder, and by 1948 the network had entertained demonstrations by Rangertone and Ampex. ABC subsequently purchased several Ampex machines and began to use them to tape other shows.[33] ABC had already abandoned the practice of airing shows live at different times for distribution to different time zones. By 1946 the network recorded the East Coast shows and distributed them on disk and, in 1948, on tape.[34] By 1947, CBS and Mutual had begun to follow suit.[35]

Local radio stations and transcription-based networks also began using tape recorders for day-to-day programming in a way that was not much different than the ways they had used disks. Many stations bought Ampex recorders for studio use, often supplemented by less expensive portable recorders made by Magnecord, a company founded by several former Armour Research employees.[36] Typical were stations in Atlanta, Georgia, where station WSB supplemented the transcription recorders in its studios and sound trucks with Ampex equipment in 1949, while its competitor WGST bought a Rangertone in 1948, as soon as it became available.[37] The Armed Forces

Radio Services, which persisted into the postwar period, was probably typical of the many new transcription networks in that it began using tape recorders in the studio, even though it continued to distribute disks to affiliated stations for several more years.[38]

The networks found tape so attractive that they sought ways to accommodate its drawbacks as compared to disks. Though the German version of the technology had been successfully transferred in whole to the United States in 1945, Americans soon realized that the Germans had not been particularly concerned with the mass production of recordings. Tapes were duplicated by the German stations simply by using two regular recorders to transfer the original to a fresh tape. The process was no faster than the duplication of disks. One of the first networks to run up against this problem was the National Association of Educational Broadcasters in Urbana, Illinois, which switched to tape in 1950. The NAEB discovered that high-speed duplication of multiple tapes was easy to imagine but difficult to accomplish. The network hired two engineers who designed a machine to make eleven copies of a tape simultaneously, or up to forty-four copies of a fifteen minute tape per hour. This limited output would have been taxed by the daily production of several different shows. In a similar experiment, the 3M Corporation discovered that "little was known about the economics involved" in tape duplication. 3M had become involved in the making of tape for the Brush Company as early as 1945, and after the introduction of magnetophon-style equipment, it became the largest manufacturer of recording tapes in the country. The company tried to promote tape recording by researching ways to duplicate recordings in quantity.

Engineers at 3M found that a machine they developed to duplicate music recordings had a theoretical maximum duplication speed of about two times the normal playback speed of 7.5 inches per second. That meant that no matter how many tapes were copied in tandem, there was a rather low absolute limit to the rate at which they could be turned out. But their machine had an acceptable output for duplication of network programming, even though it was slow compared to the stamping of disks, where a thirty minute recording on two sides of a disk could be duplicated in less than a minute.[39] The economics of tape duplication possible by the early 1950s could not compare with the mass production of consumer phonograph records, a fact that would haunt tape proponents when they tried to compete with the home phonograph in later years. But for radio, the per-unit duplication cost of a tape could be considerably less than the duplication cost of a transcription disk. After all, the duplication of transcription disks had been developed with consumer phono-

FIGURE 14. Part of tape's success in radio was due to the development of suitable duplication techniques, such as this six-tape copier. *FM and Television* magazine, January 1949.

graph markets in mind. The master disks for duplication had to be prepared like consumer phonograph records, in that the disk had to be turned into a metal stamper through a complex and expensive procedure. Once made, the stamper could be used to make hundreds or thousands of disks, but transcription records were rarely made in these quantities. Thus the economics of tape recording was well suited to the needs of networks—perhaps even better suited than the transcription disk.[40]

While tape proved to be an economical, portable, and flexible substitute for the transcription recorder, it was also the focus of considerable operational change in postwar radio. Radio stations faced severe economic pressures after the war, due to the rise in the total number of competing stations and to the virtual abandonment of radio by the major networks. Radio station profit ratios actually reached a high of over 30 percent in 1944, but immediately began to fall. The real drop came after 1947, when television began to be much more popular and the networks pulled shows and major stars out of radio. Revenues gradually fell until the mid-1950s, when network owned and operated stations were generally losing money, and independent stations showed profits of only 10 percent or less. Networks now seemed less important to a station's success, and affiliation dropped from 95 percent to about 50 percent between 1945 and 1955. Stations scrambled to replace income lost from network-sponsored shows to local advertising accounts that they maintained themselves. They slashed studio and technical personnel, cut locally produced programs, and substituted disk jockeys and popular music shows for network content. Tape continued to be used for network program distribution, but more important applications also emerged.[41]

As radio stations began looking for ways to reduce the cost of on-air and engineering staff, they also considered the use of automated equipment. Because recordings of several hours duration were practical on tape, some stations began to record their programming ahead of time. It was less expensive to pay an announcer to come in for just a few hours a day to record a series of short messages, which were then spliced into a program by a technician, than to pay the announcer to be at the station all day. In the studio, announcements and entertainment could be spliced together to make a recording that sounded much like live radio. The creative use of tape in the production studio enhanced locally produced advertisements or programs even more by making low-cost "sound effects" possible, such as echoes or pitch changes.[42]

Sometimes stations used two or more tape recorders working together to play back recorded programs. A simple electronic circuit, added to the tape recorders to detect a subaudible tone on the tapes, automatically started or stopped the recorders. In this way, a station might stay on the air all night with no announcers present, avoiding the cost of their labor. With the more elaborate electronic controls that came along by the 1970s and 1980s, some stations' programming was virtually all automated in this manner.

Other tape-based technologies complemented the style of radio programming that came to predominate in what became known as the Age of Television. Competition from TV demanded deep cutbacks in the cost of radio shows, so networks and stations looked for new types of material to put on the air. By the 1960s, for example, there were many stations that emphasized on-air "personalities " as a central part of their daily fare. These disk jockeys interspersed banter with recorded announcements and hit records to create "Top 40" and "Musical Clock" formats (the latter alternating music and time/news announcements). The fast-paced style of this type of program, combined with the repetitious broadcasting of a few commercial announcements or hit songs, provided fertile ground for the use of new types of automatic tape equipment.[43]

The most important of these technologies was based an endless-loop, tape-loaded cartridge system called the Fidelipac. Invented in the 1950s, the Fidelipac was originally intended for background music systems and had some success in that field. The Fidelipac was the invention of George Eash of Cleveland, Ohio, who made the technology available to manufacturers under license. Within a short time, a few stations in the Midwest obtained Fidelipac recorders made by the Viking corporation and modified them for automatic starting and stopping. Because the Fidelipac cartridge employed an endless loop of tape, it was relatively straightforward to build into the player circuits to detect the end of the tape and stop the machine at that point without any additional manipulation by a person. Tapes could be quickly popped into a player and played, and they would reset themselves exactly at the right spot, ready for the next play. This was a technology perfectly suited to the "Top-40" format then proliferating on AM radio, where a busy disk jockey had to operate all the controls, act as announcer, and ready recorded songs and announcements for broadcast. Some stations put virtually all their music on these "carts," since there was no possibility of a stylus jumping out of a groove or a record being started at 33 1/3 rpm rather than 45. There were even carousel-style cartridge changers holding dozens of carts, which made it possible to program a long radio show and insert or remove new selections at will. But the main uses of the cart by the end of the 1960s were for single musical selections and short announcements. For these purposes the cart was ubiquitous in American radio through the 1990s, when CD carousels and computer-based automation began to replace it.

Yet the question of whether audiences actually preferred live performances on the radio or whether they would reject that which was obviously "canned" never really came to be tested. Changes in the kinds of program materials that networks and local stations broadcast virtually eliminated the old style of radio entertainment by the mid-1950s. Even if the old style of programming had persisted, technical improvements such as the tape recorder would have made it difficult to test audience preferences, because audiences cannot distinguish live from recorded programs using purely sonic criteria. The technology is far too good to do so. The fact that recording has captured radio programming has largely gone unnoticed, even though its use has wrought such important changes in the way the radio medium delivers audio culture. More of radio originates in recordings than we may realize. What sounds convincingly like the prattle of a live announcer talking about current events, taking telephone calls on the air, and playing music may in fact be a recording made days earlier in some distant studio. A scene from the motion picture *American Graffiti* in which a disappointed fan discovers that the local disk jockey he admires is merely a tape captured the essence of radio's use of recording and the public's innocence. Thus the prewar radio networks' self-interested dismissal of recordings has effects today: records on the radio still represent an inferior form of culture to the general public. It is the live sound of today's radio programming that helps keep listeners interested.[44]

Conclusions

Broadcasters established the radio business in the United States on the basis of live transmission of program material. But a live network soon became much more than simply the best technical means to achieve the distribution of programming; it also became a part of a business strategy. NBC and CBS actively discouraged a viable technological alternative to the live network, the transcription disk recording, and denounced recordings as an inferior form of culture. These networks went so far as to adopt antirecording policies, and virtually banned the use of recording equipment in their own studios. Even though most local stations were nominally independent, network executives and managers, working in conjunction with government regulatory agencies, had systemic influence in terms of the technologies that local radio stations purchased and used. This centralization of control operated both in the United States, where recording technologies were rarely used, and in Europe, where they were used extensively. After 1945, technical innovations and the success of television broadcasting brought about rapid changes in the use of recording technology in radio. The changing economics of the industry suddenly made the use of recording equipment vitally important and made sound recording equipment one of radio's most significant production tools. However, by this time the public had come to expect spontaneous-sounding entertainment from radio, and stations found it undesirable to turn away from that sound.

Both the pre-1945 failures and the remarkable postwar successes of the sound recorder in U.S. radio are linked to the desire to broadcast (or simulate) live music and voice. In the postwar context, the radio industry faced complex technical and economic changes. The old network system virtually fell apart, and radio stations had to invent new forms of culture and new ways of doing business. Since that time, radio stations have created a very different sort of programming, one that depends much more heavily on sound recordings. Yet the charm of radio still emanates from the sense of immediacy that listeners perceive. The technology of recording has, ironically, helped preserve radio's apparent spontaneity. The legacy of obsolete network policies encouraged the adoption of technologies and practices of recording that were oriented toward a live sound. Since the late 1940s, this recording culture that emphasizes live sound has persisted, and it continues to influence the adoption of new technologies that increase, rather than decrease, stations' dependence on recordings. The history of sound recording in the entertainment industry is unique in part because of the paramount importance of aesthetic considerations in the final product. In records and broadcasting, sound recording technologies were at the intersection of commerce and culture. In many other businesses, sound recording also played an important role, but often aesthetic concerns about the final product were much less important. Where in the studio the sound recorder was both a production tool and artist's pallet, in the business offices of corporations across America, the sound recorder was an instrument of management. This development parallels the history of sound recording in the entertainment industry, and will require us to return to Edison's laboratory of the 1880s.

CHAPTER 3

"Girl or Machine?":

GENDER, LABOR, OFFICE DICTATION, AND THE FAILURE OF RECORDING CULTURE

$\mathcal{F}$or much of the twentieth century, sound recording has been a part of the daily labor not only of recording engineers and musicians but also of office workers. Executives, clerical workers and even office boys came in contact with sound recording in the form of a device known generically as the dictating machine. Dictation equipment was intended to replace the human stenographer with a desktop machine and thus streamline the process of dealing with office correspondence. The history of the dictation recorder is comparable to the histories of other technologies of office production such as typewriters and calculators, in the sense that its story can be told in the context of office mechanization (or, as it was later called, automation).[1] However, there are two basic differences. One is that the sound recorder in business was never as successful as these other office machines. "Dictating and transcribing machines," William Henry Leffingwell wrote in 1932, "though a thoroughly demonstrated success and on the market for years, are not yet so extensively used as they should be."[2]

Secondly, the success of dictation systems demanded the mechanization of executive labor as well as clerical work. Equipment manufacturers and salesmen, office managers, and others who wanted to see dictation equipment succeed tried for many years to overcome what they perceived as technical problems with the machines and achieved considerable success in improving their performance. However, the dictation machine's advocates faced considerable user resistance, some of it rooted in power, gender, and status issues beyond the scope of their influence. The most frustrating source of resistance was at the very top. The executives and managers who could have mandated dictation equipment use within companies often failed to do so, in part because the technology's promoters had not made a seductive case for it, in part because so many of these executives themselves found the machine inadequate or undesirable.

The history of office dictation necessarily addresses issues long of interest to labor and gender historians. Scholars have studied other office machines, especially the typewriter, telephone, and computer, in terms of their consequences for women workers. Indeed, much of the history of office dictation involves women's labor issues. The managerial effort to mechanize a skilled task, stenography, in a field dominated by women is at the core of the dictation machine's history. In some cases, managers simply imposed the use of dictation equipment upon office workers, who had little choice but to accept it or quit. In fact, managers' decisions to include dictation equipment in existing typing "pools" sustained the dictation machine industry for many years. Yet it is a myth that the use of office dictation technology was universal by the early decades of the twentieth century, or at any subsequent time.[3]

Growth in the industry, especially after the 1930s, would depend upon the ability of equipment marketers to convince those in the most resistant market segment, the top managers, that the use of the dictating machine would be enjoyable, that it would enhance their jobs, and that it was the "modern" way to create correspondence. Perpetuating a culture of sound recorder use would prove to be an unattainable goal.

Many American office workers were familiar with dictation machine, but that familiarity does not necessarily imply use. The alleged gains in letter-writing efficiency possible with the dictating machine did not automatically propel it to commercial success, and its sales and use were only a small fraction of that of the typewriter or the telephone (or the computer since the 1960s). Marketing campaigns for dictation equipment had to convince customers to buy the devices, yet salesmen also had to revisit old customers constantly to ensure that the machines stayed in active use. Over the course of several decades, sales were enough to keep equipment manufacturers hopeful, but manufacturers never quite conquered the vast potential market for office equipment in the United States.

As part of a system involving male managers and female clerical workers, the adoption of dictation technology depended on managerial as well as clerical acquiescence or accommodation. Unlike the typewriter, billing machines, calculators, filing systems, stencil duplicators, or most other office technologies, the use of dictating machines demanded the participation of managers, not just their oversight. Their negative reactions to the use of the machine, based almost wholly on personal preference, posed a challenge to the Scientific Management movement, as managers through their rejection prevented the replacement of skill and knowledge with a machine. Resistance to the new technology from managers not only made it difficult to implement dictation systems, but undermined what managers themselves argued was the most rational, efficient, and hence best way to do business. Every form of sound recording in use in America balances the interests of businesses selling or using recording technology against the labor of those making or using recordings. The dictation machine's history offers insights into the ways office mechanization, Scientific Management, and the politics of gender played into the creation of a new recording culture.

The Invention of Mechanical Stenography

Although many of us think of the phonograph and the tape recorder as sources of home entertainment, the first commercial application of each was for office dictation. Entertainment, in fact, appeared near the bottom of a list of possible applications dreamed up by Edison for the phonograph, whereas letter writing appeared at the very top.[4] Edison deliberately called his invention a "sound writer" because in its original form it could both record and store sounds, not just reproduce them. Being able to do both suited what he had in mind for it.

His breakthrough in inventing the phonograph is one of the most often-cited cases in the history of modern invention. In 1877–78, while experimenting with a device to record telegraph messages on a disk, Edison extended the concept to include the possibility of the recording of sound. He used a piece of tinfoil, wrapped around the outside of a metal cylinder, to receive the impression of a stylus microscopically vibrating under the influence of sound waves.

The name that Edison chose for the recorder may have been inspired by another sort of "phonography." This earlier tradition of "sound writing" also involved the transcription of the spoken word, but it had its roots early in the eighteenth century in the practice of legal or legislative reporting. The word phonography was for many years synonymous with stenography or short-hand. Phonography at that time also implied fidelity, in the sense that the hand truthfully transcribed what the ear heard. Perhaps overconfidently, Edison claimed his mechanical amanuensis would do the same.[5]

At about the same time that Edison was perfecting his phonograph, a machine to record magnetically on wire (or, a few years later, tape) appeared although it was kept secret by its inventor until the 1880s (see introduction). Magnetic recording was a promising alternative to the phonograph, yet it did not appear commercially for several more years, allowing the phonograph's promoters a head start. The telegraphone, the first magnetic recorder marketed in the United States, was invented in Denmark around 1900, and became the basis of a new office dictation system after 1910. The telegraphone sold poorly due to technical and business-related difficulties, and the American Telegraphone Company's demise after World War I marked the last attempt to market magnetic recorders as dictation machines until about 1945. In the meantime, makers of phonographic recorders had the freedom to shape the nascent field of office dictation, though the magnetic recorder would reemerge in later years as a serious competitor.[6]

The early history of the phonograph did not suggest an invention with a bright commercial future. Historians like to tell the story of Edison the "system builder"[7] who, for example, not only created a complete system of electric lighting technology, but became its most ardent promoter and commercializer. However, Edison lost interest in the phonograph after a brief round of public demonstrations in the late 1870s. Understandably, this prolific inventor could not devote his full energies to every one of his devices. He arranged for the manufacture of a few tinfoil recorders, but then turned to other projects for several years.[8]

Meanwhile, Alexander Graham Bell and several associates, including Charles Sumner Tainter, surprised Edison by entering the phonograph field and producing an improved sound recorder, which they demonstrated in 1886. Tainter abandoned Edison's tinfoil-wrapped cylinder and adopted a cardboard cylinder coated with a wax compound, which gave him better results. Instead of embossing the groove into the medium, the stylus carved out its groove on the surface of the wax cylinder, and these differences were enough to make the new "graphophone" patentable. Bell's group also saw the principal application of sound recording as a mechanical stenographer.[9] The company they formed to manufacture the graphophone sold a few machines to the United States government for the purposes of recording notes taken at congressional sessions. Sales to the Civil Service Commission, the Post Office, and the Bureau of the Republics soon followed. Edward D. Easton, the official reporter for the United States Congress, became a convert to machine stenography almost immediately. Easton took notes in shorthand, but adopted the practice of reciting his notes to the graphophone immediately after a session, while they were still fresh in his mind. By early 1891, the Columbia Phonograph Company had about sixty machines leased to various companies in the Washington area.[10]

Insulted by Bell's incursion into a field he considered his own, Edison in 1886 returned to the phonograph and in 1888 invented a thinly disguised copy of the graphophone using an all-wax cylinder and a slightly different mechanism. When he reentered the phonograph field, he turned his considerable marketing expertise to expanding the use of mechanical stenography by convincing some businessmen, doctors, and other professionals to substitute the phonograph for a live stenographer in the creation of business correspondence.[11]

In these early years, by all accounts the graphophone was the better-made machine. Though seemingly less sophisticated than the Edison phonograph (especially since it used foot-treadle power instead of an electric motor), the graphophone in service was more reliable and produced better records. But neither phonograph nor graphophone did very well in the marketplace, and both companies were struggling to stay alive even as early as 1890. An 1891 meeting of companies licensed to sell phonographs revealed that only about 1,740 business phonographs were currently in use in the entire country. Curiously, Edison chose not to divert resources from more profitable ventures to support what he would later call his "favorite invention," but instead allowed the flagging enterprise to be purchased by J. B. Lippincott, who also bought the rights to the graphophone. By the 1896, ownership of the patents and firms changed again, with Edison regaining control of his phonograph and the Columbia Graphophone Company gaining the rights to the Bell invention. In the interregnum, the business recorder market had evaporated, so Edison did not offer a new model until 1905. Columbia, with its headquarters in Washington, D.C., remained in the business machine market mainly by maintaining its federal government accounts.[12]

The 1890s were a turning point in the history of the phonograph (and after this point the word "phonograph" is used generically to describe either the true phonograph or the graphophone). Revenues from a new machine, the "nickel-in-the-slot," phonograph (a proto-jukebox) became important, as did the sale of recorded cylinders for use by consumers at home. Within a few years, sales of the entertainment phonograph and recorded cylinders led the industry, while sales of the recording phonograph dropped off to almost nothing. Sales of office phonographs slowly revived, however, and both the Edison and Columbia business machine operations remained profitable but relatively small enterprises. After the turn of the century, the marketing and sales organizations diverged, so the business and entertainment versions of the technology became the basis of separate divisions in the Edison and Columbia organizations. By 1906, when Columbia's business recorder was renamed the "Dictaphone," the division that made it was on its way to becoming a com-

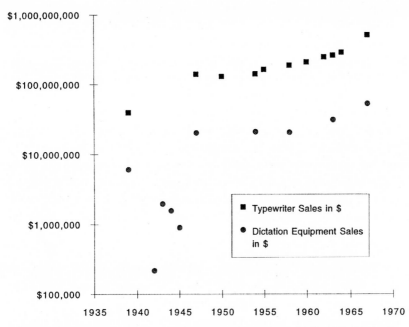

FIGURE 15. Sales of dictation equipment versus typewriters, 1939–1968. Typewriter sales remained at least ten times dictation equipment sales for much of the twentieth century. The two devices were comparably priced during much of the period. Source: U.S. Department of Commerce.

pletely separate entity. This process was complete in 1923 when Columbia went bankrupt and the Dictaphone Corporation formally split off. Similarly, Edison's National Phonograph Company established a Commercial Department in 1906, and though it never became a completely independent company, it was distinct from the entertainment phonograph business after that time.[13] The two products were nearly copies of each other, at least in terms of functionality, and they were marketed in nearly identical ways. The public understandably saw little difference, and as early as 1916, Ediphone salesmen were already struggling to eradicate the use of the word "dictaphone" to describe all dictation machines, but the term stuck.[14]

The market for business recorders at the turn of the century was smaller than that for home or arcade phonographs, but the profit margin per machine was higher, and supplies and service constituted a lucrative sideline. Sales figures that would indicate the size of the office recording market in the first decade of the century are not readily available, but the fact that the Department of Commerce saw the market as too small to report separately in the Census of Manufactures is indicative that its size was small indeed. Edison's company sold only 5,000 machines in 1910, the company's best year yet. Sales rose during the 1910s, until in 1919 the two companies sold 22,853 units. Edison's share of this business was smaller than Columbia's, resulting in 1919 sales of only about 5,100 machines and revenues of $581,760, which included income from cylinders and other supplies. But total U.S. sales fell to only 15,000 units three years later, and then dropped below 3,500. The 1930s saw a significant revival, and sales jumped during World War II, but no exact figures are available for these years. In fact, relative to sales of the typewriter, business phonograph sales were insignificant. In contrast to the 15,000 dictation machines sold in 1923, typewriter manufacturers in that same year sold a remarkable 744,000 units. Typewriter sales continued to rise somewhat during the Great Depression, as shown by sales figures of 917,290 units in 1939.[15]

Despite their small sales relative to the typewriter industry, between the 1910s and the end of World War II these two companies successfully convinced many firms to try using office recording technology. Both the Edison product, renamed the "Voicewriter," and Columbia's Dictaphone would benefit from the popularization of Scientific Management, with its stress on systemization, standardization, and the adoption of labor-saving machinery. Both companies redesigned their products to allow for the greater subdivision of tasks and to optimize the machines to the demands of correspondence production.[16] Most important was the design of separate machines for transcriber/typists and the unfortunately named "dictators." The transcribing machine had, for example, foot controls to allow a typist to repeat phrases or passages easily. This was important since the quality of an cylinder recording was pretty poor. A transcribing or secretarial machine could not record, and playback was via ear-tubes (or later a headphone set). Dictators' machines could record or play back via the speaking tube, but lacked the foot pedal controls of the transcription machine. Instead, all the machine's functions could be controlled by hand. Later models moved many of the controls to the speaking tube (replaced by a microphone in the 1930s).[17]

Wax-cylinder recording was an unforgiving process, in that a dictator's volume and enunciation had to be carefully controlled. The cylinders did not allow for the correction of mistakes. Edison Company literature admonished mumbling executives to be open to criticism from their typists. Although one could look at a cylinder to see if a recording was present, it was not possible to mark or write on the cylinders themselves to identify them. Later Dictaphones and Voice Writers included ruled paper slips and a system to mark them semiautomatically while recording. If the dictator recorded special instructions on the cylinder or made a mistake, he could press a button on the machine to make a tick mark on the slip of paper, showing the transcriber where on the cylinder to stop and listen. At the end of a recording, the dictator wrote any other instructions on the slip, which accompanied the cylinder from station to station around the office. There were always opportunities for slips to get lost or for cylinders to fall and break.[18]

A feature of the office dictation "system" that had emerged by the teens was the further subdivision of the labor process to include recommended procedures for the transportation of cylinders and their recycling. Typically, office boys performed both of these tasks. They picked up cylinders from the desks of the dictators and delivered them to typists or to a box in the typing pool. Later, they picked up spent cylinders and brought them to a third machine, which "shaved" off the top layer of wax. A cylinder could be reused dozens of times, and even the wax shavings could be returned to the factory to be made into new cylinders. Wax-cylinder dictation systems thus involved the integration of technology with both men's and women's (and, incidentally, children's) labor.[19]

Ediphone and Dictaphone, vigorously competing in the United States in the 1920s,[20] had their greatest successes in large, highly rationalized offices and in government bureaus. William Taft's Commission on Economy and Efficiency in 1912 endorsed the use of dictation equipment in government offices, and many agencies remained top customers in later years. Major users also included industries compelled, partly by changes in government regulatory practices, to keep more detailed financial records, such as insurance companies and railroads. Having accomplished the mechanization of accounting and record-keeping, managers in these organizations tried to rationalize the process of business correspondence. The use of the dictation machine grew wherever large volumes of routine correspondence needed to be generated. Insurance companies, for example, employed large numbers of low-ranking men as agents, and a significant part of their duties included the creation of rather standardized correspondence, forms, and reports. Their managers bought dictation machines for them and saw to it that they were in regular use. Similarly, typists in these organizations (often already organized into centralized pools) were hired with the understanding that they would use dictation transcribers heavily.[21]

Major dictation equipment consumers also included state and local governments and some of the largest manufacturing and mail-order operations.

FIGURE 16 through 19. Four aspects of phonograph office dictation at the turn of the century. Clockwise, an executive dictating a letter; a young man, probably a clerk, speaks into the horn; office boy delivers cylinders to the typing pool; a typist transcribing recordings. *Splitting the Other Four-Fifths* (1911).

FIGURE 20 and 21. The telegraphone wire recorder came into use just as male typists were being replaced by females. American Technical Publishers, Inc.; U.S. Department of the Interior, National Park Service, Edison National Historic Site.

Thus, Dictaphone reported in the early 1950s that certain customers from these categories had been important clients since the 1890s, including the federal government and many municipal governments, Sears, Roebuck, and Westinghouse.[22]

The typewriter and certain other office machines thrived in nearly every office environment, but dictation systems never became widespread. One reason for this was the way they were marketed. The typewriter's early promoters had emphasized the greater efficiency of the machine versus longhand for producing correspondence. However, once typewritten letters overcame a short-lived public opposition to "machine made" letters, the device became standard equipment everywhere. People began to buy the technology not just for the sake of efficiency but because handwritten letters came to be seen as unbusinesslike. Any new business or office being furnished after the early 1920s always provided a typewriter for every full-time secretary. Many smaller offices or departments which did not handle a large volume of letters nonetheless kept a typewriter or two on hand, even though the machines might be underutilized, because by the 1920s it was expected that business letters would be typed. The efficiency justification of the typewriter was thus only one factor determining typewriter usage. Because dictation equipment had not attained the status of standard office fixture, salesmen's pitches remained chained to arguments of the machine's greater efficiency versus longhand or stenography. Unlike typewriting, machine dictation never became an accepted practice in many offices, and since companies usually consumed the products of the dictation system within their own offices, there was less chance that a manager who chose to stick with longhand or stenography would be seen as unbusinesslike.[23] By 1945, after decades of marketing effort, Dictaphone estimated that only about 15 to 25 percent of the potential market for dictation equipment had been won.[24]

There were many reasons for this failure, some purely technical. Much resistance was rooted in the perceived shortcomings of the machines themselves, for despite some major improvements, wax-cylinder recording through the 1940s was difficult to master and often resulted in recordings that were virtually unintelligible. The recording process remained "acoustic" until the late 1930s, meaning that one had to shout down a somewhat ineffective "speaking tube" to cause the recording stylus to vibrate sufficiently. The distortion induced by this crude system, and the difficulty of holding the mouthpiece just close enough to the face while speaking at the correct speed and volume level aggravated the inherent problem of intelligibility. Transcribers frequently complained that they simply could not understand cylinder recordings, that the machines were difficult to operate, or that the ear tubes (later replaced by headphones or headsets) were uncomfortable and made it difficult to answer the telephone. Secretaries' machines saw many changes in design, but some of these objections simply could not be avoided. After years of development, the basic recording process still produced only marginally intelligible records. Even when Edison and Dictaphone added electronic amplifiers and modern microphones to their wax-cylinder machines in the late 1930s, intelligibility remained a problem.[25] A secretary who had worked for a prominent engineer in the early 1940s recalled that

> Sometimes before taking off on a trip, he went into the lab . . . and dictated gobs of material on the Ediphone. . . . He was a smoker in those days; and when he took a puff and exhaled, he'd turn his head away from the microphone of the machine. The exhaling sound combined with the turning away from the microphone frequently made it difficult to make out what he was saying.[26]

Wax-cylinder recording had some advantages over other recording methods. The use of a cylinder allowed the machines to record at a constant linear speed, eliminating the "slowdown" effect inherent in the inner grooves of a disk recording. Having a constant speed, in theory, diminished one of the sources of noise and distortion in a sound recording. With the cylinder, it was also easy to see where a recording had been made. Still, it was too crude and clunky for many users. Dictators had to receive training and practice in order to make a good recording, a requirement so off-putting to many that it seriously affected sales and relegated many desktop machines to an early retirement. Managers who inherited machines from their predecessors but did not receive training from the company representative often broke the machines inadvertently or got so frustrated that they abandoned them. Others found the ritual prescribed by dictation salesmen too complex and time-consuming. "You know how we have to hammer at some of these dictators to get them to use [it] correctly," an Ediphone salesman admitted in 1912.[27]

More difficult to address were nontechnical objections to the dictation machine. Businessmen who tried the equipment and rejected it reported that they got felt awkward or silly talking to a machine, or that when they checked their recordings, they found that they intensely disliked the sound of their own voices coming from the cylinders. Manufacturers, borrowing terminology from radio, called this phenomenon microphone fright; a potential user found that his mind "went blank" and he became anxious when the time came to record. Compounding this discomfort, users complained that the dictation machine was inherently incapable of thoughtful interaction with its user. If a dictator was hunting for the correct name or word, a human stenographer might be able to provide it, while a dictating machine could not.[28] Machine dictation's champions encouraged managers to change their habits in order to take advantage of the technology:

> Too many men in the executive echelons are dependent on the *personality* of the secretaries or stenographers to whom they dictate for a cold machine ever to replace the human presence. They are accustomed to secretarial thinking, memory, interpretive ability, understanding of the boss's peculiarities, correction of the boss's mistakes, filling in his omissions. [emphasis in original][29]

Curiously, secretaries are less often noted as being afraid of the machines. Probably this is due to the smaller body of evidence documenting their opinions of them, but it is also likely that secretaries had more familiarity with office machines when they were first hired. The influence of both the Dictaphone and the Edison companies reached the labor supply even before women workers took their first jobs. Edison as early as the 1930s began a major advertising campaign in the leading U.S. shorthand magazine, the *Gregg Writer*, and both Edison and Dictaphone launched aggressive campaigns to sell dictation equipment to vocational schools. The fact that women often had some exposure to dictation equipment by the time they became secretaries, and had learned to use the devices at a young age in the atmosphere of the classroom, may have reduced their technophobia as compared to managers, who were expected to teach themselves or learn from a sales demonstration.[30]

In response to the complaints of managers and secretaries, manufacturers argued that the machines could overcome some of the problems that managers encountered in dictating to a secretary or stenographer. The manager's primary business machine, the telephone, often interrupted a dictation session, forcing the stenographer to wait idly. Sales literature promised that the dictation machine would free a man from the limitations of a stenographer, allowing him to nail down an idea whenever it occurred to him. It did not grow impatient while dictators searched through notes and records for needed information, as supporters claimed that secretaries did. Nor did it take coffee breaks or leave the office at 5 P.M. There were also claims that machine dictation would cut down on frivolous socialization by keeping clerical workers at their stations.[31]

The Scientific Management movement's great booster, William H. Leffingwell, thought dictation equipment was a godsend that would prove to be a standard fixture in all offices. Many corporate executives eagerly employed machine stenography in their own work. More striking, however, is the list of famous writers, politicians, musicians, and others who became ardent fans of dictating devices. Mark Twain, for example, who had earlier been one of the first authors to adopt the typewriter, dictated some of his later works on an Edison recorder. Edgar Rice Burroughs lavished praises on his dictating machine, claiming it doubled his output. L. Ron Hubbard also adored his recorder, through which he "rolled out" his book *Dianetics* in "almost no time" in 1946. Melvin Kranzberg, a prominent historian and prolific letter writer, spoke volumes into his "dictaphone." Even the enemies of capitalism could be seduced by the charms of these labor-saving machines, as when Leon Trotsky dictated his biography of Stalin into an Ediphone while in exile in Mexico in the late 1930s. The list of writers who used dictation equipment is long indeed, suggesting that the machine offered a considerable boost to productivity, even outside the normal office context.[32]

FIGURE 22. Dozens of dictation machines in use in a large typing pool at the Sears, Roebuck and Company headquarters in the 1910s. Stereoscope card from the author's collection. Courtesy of the Sears, Roebuck and Co. Archives, Hoffman Estates, Illinois.

Dictation machines had few supporters among secretaries and typists.
Women clerical workers denounced dictation machines as a threat to their sten-
ographic skills, which were the basis of their claim to higher wages than other
office workers such as filing clerks. Part or all of a cylinder might be unintelligible. A typist was expected to listen patiently all the way through a recording before beginning to type, in order to be sure of the length and content of
a letter. The difference in letter length represented by just a few seconds of
recording might throw off the centering or spacing of the typed product. Early
machines took up a lot of space on a desk, or required a separate cart, and
because of their shape nothing could be stacked on them.[33]

Gender and Status in the Office

Like the typewriter, the dictation machine had an important role in mechanizing women's labor. The typewriter was initially rejected by office workers, at that time primarily men, who saw it as a threat to their skills. Edison and the National Phonograph Company, aware of this resistance, hoped to overcome it by promoting the idea that male stenographers could use the product to transcribe their own notes while they were still fresh. At that same time, Edison-sponsored publications like the *Phonogram* subtly suggested that the real way businessmen would profit from the phonograph was to displace skilled stenographers and hire phonograph operator/typists at lower wages. However, the first real boom in dictation equipment sales took place after male clerks had already been displaced by women.[34] There were, therefore, not significant sales when male stenographers dominated the profession, and women were not hired in order to complete the transition. The real conflict between labor and dictation equipment occurred later as women, already working in offices as stenographers, struggled to preserve their status as skilled workers.[35]

Ironically, office managers could in some instances present a new dictation equipment installation as an opportunity for women. Women employed solely as typists were common, and the acquisition of dictation machine operation skills sometimes resulted in upgrading. But more women affected by the dictation machine were employed as stenographers, stenographer/typists, or personal secretaries. These women rightly saw the installation of dictation equipment as an attempt to de-skill their jobs, and resisted its use as much as possible.

As low-ranking workers within organizations, most women had little choice but to accept the use of dictation equipment. In some businesses, dictation machines and typewriters were placed in the central typing pool, where women's labor was most highly subdivided, mechanized, and supervised. But companies acknowledged that few women preferred to work in the typing pools, so that typically they promoted good workers out of the pool and into private offices, where the volume of correspondence was lower and dictation equipment was less frequently present.[36] This created the impression that dictation equipment operation was a low-status skill that one needed to get a foot in the door, but which might soon be left behind. Accordingly, personal secretaries' disdain for the dictation machine was not only based on a fear of de-skilling, but also reflected their sense that they had a higher status than the women in the typing pool.

Such a low opinion of dictation equipment made it necessary for salesmen to pitch dictation machines to both the manager and the secretary, a task that could not easily be done with both parties in the same room. Pamphlets prepared for Dictaphone and Ediphone salesmen addressed men and women separately, and presented the case for machine dictation in very different terms. In particular, equipment manufacturers tried to convince secretaries that stenography was drudgery that took up too much of their time. With machine dictation, they would have more time to spend on important tasks. The Edison Company in the 1930s promised to make such liberated secretaries less like wage slaves and more like "junior executives." When addressing the men who made company-wide purchasing decisions, dictation machinery's promoters portrayed the machines as labor-saving devices capable of mechanizing work that was, in a literal sense, hand labor.[37]

Men's resistance to dictation machine technology also reflected gender relations and office politics. Many of the men whose jobs justified an expensive piece of equipment such as a dictation machine were at the middle or upper levels of management. But these same men frequently desired personal secretaries, not only because they needed them but because a personal assistant "went with the job," and was a status symbol, especially when the secretary was young, attractive, and single. The dictation machine had none of the attractions of such an "office mistress": neither a pretty sexual object to look at, nor the fantasy (or reality) of a romantic partner. The prospect of purchasing and using a dictation machine instead of having a secretary threatened one of the most visible signs of corporate success available to many men. Indeed, managers sometimes avoided putting a dictation machine on their desks at all merely because it suggested that they did not have a personal secretary. As a manager moved up the corporate ladder, the dictation machine was one of the things he left behind.[38]

Technological Change before 1945

The technology of office dictation would not change dramatically until the end of World War II. The Edison and Dictaphone systems reached a stable form in the 1910s that they would retain through the 1940s, even though competitors appeared to challenge the basic technology of the wax cylinder. Magnetic tape and wire recording, invented by Oberlin Smith in the 1870s, developed into a commercial product by Valdemar Poulsen around 1900, and first marketed in the United States between 1900 and 1915, posed a real threat to wax-cylinder recorders. Poulsen's system, embodied in the American

Telegraphone Company's wire recorder dictation network, employed a centralized recorder linked to the desks of dictators by satellite telephones. American business culture, seemingly addicted to the notion of efficiency through centralization and rationalization of operations, might have embraced these centralized dictation systems if American Telegraphone had been more effective in manufacturing, marketing, and servicing its products. While one customer, Dupont Corporation, did experiment with a telegraphone messaging system from 1913–1917, it abandoned it when the American Telegraphone Company failed to fulfill its obligation to provide replacements for worn-out machines. A handful of companies in Europe struggled through the 1920s and early 1930s to sell wire- or tape-based central dictation systems, but in the United States this technology temporarily vanished after about 1915. It would return after World War II and become an important competitor to desktop systems.[39]

Dictaphone and Ediphone competed almost unchallenged in the U.S. before 1945, and their corporate sponsors made little effort to change their products. One manifestation of this was the continued use of a wax-cylinder recording medium, which became an anachronism by the 1940s. The wax cylinder for home entertainment had been in decline even at the turn of the century, and wax recording was completely gone by about 1906, when the Edison Company introduced its last recording phonograph for the home market. Edison's company was virtually alone in supplying recorded cylinders for the entertainment market in the 1920s, and even these disappeared before 1930.[40] Only in dictation equipment did it survive nearly unchanged through the early 1950s, when Dictaphone and Ediphone finally stopped supplying them to customers. Through 1939, all Ediphones and Dictaphones used "acoustic" recording (essentially the same process used in Edison's original phonograph of 1878), and even after electronic versions arrived, older acoustic machines were still widely in use. Electronic vacuum-tube amplifiers added in 1939 came about two decades after amplifiers had appeared in radios. Electronics improved sound quality somewhat, but did not fundamentally change the technology of wax-cylinder recording, which had been pushed to its physical limits.[41]

Other companies were at work as early as the 1930s developing new types of dictation technologies that promised better recordings and more convenient operation. The Gray Manufacturing Company, a maker of telephone equipment, developed its "Audograph" around 1939, which used a thin vinyl disk and could record directly from the telephone if desired. Gray did not offer its product to the public until after 1945, because its successful bid for the

U.S. Navy's dictation equipment needs consumed its entire output. Another company, Soundscriber, also began selling vinyl disk-type dictation machines around 1940.[42] These companies would emerge in the postwar period as major competitors to Edison and Dictaphone.

Another important technology applied to postwar dictation was magnetic recording. Radiotechnic Laboratories, a Chicago manufacturer of magnetic wire recorders, offered a new office dictation unit after World War II that used advanced electronics and the new erasable medium. Magnetic wire recording had some important advantages for office dictation, particularly because mistakes could easily be erased and rerecorded, something not possible with other media. Radiotechnic, renamed the Peirce Wire Recorder Company by 1945, joined Gray and Soundscriber as competitors to the established oligarchy.[43]

Gray, Peirce, and several other entrants in the early 1940s revived some of the ideas pioneered by makers of centralized, magnetic recording systems of the period before 1920, such as the telegraphone. Because the new machines were electronic, one central recorder could be linked by wire to one or more users (dictators and transcribers) located in different parts of an office building. Centralized banks of such recorders could be the basis of large dictation systems linking dozens of offices with a typing pool or individual typists. Since dictators often used the machines for only a few minutes at a time, three or four of them could share a single recorder. Further cost reductions came through the use of telephones or desktop microphone controllers for access to the central dictation machines. These centralized systems, because they employed fewer recorders, promised lower first costs as well as reduced maintenance expenses. But the machines were unproven, and the cost savings could be negated if the system required a great deal of rewiring inside the office. They would nonetheless appeal to companies already familiar with dictation technology and convinced of the value of centralization. Although AT&T and the local telephone companies for some years prohibited the use of the same desk sets for dictation and telephone purposes, some central machines were accessible from relatively inexpensive desktop microphones or telephones. Dictaphone already had a product called the "Telecord," introduced in 1926, for telephone recording, and the company soon adapted it for central office dictation. Soon Edison was forced to fall in line. Central dictation systems became one of the fastest growing forms of office dictation in the postwar period.[44]

To counter the technological threat, Dictaphone and Edison quickly developed new recording technologies. Dictaphone invented a machine to record

POWER

...in the palm of your hand

The Dictaphone TIME-MASTER dictating machine now brings you *revolutionary finger tip power control* of dictation.*

Nestle the mike in the palm of your hand . . . speak in your usual voice . . . and you discover new-found power.

Power to get ideas across more quickly, more easily, with greater force.

Power to dispose of routine work swiftly . . . anywhere, any time.

Power to capture ideas instantly with mistake-proof clarity on *Dictabelt* records.

Power to write with the vigor and impact of living speech.

Power to make full use of *all* your ability and knowledge—not just a part of it.

* Simple and foolproof. Dictaphone's exclusive power controls respond to a touch of your thumb . . . for the most nearly automatic dictating possible. (Power Control model available at small extra cost.)

Mark Length of Letter—by pressing button "L."
Indicate Corrections—by pressing button "C."
Start and Stop—by pressing this bar.
Continuous Recording—press in and up to lock bar.
Automatic Playback—by pressing button "P."

For an illustrated booklet telling about this latest advance in electronic dictation, write Department H15, Dictaphone Corporation, 420 Lexington Avenue, New York 17, N. Y.

DICTAPHONE®
CORPORATION

DICTAPHONE, TIME-MASTER AND DICTABELT ARE REGISTERED TRADE-MARKS OF DICTAPHONE CORPORATION

Mention the National Geographic—It identifies you

FIGURE 23. Dictation equipment manufacturers tried to entice busy executives by promising a device that would enhance their efficiency. If there was any doubt as to whether the device benefited management or labor, this advertisement settled the issue. Author's collection.

on a thin plastic cylinder, usually called a belt, in 1940, although these machines were only available to government accounts until 1947. They were reintroduced to the public as the popular Time-Master series, and the medium named the Dictabelt. By 1952, 90 percent of Dictaphone's sales were Dictabelt machines. Edison was the last holdout in the wax-cylinder business in the early 1950s, but eventually introduced a vinyl disk recorder.[45]

Changing Economics of the Industry and the Challenge of Imports

Traditionally, dictation equipment was sturdier than the ordinary consumer phonograph. Its price was correspondingly much higher. From its introduction until about the 1950s, Dictaphone and Edison priced their machines to be competitive with an office typewriter. By 1945 the cost of a basic Dictaphone or "Voice Writer" was over $300, compared to less than $20 for the average home phonograph. The emergence of a fast-growing market for low-cost, less-complex dictation machines caught U.S. manufacturers completely off guard. The pioneering products were the consumer wire recorders manufactured by companies such as Webster-Chicago, a maker of phonographs and radios. The "Webcor" and similar machines sacrificed heavy-duty designs, fast operation, and some other features, but the machines sold for only $150. These machines appealed to individuals who would otherwise not have bought any dictation equipment because of the cost. Typically a single unit was used for both dictation and transcription, making the wire recorder significantly less expensive than the three-unit wax-cylinder system. Some manufacturers also marketed the wire recorder for home entertainment, but these were much less popular than the dictation versions. This product was available for only a few years, from 1945 to about 1955, and peak sales of about 20,000 units per year lasted about two years (from 1947 to 1948), after which another innovation, the tape recorder, displaced the wire recorder.

Another surprisingly aspect of the low-cost dictation machine market was its domination by foreign firms. In 1955, the German manufacturer Grundig struck a deal with a Long Island-based camera distributor to market its "Stenorette" dictation machines. The Stenorette utilized the new technology of magnetic tape, employing a standard, inexpensive, quarter-inch-wide tape. The machine was compact, very well made, and could match the performance of any American desktop dictation system in almost every category. It lacked the long-term reliability of the Dictaphone or Ediphone, but many potential users did not require such ruggedness. It also lacked some of the features of the American products, particularly since it was a combined dictator/transcriber. But this was less important to potential customers than the fact that it cost about half as much as its competition, and, like the wire recorder, it appealed to individuals who otherwise would not purchase dictation equipment. Within a few years, the Stenorette had expanded the U.S. market for dictation equipment by 25 percent, although this expansion did not take away many sales from Dictaphone, Ediphone, Gray, Soundscriber, or the other manufacturers of traditional office dictation machines.

New technologies of the postwar period overcame one of the most pressing technical problems, that of intelligibility and ease of recording. Users found it easy to get consistently good sound quality using the new belt and disk media, and in particular magnetic media. However, the appearance of over a dozen new types of dictation machines created a new problem, that of media compatibility. Whereas only cylinders had been available before 1945, in the 1950s and 1960s manufacturers developed machines to record phonographically on disks and plastic belts, as well as magnetically on wires, belts, cards, grooved disks, smooth disks, and various widths of tapes. Two manufacturers even recorded onto a wide roll of magnetically coated paper, which the dictator tore off at the end of a recording session and fed into the transcriber's machine. Large buyers of equipment had to pick one technology over another or face the problems of noncompatibility between the typing pool and individual dictators. The fact that some companies offered machines in two or more formats reinforced the widespread feeling that office dictation had to achieve some standard, and this seemed to slow the growth of sales.

Dictation Moves out of the Office

A new technology for portable dictation applications provided the unexpected answer to the media compatibility problem. In the late 1950s, several companies, mostly European, had entered the field, including the Philips Company of Eindhoven, Holland. In 1958 Philips introduced a portable, tape-cartridge dictation machine with a low price and a minimum of features but with high-quality construction. Philips' positive experience selling this inexpensive dictation machine in the U.S. encouraged the company to develop an even smaller, simpler, and less expensive cartridge, known as the Compact Cassette, in 1962. The Compact Cassette would come to have great significance in the entertainment field, because it was the basis of today's audio cassette. But in dictation it signaled the appearance of a market for portable business recorders. Not only was the technology of dictation changing, but it was moving out of the office.

This explosion in sales of portable dictation equipment was yet another surprise to the American companies making traditional office dictation systems. Dictation for businessmen on the road had always been a difficult proposition, although regional sales offices tried to encourage it. In 1926, Sir Edward Lund traveled across Europe, North America, and Asia, recording his impressions on a Dictaphone office recorder. His plans had to be carefully coordinated with local representatives of Dictaphone, who set up machines for him in his hotel rooms. Lund's use of dictation equipment on the road probably cost Dictaphone plenty, but he rewarded them by titling the resulting memoir *Round the World with a Dictaphone.* Both Dictaphone and Ediphone operated such hotel services in the U.S., where local sales offices maintained equipment for patrons of the larger hotels. Years later, Dictaphone also struck a deal with American airlines to make small Dictabelt machines available in-flight. But portable dictation equipment was only rarely used before the late 1940s.[46] Technical obstacles to portable dictation abounded, and among the most important was the bulk of the machines and the batteries necessary to operate them. But operationally, traditional dictation made little sense outside the context of the rest of the system where cylinders could be transported to typists easily and turned into correspondence promptly.

After 1945 that situation was changing. With the advent of tape recording and transistor electronics, miniaturized voice recorders became possible. Some of the customers for portable recorders came from the ranks of the upper-level managers and executives who already used dictation in the office. With the geographic dispersion of plants and offices and the emergence of reliable air travel, upper-level managers and executives were away from their offices and their office machines more than ever before. The new machines supplemented the recorders that current dictation equipment customers had in the office, and there was some indication that new customers were attracted to the equipment as well.

With the increase in business travel in the 1950s and early 1960s, executives turned increasingly to these dictation machines as a way to conduct business on the road. The machines they chose were not simply portable versions of office equipment. Instead, they were typically small, lightweight tape recorders sold by companies such as the Mohawk Business Machines Corporation of New York. But the portables offered by established companies were frequently incompatible with the recording media of existing

ELECTRONIC WONDER!

Amazing New Dictaphone TIME-MASTER records on plastic belt!

The electronic TIME-MASTER is the neatest, most compact dictating machine that ever took a letter or trapped a thought!

And you can mail that voice letter as easily as you can any business correspondence. For the TIME-MASTER records on a small plastic Memobelt—just the right size for your business envelope!

Twelve plastic belts—or three hours of dictation —will fit into your billfold. Hand them to your secretary for the easiest transcriptions she ever made.

DICTAPHONE
Electronic Dictation

Only Dictaphone Corporation makes Dictaphone* Machines.
(*Reg. U. S. Pat. Off.)

Yes, this new dictating development means greater convenience in *every* way for you and your secretary. Nothing can match the TIME-MASTER for *all* dictation—in your office or home and on trips. Its recording is *outstandingly* clear and transcribable.

That's because the famous Dictaphone principle of *cylindrical* recording still applies. The Memobelt is the *only* plastic dictating medium that assures *both* uniform tonal clarity and quality from beginning to end.

No other dictating machine has *all* these advantages: Lightweight, all-metal construction, easily mailable and fileable plastic belt recordings, voice-perfect recording, constant groove speed, uniform backspacing, rapid place-finding! Every facility for easier dictating and transcribing—*plus* famed Dictaphone dependability!

FOR A DEMONSTRATION of the revolutionary new TIME-MASTER model, call your local Dictaphone representative or fill in the coupon below.

Dictaphone Corporation
Department B-5, 420 Lexington Ave., N. Y. C.
☐ Please show me the new TIME-MASTER.
☐ Please send TIME-MASTER literature.

Your Name_____

Company_____

Street Address_____

City & Zone_____State_____

FIGURE 24. Post-1945 marketing strategies emphasized the convenience and advanced technology of the new machines. Dictaphone replaced its aged line of wax-cylinder machines in 1947 with equipment that recorded on a thin plastic belt. Author's collection.

FIGURE 25. The Peirce wire recorder was one of the first challengers to the established technology of phonograph recording. Paul V. Galvin Library, Illinois Institute of Technology.

office systems. Dictaphone's most popular portable was its tiny "Dictet," a three-pound tape recorder with a cassette-like tape medium that could not be played back on any Dictaphone office transcriber. Dictaphone's "Travel-Master" Dictabelt portable of 1962 had recording media that could be transcribed on an office machine, but most others were incompatible, and this sharply limited their utility.[47]

The greater use of portables and the glamour of the miniaturized machines hinted that attitudes toward dictation equipment might be changing. The association of the portable recorder and the executive, for example, was readily apparent in advertising of the day. During the 1950s the miniaturized dictation machine was, at least in ads, transcending the boundaries of sheer utility and becoming a symbol of corporate status, comparable to the cellular telephone today. Advertisements for airlines, luxury cars, office furniture, and other items began to portray successful businessmen using miniature dictation machines in autos, airplanes, or on job sites. These ads reflected that fact that more and more businessmen were seen in public with these machines, but they also provided models for real businessmen to emulate. In contrast to the desktop dictation machine's stigma as a mark of low rank, the portable seemed to be emerging as a symbol of achievment.

Certain portables had quite a measure of success, including the Mohawk Midgetape, the Dictaphone Travel-Master series, the IBM Executary introduced in 1960, and the Minifon, a German import sold through the middle 1960s which was probably the last wire recorder available on the market.[48] But for several years no company could fulfill the opportunity offered by the growth in the portables market by overcoming the problem of media compatibility with office machines. Dictaphone, Edison, Gray, and Soundscriber, the four largest U.S. companies, were at a particular disadvantage because their office machines all used variations of phonograph recording, which required more power than magnetic recording and made the battery life of miniaturized portables short. The American firms for many years struggled to adapt phonograph recording to the new demands, with limited success. Even in the early 1960s it appeared that all would have to adopt some form of magnetic medium, probably the same medium for both office and portable machines.

Only after 1962, when Philips introduced the cassette tape recorder, did the industry begin to move toward portable/office compatibility. Yet the cassette's success in dictation could not have been easily predicted. Several other companies introduced small, convenient tape cartridges in the late 1960s and 1970s, such as Dictaphone, Westinghouse Grundig, and Stuzzi, an Austrian firm. Further, Philips already had a cartridge tape dictation system on the market, and the cassette was intended to be a general purpose audio tape technology, not necessarily a dictation technology. At least a part of the explanation for the cassette's success is economic; its rise in the late 1960s as a consumer tape medium lowered the cost of recorders and tapes considerably. The original Philips/Norelco consumer cassette recorder cost about eighty dollars, but within a few years the cheapest cassette recorders could be had for under thirty dollars. Tapes that initially cost under two dollars soon dropped as low as seventy-five cents. Convergence on the cassette was also partly the result of the consolidation of the industry under new ownership which was less committed to the traditional media. By 1970, the Lanier Corporation of Atlanta had purchased the dictation divisions of Edison, Gray, Soundscriber, and Nye, the latter a maker of a centralized system. By working with a Japanese manufacturer, Lanier introduced the Edisette, the first widely available office dictation transcriber based on the Philips cassette. It was not an inexpensive machine but was an office-quality recorder competitive in price with comparable products using other media. These cassette-based machines were instantly compatible with the wide range of office and consumer dictation machines, particularly the tiny, handheld cassette recorders marketed by Sony and other Japanese firms. Along with microcassette transcribers offered by several other companies in later years, the cassette dictation machine virtually monopolized the stand-alone dictation market by mid-decade. Companies with other media standards had virtually disappeared by 1980.

While the cassette has remained the basis of stand-alone dictation products, its adoption did not correspond to the universal acceptance of office dictation as a way of doing business. Expanding markets for office dictation by the 1980s were almost certainly a product of other developments in technology and business operations. Stemming from the office automation movement that began in the 1950s, the labor of the corporate elite fell under closer scrutiny. Managerial labor had been virtually untouched by the office mechanization movement of the early twentieth century, as productivity measures applied to management's own labor usually entailed organization and changes in personal habits, not mechanization. A new wave of managerial reform in the 1960s was reflected in some management textbooks and self-help guides, which admonished their readers for continuing to resist the automation of one of their most basic tasks: correspondence. Particularly as computers began to revolutionize office procedures in the 1960s, even upper-level managers felt pressure to change their habits. Many technical objections to dictation machines no longer rang true in the age of the cassette, yet managers still seemed to prefer a live stenographer. In one 1970 management guide, *The Turned-On Executive,* the authors posed the question directly: "Girl or Machine?"[49] The book concluded that each had certain advantages. However, before the question could be settled, a new generation of office technologies would undermine the arguments for keeping either the girl or the machine.

The End of the Office Dictation Machine

The drive to automate business letter writing had its greatest champion in the 1960s in the IBM Corporation. The computer company entered the dictation field in 1960 with the purchase of Peirce Wire Recorder Company of Chicago. Peirce had managed to wrest about 15 percent of the U.S. market from Dictaphone and Edison in the 1950s on the basis of the quality of its equipment and some aggressive selling. Company founder Charles Peirce saw the end in sight for wire recording, which had disadvantages as compared to the disks or belts used by others. A wire made better recordings than a wax cylinder or a vinyl disk or belt, and could be easily erased and reused, but it took too long to access any particular passage on the wire. The wire was also easily tangled and broken, making the machines too untrustworthy. Peirce in the early 1950s set his engineers to work on a new magnetic recorder using a wide plastic belt. It was this product that became the basis of IBM's first dictation line.

IBM's aggressive sales and service organization quickly captured nearly half the total U.S. market, cutting deeply into Ediphone sales (Edison sold the division in 1970) and nearly wiping out Gray and Soundscriber. Its popular miniaturized Executary portable even had a medium that was compatible with office transcribers. Virtually the only companies unaffected by IBM's ascendance were the European firms, now joined by several in Japan, selling "low-end" personal dictation products. IBM's marketing people encountered the familiar managerial resistance to dictation equipment. Sam Kalow, an IBM sales manager who came into the firm from Peirce, actually had to start his selling campaign within the company's sales organization, for few IBM managers seemed willing to use the company's own products. But company president Thomas Watson Jr. was a long-time dictation equipment enthusiast, and with his support Kalow began changing the internal culture of the organization. Through the efforts of the company's substantial Office Products Division sales force, IBM soon found itself leading the industry.[50]

By the late 1970s, IBM, along with Dictaphone, Sony, Lanier, and others, were working on the integration of the dictation machine and the typewriter. By this time, IBM had introduced an early form of word processing machine, the magnetic card "Selectric," a semiautomatic, correctable version of its famous Selectric typewriter. IBM's magnetic card Selectric and competing word processing typewriters could act as correctable electric typewriters, or could rapidly print form letters, pausing only for input (such as an address) from a typist. Information could be stored on a medium the size and shape of an IBM punched card, but coated with magnetic oxide. IBM's management and engineers believed that the next step would be to use a dictation machine as the input to the typewriter, perhaps using electronic voice recognition.[51]

This development program encountered many obstacles. Engineers never achieved a completely satisfactory voice recognition program, for example. But even the effort to link electronically the new generation of word processing typewriters with dictation equipment failed to go smoothly. IBM's market share in dictation equipment was slipping in the late 1970s and early 1980s due to the failure of an ambitious new line of noncomputerized desktop dictation equipment and flagging interest within the company. Promoters of the new line were criticized within the company for their choice of a magnetic disk-type medium instead of tape, a decision apparently based on the superficial resemblance of dictation disks to computer disks. While the rest of the industry was moving toward the standardization of the cassette for both portable and desktop machines, IBM's managers chose to develop this entirely new format, believing that it would be more compact and convenient. Sam Kalow, who had built up the division in its early years, had now moved on to another position.

IBM's own Watson Research Center had undertaken studies that seemed to show no sizable increase in the efficiency of conventional machine dictation versus speaking (to a stenographer) or even longhand. Large differences in letter-writing speed had more to do with compositional skills, intellectual processes that were obviously not addressed by dictation equipment at all. What also emerged from these studies was a revelation that while almost anyone could be trained to use a dictation machine well, a small fraction of people found it exceptionally useful. They were "verbal" thinkers who could articulate their thoughts verbally as easily as they could write or type them. This, IBM's scientists realized, was part of the reason why some people took an immediate liking to dictation equipment and used it heavily, but others found it repellent. From that time on, Sam Kalow recalled, he "never pushed dictation within the company."[52]

In the late 1980s, with the explosion in computer technology, the market for dictation equipment radically changed. Traditional markets for desktop machines faded away, leaving only the centralized systems that had competed with desktop machines for eight decades. However, these central systems employed digital technologies to link telephones, switching systems, and a personal computer. Messages were recorded in digital form on the computer's hard disk and could be accessed remotely by the transcriber. Such systems completely changed the economics of office dictation systems by making it possible for everyone in an office to access a single machine that was part of the existing telephone network. No longer necessary were stand-alone desktop units or the special wiring, microphones, and other hardware associated with older centralized systems.

The personal computer displaced the desktop machine for another large market segment. Those who previously had generated relatively low volumes of correspondence often took to keying in their own letters on a personal computer. More and more managers knew touch typing, and even without this skill many found that word processing programs could make up for a lack of typing proficiency. Field agents and other customers for miniaturized portables turned increasingly to laptop computers. High-volume letter writers had other options. For many managers and secretaries, the use of personal computers and high-speed printers replaced many of the older tasks involved in routine correspondence. While managers remained managers and secretaries remained secretaries, the power and gender issues related to correspondence disappeared or changed radically.

Particular dictation equipment markets remained, though increasingly customers turned to the new centralized systems, often in conjunction with new technologies like voice recognition software, which steadily improved during the 1980s. The persistence of these markets may be linked to the fact that in some organizations the relationships between high- and low-ranking employees and the uses of sound recording equipment were different than those in the typical business. Hospitals, for example, had been one of the most important customers for dictation systems for decades, and after 1945 invested heavily in centralized dictation systems. However, the use of dictation in hospitals was remarkably different than that in offices. High-status employees such as surgeons were obligated to file many routine reports per day. These reports, because they involved a patient's health, had to be completed by the doctors themselves, and thus stenographers were rarely required. Doctors, sometimes fresh out of surgery, preferred to dictate reports via a centralized system immediately after treating their patients. This activity had never engaged the traditional boss-secretary relationship, and thus did not involve the same issues of status and gender. Nor did the technology seem to generate "mike fright" or the other anxieties that had led to resistance among business users. The information transmitted was of a technical nature, the result of a scientific rather than a primarily creative thought process. Women using the machines had never acted as stenographers to these doctors and were not threatened by it. Doctors welcomed dictation technology as a way to lessen the burden of a task that they were required to complete themselves. Often, they did not know or even see the typists who prepared the reports; sometimes the typists did not even work in the same building. It is this environment in which office dictation continues to thrive. However, after over a century of existence as a desktop device, the familiar dictation machine had virtually disappeared by 1990, replaced by computer software or merged into multifunction office communications systems.[53]

Conclusions

The American business office of the period from 1900 to 1990 was not an ideal environment to establish and maintain the practice of sound recording. The use of recorders with the desires and prerogatives of office workers. Though the dictation machine enjoyed a significant measure of commercial success during its long history, this triumph was minor compared to that of the typewriter, the telephone, or the word processor. The practice of office recording in many business situations simply did not persist over time in the manner of other office appliance usage. In most companies, promoters of dictation equipment had to begin their selling efforts all over with every turnover in management to keep existing machines operating and ensure sales of new ones. Promoters of office dictation machines, either within businesses or as representatives of equipment manufacturers, faced both technical and social obstacles. While the technology of office dictation gradually made it easier to use, the nontechnical obstacles remained.

Machine dictation had (and still has) greatest acceptance where it appeals to the personal preferences of individual managers, or where the task of recording is most rigidly defined, as in hospitals. Men who filled large portions of their days by composing a few standardized types of letters also found the dictation machine an acceptable labor-saving device and tended to use it. It is true, though, that often these men were virtually compelled to use the machines by their own bosses, so it is difficult to know if they truly preferred the machine or merely tolerated it.

Electronics and tape recording overcame most of the technical problems of making of recordings by the 1950s, but these improvements did not lead to the universal application of dictation technology. One reason is that better desktop technology, low-cost portables, and improved centralized systems arrived too late. Even in the early 1960s, the first generation of office automation technologies was in place. Additionally, the new technologies eliminated the work involved in the simplest correspondence tasks, undermining the core market for office dictation.

Even where the practice of using dictation equipment survived, it failed to spread. Early in the century, this could have been attributed to dictation's failure to attain the status of a "standard business procedure." Because the products of dictation systems, the cylinders, disks, tapes, or belts, remained inside the office, firms felt less pressure to use dictation equipment than technologies such as the telephone or typewriter, which connected the corporation to the outside world and signaled "professionalism." Offices adopted the telephone and typewriter in part because outsiders came to expect them, but the impetus to buy and use dictation equipment was purely internal. Its use throughout a single firm therefore depended heavily on the culture within that company rather than on the desire to imitate other organizations. Only in a few cases did most firms in particular industries, such as insurance or hospitals, widely adopt dictation equipment. Even so it was often the case that many individuals still did not use the dictation equipment their employers purchased for them and felt little pressure to do so.

One of the incidental reasons why telephone-accessible designs proved appealing to some businesses is that their use could be easily reassigned to new employees. Desktop machines could be picked up and moved in and out of offices, corresponding to the occupant's willingness to use them. But often, with employee turnover in an organization, the new occupant of an office saw no need to use the dictating equipment he inherited from his predecessor. Such idiosyncratic utilization of the available technology was not the pattern with more successful machines such as the typewriter or computer.

A varied and interesting response to machine dictation came from mid- and high-level managers and their secretaries. Managers and executives had, as IBM put it, "discretion to choose among a variety of alternatives."[54] Some of these men were infatuated with the machine and used it constantly, but more of them resisted salesmen's efforts or let the machines their companies bought for them gather dust in a desk drawer. From the perspective of secretaries, the dictation machine was a "speed up," an attempt at de-skilling and a threat to hard-won privilege. Women's resistance to it was an effort to preserve the skill of stenography and the social networks available to stenographers. The use of the dictation machine also represented low status both for women and men, because it was associated with low-level, unimportant work. For many, a dictation machine on the desk signified that one had not yet "made it." Even the act of recording proved intractably unpopular, because of factors such as mike fright. Contradicting the usual assumption that men are technophiles, advertisements for dictation machines sometimes portrayed male resistance in ways that made the managers and executives of America's largest corporations look like cowards when faced with a recording device. Underlying the general distaste for self-recording, according to IBM's social scientists, was the fact that dictation equipment could not automate the most important part of letter writing; the intellectual process of composition itself. Thus the more original or complex the letter to be written, the less helpful the dictation machine would be. However, new technologies such as the word processor were far more damaging to the dictation machine's career than IBM's findings, taking over simple letter writing or giving managers an easier way to type letters and reports themselves.

For these reasons the dictation machine's history holds much insight into our understanding of how and why Americans came to use or reject the use of sound recorders generally. Gender, status, and psychology were powerful forces, but in this case so was the relentless drive for "efficiency" in the office. As a business machine, dictation equipment was not a consumer technology in the normal sense of the word. Yet in the final analysis, it was the collective choices of consumers which made the difference in dictation equipment's commercial success. So many people had the power to decide for themselves that their negative decisions overcame corporate imperatives. Ultimately, technology did revolutionize the process of creating correspondence and paperwork, but it was not the technology of sound recording. The history of office dictation also highlights the fact that sound recording technology is not simply a means of mass communication, as it is in the record industry and radio broadcasting. As a dictation machine, sound recording also became a form of interpersonal communication, one with a unique cultural importance. Where it was used, the dictation machine complemented or transformed other forms of communication, such as the business letter and the typewriter. This suggests that there are other cases in which recording played into the history of interpersonal communication, and indeed there are many.

CHAPTER 4

The Message on the Answering Machine

RECORDING AND INTERPERSONAL COMMUNICATION

The telephone answering machine is one of numerous communication devices that has permeated American life in the last two decades. Along with the cassette tape recorder, answering machines are the most widely used of all sound recording technologies. Whether Americans find them to be a convenience (perhaps even a necessity) or an annoyance, they cannot help but come into regular contact with them. Answering machine users may value their machines, but they do not often place permanent value on the recordings they create, which are typically soon erased and forgotten. Yet the use of telephone recording devices on such a regular basis is significant in our society, constituting an important adjunct to the telephone system and perhaps even a new form of communication.

Although most Americans recorded their first telephone messages only after 1980, the equipment to do so has been available for a century. The ownership and use of answering machines was a hotly contested issue at the turn of the century. Today's answering machine reflects a long history of struggle among corporations and consumers to define this technology and the ways people use it. Because the answering machine is not a general purpose sound recorder but a specialized *telephone* recorder, its development necessarily took place in the context of the American telephone system. In the United States, telephone service was dominated for many decades by the looming presence of American Telephone and Telegraph Company. For most of its history, then, the technical evolution, manufacture, distribution, and even use of the answering machine was dependent upon the actions of AT&T personnel.

Although in more recent years the telephone answering machine's commercial success depended on widespread consumer acceptance, for much of its early history it was not something that consumers could simply buy, bring home, and use. Like the ordinary telephone sets that AT&T customers used in their homes, the answering machine was the property of the Bell System, its use contingent upon the good behavior of the customer, and the company could deny its use quite arbitrarily.

AT&T became so concerned about the possibility of the answering machine coming into widespread use that it virtually banned the technology. Thus one of the most remarkable aspects of answering machine history is the explanation of how such a seemingly innocuous device as a telephone answering machine could generate so much distrust among AT&T's policy makers. Interestingly, the controversial nature of the device preceded its first use in the Bell System. Even in 1930, before the first answering machines were in production, they were the focus of a vigorous internal debate at AT&T over which telephone customers would be allowed access to it and how they should use it. Inventors, corporations, consumers, and other groups also had a stake in determining the design of the technology, and all played a role its commercial fortunes. These same groups, often in subtle ways, tried to redefine what would, could, or should be communicated through the answering machine, sometimes in opposition to the telephone company. While the telephone company arguably was a powerful force in this debate, all these groups had to reach a compromise before the technology would succeed. In the last two decades, as AT&T has relinquished its monopoly on long-distance service and cut loose its local operating companies, telephone machines have become quite popular, and consumers have taken over the dominant role in determining the course of the answering machine's commercial development. In particular, Americans have invented their own set of practices associated with answering machine use, a process that continues today. These practices have often ignored the boundaries for answering machine usage set by telephone companies and manufacturers. Consumers, unfettered by corporate restrictions, have been adept at redirecting the technology to their own ends, some utilitarian, some playful.

The American Telegraphone Company

Representatives of Valdemar Poulsen, the Dane who invented the first viable telephone recorder, traveled to America in 1901 in an attempt to attract investors, but to little avail.[1] The machine they brought with them, called the telegraphone, operated somewhat like today's answering machines in that it used a magnetizable medium (steel wire) to record messages and an electric circuit to detect an incoming call and put the machine in motion. The main difference was the lack of an "outgoing" message. When the Danes later drew the attention of the American Bell Company as a potential investor, success seemed near, but the deal fell apart when Bell suddenly withdrew. Finally by 1903 an American succeeded in attracting a new group of investors and formed the American Telegraphone Company in the District of Columbia, uncapitalized as yet, but in possession of the American rights to Poulsen's inventions.[2]

While the company geared up to produce the telephone recorder, it did not fill any significant orders until 1912. In the meantime, a new director had moved production from its original location in Wheeling, West Virginia, to Springfield, Massachusetts, and set up the Telegraphone Sales Company, with offices in Washington, Boston, Chicago, Philadelphia, and New York.[3] The new production facility occupied some 75,000 square feet, and the company announced in 1910 that "the machines are about to go on the market in large quantities."[4] But the firm, probably for lack of good management, never got the factory into full production, and lapsed into bankruptcy by 1915. In the interim, however, American Telegraphone sold enough telegraphones in the United States to make a lasting impression on potential users or buyers of telephone answering devices.

Weaving Telephone Recording into the Telephone System

Emile Berliner, the famous inventor of the disk gramophone, rejected the telephone recorder as an outlandish proposition, claiming in 1900 that "There is practically no demand for a recording attachment to telephones."[5] But others weren't put off so easily. American Telegraphone's leaders believed that the communications network being created by AT&T could simply absorb the technologies associated with telephone recording. However, the company's efforts to effect this conflicted with AT&T's internal program of national telephone standardization. Today, ordinary consumers can use the telephone system for a variety of things besides voice communication (such as fax and the Internet), but AT&T's policies before the 1960s were aimed at limiting rather than expanding the consumer uses for the telephone system. The company was struggling at the turn of the century to integrate the technologies of a diverse group of local operating companies using different brands and designs of switchboards, telephones sets, and other equipment, and AT&T had little interest in allowing unfamiliar new devices to be attached to this system. The sale of telephones and related equipment was also a lucrative business for AT&T's subsidiary Western Electric, and AT&T

FIGURE 26. The telegraphone in use as a telephone recorder around 1910. American Technical Publishers, Inc.

strongly encouraged local companies to purchase Western Electric equipment rather than anything made by outside suppliers like American Telegraphone. Outside manufacturers sometimes acted as Western Electric's subcontractors or sold their own designs to local companies, but in most cases AT&T referred to all non-Western Electric equipment in a pejorative tone as "foreign attachments."

Nonetheless, AT&T engineers and executives flirted with the idea of bringing the telegraphone into the company's technical stable as early as 1900, but ultimately declined to buy the rights to the Poulsen patents. AT&T did purchase several telegraphones between 1900 and 1910, using them for testing and evaluation purposes.[6] Frank Jewett, the Western Electric engineer who would soon head AT&T's Bell Telephone Laboratories, remarked that "the telegraphone is, from a physical standpoint, so striking in its method of operation, that it is difficult to convince one's self that it has not important possibilities."[7] Jewett was not alone in his cautious praise—Hammond Hayes, an AT&T engineer who produced an extensive report on the telegraphone in 1901 and who more lavishly complimented its performance, still could not wholeheartedly recommend that the corporation attempt to exploit the invention. Sound recording, he felt, could be usefully employed in voice communication in many ways, but it did not fit well into the corporate plan.

Some engineers suggested, for example, that by using a telegraphone customers might save considerable money on long-distance calls. The calls could be recorded, transmitted at high speed, and returned to the normal speed at the receiving end. Yet this was not technically feasible before World War I—without any electronic signal amplification, the telegraphone could not adequately record the weak currents of a long-distance transmission.[8]

After the turn of the century, as the use of the telephone continued to spread, new proposals and patents for telephone recorders continued to appear.[9] Even at this early date, businessmen (who constituted a major group of telephone users) dearly wanted to find a way to respond to telephone calls without having to tend the device constantly. Many of them had telephones installed in their homes, for example, but did not want to be constantly interrupted and could not justify the expense of a secretary to answer them. Owners of small businesses such as pharmacies or stores appreciated the additional business a telephone brought in but feared that failing to answer it would anger customers. Doctors, many of whom were the first in their communities to purchase telephone service, found it both a blessing and a curse because of the attention it required.

Thus it was not too surprising that other mechanical telephone answering devices had appeared even at the turn of the century. Edison, in fact, announced the possibility of telephone recording and reproduction even before demonstrating a practical tinfoil phonograph in the 1877, predicting that it would be done on strips of wax-coated paper. When telephone recording proved to be more difficult than he anticipated, Edison turned to an acoustic recording process, and the result was the familiar tinfoil phonograph rather than the answering machine. However, his continued experiments led to a crude electro-mechanical telephone recording device, called the Telescribe, by 1914. He had his publicity experts write press releases and print up promotional pamphlets for the Telescribe, although the device itself was still technically immature. Such a device, he thought, would be just the thing for businessmen who did not want to miss their calls. But unfortunately for Edison, he was not able to make the Telescribe work very well, and eventually withdrew it from the market.[10]

The Perceived Threat of Telephone Recording

After 1900, AT&T usually discouraged inventors who came to the company with new telephone answering machines, and while the company rejected American Telegraphone's proposals to sell telegraphones to telephone customers, it nonetheless took the technology on which it was based, magnetic recording, under its wing after Poulsen's patents expired in the 1920s. Sound recording in the late 1920s became one of the major research programs of the new Bell Telephone Laboratories, the recently created industrial laboratory for the company. With the huge resources of AT&T available, engineers were able to make many improvements to Poulsen's machine and investigate the physical basis of the magnetic recording process.

Bringing the telegraphone into Bell Laboratories, a self-contained "invention factory" with its own financial resources, technical expertise, and captive markets for its products, was the first step in controlling public access to telephone recording and to redefining it to suit corporate needs. In 1900, when the telegraphone first appeared, individual inventors and promoters presented it to the public via the technical press and encouraged the public to imagine the possibilities for this new invention. Over the course of fifteen years, promoters of the telegraphone demonstrated it in numerous public venues, beginning with the 1900 Paris Exposition and continuing to the 1915 Panama-Pacific Exposition in San Francisco. During that same time, articles, editorials, and letters about the various telegraphone models appeared in newspapers, popular magazines, and scientific journals in the United States and Europe. No less than seventy-five such articles appeared between 1899 and 1915, and descriptions of the telegraphone continued to appear in radio and telephone textbooks into the 1930s, despite the fact that the machine's sponsor, American Telegraphone Company, was effectively defunct after World War I.

After 1930, this public forum disappeared, and the answering machine's promoters were replaced by corporate engineers working within AT&T, speaking mainly to each other. Inventions made at Bell Laboratories, while not necessarily hidden from the public, were not subject to the same public exposure as those made by independent inventors or smaller companies. Most of the products of the laboratories were transferred to an AT&T subsidiary, Western Electric Company, for manufacture. Further, the primary market for Western Electric equipment was the local Bell Telephone operating companies. With such an internal market already established, there was less incentive to publicize Bell Labs' innovations to the same degree as companies looking for investors or new customers. The telephone company's own technical and scientific publications, the *Bell System Technical Journal* and the *Bell Laboratories Record,* carried only five articles on tape recording between 1933 and 1948. As a result, magnetic recording technology, upon which the telegraphone was based, was virtually forgotten by other engineers and members of the general public. The transition from being a technology in the public's eye to being an obscure project within a single company was important, because it gave AT&T the opportunity to reshape the concept of the telephone recorder to suit its own goals, free from the demands of the market and beyond the reach of public input and criticism.[11]

AT&T took a stronger interest in the telegraphone after 1930 because of the belief among its top management that it was of considerable importance to the company. They believed that it was a breakthrough in a technical sense, but that its unrestrained use might decimate the telephone business. The main objection within AT&T to the telephone recorder was the fact that it threatened the privacy of calling. Executives knew from experience that many people relished the idea of listening in on others' conversations but at the same time hated the idea that they themselves might be the subjects of eavesdropping. Wiretapping, listening in on party lines, and even eavesdropping by AT&T's own telephone operators were all serious problems that undermined the public's trust in the telephone system.

To AT&T, the sound recorder was a dangerous weapon in the hands of unscrupulous members of the public. The making of secret recordings (whether from the telephone or not) without the knowledge of the person being recorded had a notorious history that dated from the earliest years of the phonograph. Turn-of-the-century magazines and newspapers were replete with tales of the phonograph being used surreptitiously to capture the words—and usually the embarrassing or incriminating words—of the unsuspecting villain, adulterer, or rube. But there are more documented examples of ordinary telephone eavesdropping than of the making secret recordings from the telephone, simply because the phonograph was not sensitive enough or small enough to be used discretely. While the talking machine could repeat the intonations of those who directed a loud voice into the recording horn, it was unlikely that someone shouting down a horn would have no idea that they were being recorded. So despite all the apocryphal tales of phonographs deviously hidden under furniture at parties, anyone familiar with the machine knew that only a concerted vocal effort directed at recording horn or speaking tube could produce an intelligible phonograph record. Making a phonograph recording of a telephone conversation was even more difficult, since the sound from a telephone was so faint.

Though the phonograph posed no real threat to AT&T or to telephone privacy, the telegraphone certainly did. Because it could record directly from telephone lines, its presence could easily be concealed by locating the recorder out of sight of a telephone user. It was sensitive enough to record the faint impulses of a telephonic transmission without the need to convert those signals to sound first, a step that dissipated some of the energy available. If anyone at AT&T had doubts about the possibilities of the telegraphone, the publicity stunts staged by the American Telegraphone Company put them to rest.[12]

Telegraphone advertisements and pamphlets glorified the invention's potential for telephone surveillance and trickery, and suggested its additional utility for purposes of entrapment or even blackmail. American Telegraphone's promoters were clearly aware of the controversial nature of such telephone recordings, but it is debatable whether they were trying to taunt the telephone company, or whether they simply did not anticipate AT&T's negative response. Either way, the message American Telegraphone sent to telephone users was clear:

Said Mr. Brown to Mr. Jones:

"I never in my life agreed to do anything of the sort!"

"And I say that you did!" Mr. Jones replied flatly.

"And I say again that I did not!"

Just here Mr. Brown brought his fist down with a slam that made things rattle on Mr. Jones's desk. He faced him with a glare of defiance and perhaps a little cunning.

"Then I must repeat that you did!" Mr. Jones pursued smoothly. "Last Thursday morning, when we discussed the affair over the telephone, you agreed to do precisely that and nothing else. My plans have been made accordingly, and the fact that you have changed your mind doesn't alter matters a particle."

"Jones!" thundered Mr. Brown, "I defy you to prove—"

"Hold on!"

There was something odd about Mr. Jones's voice. Mr. Brown started a little and stared more. From the queer machine on the desk across the room, the cover was removed, to reveal an instrument of most unusual appearance. Mr. Jones stepped to his own desk and extracted from a drawer a big spool of fine, shiny wire. He hurried back and slipped it into the machine; he pressed the button and the spool began to spin rapidly; he picked up a pair of telephone receivers and listened for a minute. After which, he smiled slightly and said:

"If you'll just come over here and listen for a minute—?"[13]

Machines that American Telegraphone provided to celebrities were used for this purpose, with the company's full knowledge and approval. The *New*

York Evening Journal in the late summer of 1907 reported how "Miss Robson Laughs at the Bunco Trader." The "bunco trader" was a dishonest grocer who substituted higher-priced goods in an order placed by telephone. "Miss Robson" was Eleanor Robson, an actress who secretly had recorded her order on the telegraphone and then played it back to the flabbergasted shopkeeper, who promptly apologized.[14] The famous private detective William J. Burns had helped convict criminals in 1912 by recording their telephone conversations on the telegraphone. "Romance and commercial interest are combined in the plans of the American Telegraphone Company," maintained the *Springfield (W.Va.) Daily Republican*. Burns was given a recorder for use in his personal office and subsequently used it to gather evidence to be used in the Rosenthal case, a highly publicized murder trial in New York.[15] The American Telegraphone Company's own sales organization reported that the mayor of Pittsburgh, enraged by the discovery that his office boys made expensive telephone calls to their girlfriends, installed a telegraphone in order to catch the culprits. The company claimed that the telegraphone could prevent such abuse, "all this being done secretly, if so desired."[16] In each of these cases, the telegraphone was not used as an answering machine but simply as a way to record telephone conversations. It was this very use that terrified the managers at AT&T the most.

The Clash between AT&T and Bell Labs over Magnetic Recording

The telegraphone's capability to make illicit recordings would pit AT&T's corporate managers against Bell Labs engineers who, by the late 1920s, enthusiastically promoted telephone recorders within the company. The controversy would highlight the moralistic aspects of official corporate policy regarding telephone use. AT&T in these years walked a fine line between its role as impartial "common carrier" and steward of telephone propriety. On the one hand, the company's leaders had over the years repeatedly threatened to cut off service or even prosecute customers who did not use the telephone in the "proper" way, or made harassing calls, or used profane language.[17] At the same time, they recognized that a large percentage of their business came from people engaging in very private conversations, such as husbands and wives, or lawyers discussing their clients' cases, and that the secrecy of these discussions must be maintained. If customers believed that there was a real risk that these private discussions could be made public, use of the telephone might decrease considerably. The company's preferred role was to try to protect telephone privacy and the right of all customers to discuss whatever they liked on the telephone, as long as it did not conflict with the values of corporate executives themselves.[18]

Yet the line between content provider and common carrier was not as easy to draw as the leaders of the corporation would have had the public believe. Many technical decisions made in the process of network building also acted to define the content of the telephone medium, or to restrict the kinds of information that could pass through the network. Simply by separating its telephone and telegraph services into two distinct physical wire networks, for example, the company had taken the first steps to narrow the varieties of content that would pass over its wires. Another way the company shaped the general nature of telephone content was through the practice of leasing telephone sets to customers rather than allowing customers to buy their own. This gave the company the power to standardize the customer's interface with the rest of the network, but it also ensured that companies or experimenters did not use the telephone network for unauthorized applications such as facsimile or teletype. A further example was the company's practice of leasing special lines to businesses (mainly radio networks) for the transmission of music or other audio material requiring a frequency bandwidth greater than the minimum needed for intelligible voice conversations. Such policies put the firm into the gray area that existed between merely transmitting the content of communications and determining what the content would be, if only in a general way.

A much more blatant attempt to delimit and define communications content through technical means resulted from AT&T's research and development effort in telephone recording devices. Rudolph Mallina, a senior Bell Labs researcher, opened a new investigation of telephone message recording in 1929. The Labs had just successfully commercialized the products of its sound recording research in the motion picture industry, giving impetus to additional research efforts. Engineers at Bell Labs were also aware that the technology of magnetic sound recording, which had languished in the United States for some years, was the basis of moderately successful products in Europe. Mallina traveled to Germany and England to gather intelligence on the things companies in those countries were researching, and there he learned about several efforts to develop and commercialize magnetic wire and tape recorders. These machines had been in use, experimentally at least, for several years as general-purpose audio recorders for radio stations, as dictating machines, and as telephone recorders.[19]

Mallina, Christopher Wente, and Clarence N. Hickman experimented with telegraphones obtained some years prior but soon designed their own recorder. A simple prototype magnetic tape recorder demonstrated in 1931 proved sufficiently promising for Bell Labs managers to recommend further research. By the time of the demonstration, the engineers imagined that magnetic recording might become the basis of an automatic telephone answering machine of the sort demonstrated by Poulsen thirty years earlier. "It would be well worth while," Rudolph Mallina wrote, "to build a model of a message recorder, and determine its usefulness by trying it out in various offices and homes." The team made many technical improvements over the next few years, switching permanently from the wire used in the telegraphone to a specially prepared steel tape, inventing machines to mass-produce that tape, and employing vacuum tube amplifiers in the recorders themselves to improve the sound quality.

The need for a telephone recorder manufactured within the Bell System seemed obvious to Bell Labs engineers, considering the competing European equipment and a new, American-made product from the Dictaphone Corporation. Dictaphone first showed Bell Labs engineers its "Telecord" in 1923, a product that could act as a telephone recorder or a remote-control dictation system. Though it employed the new technology of electronic amplification, it used the wax cylinders like an old-fashioned phonograph and did not function as a fully automatic answering machine. While AT&T politely refused to let Dictaphone sell the machine to telephone customers, Western Electric engineers quietly began copying the machine and evaluating its potential for production. On several occasions in the 1920s and early 1930s, Bell Labs also invited other inventors, sales agents, and representatives of various manufacturing firms to demonstrate similar telephone recording machines, offering no encouragement but taking note of advances in the field. Public announcements of telephone recorders came regularly, but commercial interest receded immediately. The International Telephone and Telegraph, for example, publicly announced the availability of its "Echophon" telephone recorder in the United States, and while the machine sold fairly well in Europe, it could not be adopted here. The company's official public position remained that equipment of "foreign" (i.e. non–Western Electric) manufacture would not be allowed to be attached to AT&T's public telephone network.[20]

Answering Machine Use at the
Margins of the Telephone Network

Despite AT&T's strong corporate presence in telephone communication in the United States, it did not have absolute control. Persistent inventors devised ways to circumvent company rules about the connection of foreign attachments directly to the telephone lines by using inductive or acoustic coupling, and AT&T had to approach the FCC several times in the 1920s and 1930s to suppress these devices.[21] Yet, because AT&T did not maintain a single set of rules and restrictions for all customers, there was room for some answering machine use. The company sold and maintained private telephone systems where foreign equipment rules were not enforced. Thus the Dictaphone and Edison companies could sell telephone call recorders to these customers, which they did as early as 1925. Many of these private line installations in the late 1920s were for power and rail companies, where telephones were used to communicate between stations. AT&T estimated that the ultimate demand for call recorders on private lines would total about a thousand installations. Early customers for the call recorder used them more heavily than expected, and Dictaphone reported this fact enthusiastically in trade and technical magazines. The Public Service Company of New Jersey, a major electric utility, reported in 1930 that it was filling eighty to ninety wax recording cylinders each day with messages captured by the Dictaphone Telecord. Public Service and other customers often used their equipment to help simplify routine record keeping that ordinarily would have to be written by hand. Messages recorded on Telecord cylinders could be transcribed at a later time on an ordinary dictation machine.[22]

The use of these machines spread, and by 1930 AT&T managers noted an increase in requests from its own local operating companies to install Dictaphone and Edison call recorders, sometimes for new purposes. Some customers, reading reports of telephone recorders in the press, believed that the equipment might now be available to all customers, not just those with private lines.

Soon, the company actually faced the threat of the telephone recorder being used for surveillance purposes. The U.S. Department of Justice contacted the Chesapeake and Potomac Telephone Company in the District of Columbia in 1930, expressing an interest in installing a Telecord in its offices. The local operating company dutifully passed on several such requests to AT&T's head office in New York. AT&T executives at first instructed C&P to promise a superior recorder of Western Electric manufacture soon. Then C&P was told to stall as long as possible in hopes that the Justice Department would lose interest. Finally, after several months, the telephone company refused the request outright.[23]

Suddenly, engineers and Bell Labs managers imbued with enthusiasm for the new technology, and working on applications that seemed to have immediate commercial prospects, found themselves in conflict with a different corporate culture of which they apparently had been unaware. AT&T executive Elam Miller lashed out at Bell Labs' magnetic recording project, stating that "among other objections, the connection of recording equipment might tend to break down the public's faith in the secrecy of telephone conversations. Our position is and will continue to be that it is highly undesirable to permit recording equipment furnished by others to be connected to telephone lines and we suggest that all requests for such connection be refused." Another senior manager, Bancroft Gherhardi, circulated a memo in 1930 claiming that "all of this [informality and privacy] would be changed if in our day-by-day conversational contacts we were always to have a permanent record made either by machinery or by a stenographer, or if we did not know whether or not such a record was being made. . . . It would change the whole character of the words 'conversational contacts.' " Most of the presidents of the local operating companies echoed these sentiments when AT&T Vice President E. F. Carter polled them late in 1930.[24]

Such opposition almost immediately killed the Bell Labs automatic telephone answering machine, already in prototype form by 1931, and intended to be used at the premises of small businesses. E. F. Carter, in addition to recommending the termination of the project, insisted on refusing all future requests for the connection of the Telecord or similar machines. He also suggested avoiding any engagement with the public in the debate over their use.[25]

Yet enthusiasm for magnetic recording, the technical basis of the answering machine, remained strong at the highest levels of Bell Labs' management, so these executives looked for a new path to commercialization for this promising technology. They found one that allowed the corporation, in fact, to exercise a great deal of control over the information content of the recordings made on telephone recorders: by designing machines to their specifications and by marketing them within AT&T-controlled companies.

A "Legitimate" Telephone Recorder

Bell Labs president Frank Jewett came to the rescue of the telephone recorder soon after top management's attack. In December of 1930, he reminded top executives of the fact that such equipment was being manufactured by competitors in the U.S. and Europe, and this competition would almost certainly force AT&T to offer its own version. Other Bell Labs managers knew that telephone recording had in the past ten years become common in the railway and electric power industries and thought that a properly designed answering machine would not be a threat.

An "abuse-resistant" telephone call recorder proposed in 1932 employed human operators, trained by AT&T, who would manually connect a caller to the recording mechanism and make it clear that a recording would take place. If that were not enough, the recorder innovated the use of a faint background "beep" issued to both parties at regular intervals along with a message that a recording was being made. The first trials of the new machines took place in 1935 at the offices of the Associated Press, United Press International and the New York Times. Six machines constructed by Western Electric were distributed amongst the three news organizations and connected to telephone lines with unlisted numbers, with the understanding that the lines were to be used only for recording the incoming news reports of journalists. The limited usefulness of such a device, and the high cost of leasing and staffing it, doomed the so-called News Bureau Recorder.[26] But the main effect of AT&T's criticism was to stimulate an imaginative effort to turn Bell Lab's magnetic recording project away from answering machine development entirely.

Almost all subsequent developments at Bell Laboratories aimed either at sound recorders for use within telephone system switching offices (rather than at customer premises) or for military markets unrelated to telephony. One such line of development was for call announcers, machines to perform various announcing tasks automatically. Within AT&T's "Long Lines" or long-distance division, for example, automatic machines playing voice recordings of single digits were in place by 1930. By playing a sequence of recordings, the machines transmitted a telephone number to a distant human operator, thereby automating one of the repetitive human tasks needed for long-distance calling before the advent of direct customer dialing.[27]

Another typical application was the installation in urban switching offices of equipment to replace human "time of day" announcers. By the early 1930s, cities such as New York and Chicago offered a time-of-day service, relying on human operators in what must have been a very tedious assignment. The experimental use of the Bell Labs News Bureau recorder for such services apparently began in the later 1930s, but there was no specialized time-of-day announcer until 1960. Like virtually every other application of sound recording in the Bell System, the time-of-day equipment was installed on telephone company premises, and could be operated only by Bell System employees who regulated the content of recordings.[28] Ordinary telephone users experienced these technologies only indirectly, as they listened to the information provided or approved by the telephone company.

One effect of managerial objections to telephone recording was to turn Bell Labs' magnetic recording project away from devices intended for use in the Bell system. A few examples are necessary to appreciate just how far the line of invention and development begun at Bell Labs with the investigation of the telegraphone strayed. While the news bureau announcer and similar tape recorders found little commercial success through the end of the 1930s, the outbreak of World War II offered AT&T new possibilities. One of the most successful products was a gun locator that used a tape recording to help artillery crews locate the source of distant enemies. Another product was the Heater, a public-address system, used by the Psychological Warfare divisions of the army to broadcast fake battle sounds to the enemy. Most land-based Heaters apparently used phonograph records, but in 1946, too late to see service in the war, Bell Labs tested the Water Heater. This bizarre device incorporated a magnetic recorder and public address system inside a torpedo casing. Fired from a boat toward the shore, the Water Heater would stop at a predetermined distance, drop anchor, and right itself in the water with the tip of the torpedo standing above the water. Then off came the nose cone, out popped a loudspeaker, and the show began. Although the Water Heater never went into production, gun locators sold in significant numbers. They proved to be the only viable tape recording device to emerge from Bell Laboratories after more than a decade of product development.

Control and Consumers

Though AT&T continued to develop sound recording equipment according to its own internal goals, and its concern for privacy had a long-lived influence, the company subsequently played a lesser role in developing the modern answering machine. Telephone recorders and answering machines made by other companies continued to appear after the 1930s, and some were put into use at the margins of AT&T's business. By the 1940s and 1950s, the use of these machines began to spread to more mainstream customers. Gradually, AT&T's leaders came to see the distinction between general purpose devices capable of recording telephone calls, which were indeed subject to abuse, and specialized machines for the storage of telephone messages recorded knowingly by the caller.[29]

In the interim, however, the company offered its customers an alternative technology, one that had the unexpected effect of increasing demand for call recorders. As early as 1935, AT&T began to lease its customers equipment that made off-site, live answering services possible. Customers could rent a small add-on called a "key" that operated in conjunction with a standard telephone. When activated, the key would automatically transfer calls to the switchboard of a commercial answering service, where operators would answer the telephone and take messages.[30]

Answering services took years to catch on, perhaps because the economic depression discouraged spending among the prime customers, small businesses and professionals. However, the services began to be much more popular in the early 1950s. Among the leading customers were doctors, pharmacists, dry cleaners, and repair shops, but also "call girls," the prostitutes whose livelihood depended on the telephone but who were too busy to wait for calls from customers. Through films such as *Butterfield 8,* starring Elizabeth Taylor, the public knew about this association between answering services and prostitution, but the telephone company did little to discourage it.[31]

AT&T and its subsidiaries benefited economically from the operation of these services in several ways—AT&T most directly through the sales to the operating companies of answering service switchboards and customer-premises equipment. The local telephone companies in turn charged the customer for the rental and installation of the special equipment, and charged the answering service for switchboards, lines, and other equipment. This income must have further justified AT&T's anti–answering machine sentiments.

The company nonetheless began to realize that automatic answering machines were becoming more popular, particularly after World War II. The public was certainly becoming more aware of them, especially following the introduction of a number of new answering machines after 1945. One Swiss telephone answering machine dating from the 1930s, a magnetic recorder called the Ipsophon, emerged in the U.S. after 1945 and was the subject of a widely read article in *Life* magazine. The Ipsophon even introduced the notion of remote access; filtering circuits in the machine could detect a spoken code sequence, allowing the machine's owner to access recorded messages from any public telephone. Like many technologies, the answering machine in the postwar period was presented as an ultra-modern advance that ordinary Americans would soon be using on a daily basis.[32]

One of the most successful early entrants into the postwar answering machine business was Electronic Secretary Industries of Chicago. Joseph Zimmerman, an electrical engineer and the company founder, combined the newly available magnetic wire recorder (for recording messages) with a

78-rpm record player (later RCA's new 45-rpm player) to create the device. Faced with telephone company restrictions, Zimmerman initially equipped the Electronic Secretary with a mechanical arm to physically lift the telephone receiver from its cradle and place it near the machine, making no electrical connection to the telephone circuits. Only in 1952 could Zimmerman redesign the machine to allow direct connection to the telephone lines.[33]

In opposing telephone answering machines, AT&T did not distinguish between devices to record only incoming messages and machines capable of recording both sides of a conversation. It was the latter that the company had always feared, but the two types of devices had very different uses. Customers could use automatic answering machines to collect harmful or embarrassing information to be used against telephone customers, but the likelihood of this happening was smaller than with two-way telephone recorders. Such devices were at this time also coming into more widespread use among police organizations, the military, journalists, politicians, and businesses. In Washington, D.C., for example, Franklin D. Roosevelt allowed RCA to install a sound recorder in the basement of the White House capable of recording telephone messages. The machine could also record voices in the Oval Office via a hidden microphone. Apparently many presidents since his time have had similar equipment installed for the purpose of recording conversations. Harry Truman used an Amour wire recorder for a short time, for example, and John Kennedy used a variety of dictating machines and tape recorders in his office. The most famous, of course, was Richard M. Nixon's use of a German-made tape recorder in the early 1970s to collect information that would later be used against him. The practice of telephone recording was apparently quite widespread in Washington. The first public official who publicly admitted to making office or telephone recordings for record keeping or to prevent misquotes in the press was Treasury Department secretary Henry Morgenthau in the early 1930s. He had a switch hidden under his desk that allowed him to record his telephone conversations. Military regulations regarding telephone record keeping, already in place in the early 1940s, encouraged the widespread use of telephone recording during World War II, which apparently shocked the public when some of these recordings became part of an investigation in 1946. The public's fear of having their calls secretly recorded was very real, but there was no evidence that the public would have construed the use of an answering machine as a secret recording.[34]

Commercial pressure helped change the telephone company's attitude. By 1949, key individuals within AT&T and Bell Labs were beginning to change their negative stance on answering machines. Lloyd Espensheid,

FIGURE 27. One of the many telephone answering devices that appeared shortly after World War II. *Popular Science Magazine*, April 1947. Reprinted by permission.

one of Bell Labs' most prominent engineers, wrote a long memo to management on the virtues of customer answering machines.[35] Espensheid's argument did not mention privacy issues but was purely economic and technical, focusing on keeping up with the "march of progress." One indication that AT&T's opposition did not have overwhelming support among its subsidiaries was the first official trial of a telephone answering device in New York and Cleveland, Ohio, in 1950. The machine itself was a disk-based device called the Peatrophone, made by the Gray Manufacturing Company, a maker of telephone and dictation equipment.[36]

Though AT&T's ability and desire to restrict the use of answering machines was eroding, managers launched a belated effort to regulate the design of the equipment then being manufactured by others. In 1946 and 1947, in response to pressure from Dictaphone, Thomas A. Edison, Inc., and Sound-scriber Corporation (a maker of dictation and telephone recording equipment) as well as a major institutional user, the U.S. Navy, the FCC ruled that telephone recording devices could be attached to AT&T's lines, but the company insisted that they issue a "beep" at regular intervals to make it clear to both parties that the call was being recorded. The vestige of this regulation is the universal use of a beep to signal the beginning of a recording on current answering devices.[37] The local operating companies also retained the right to supply, install, and maintain the equipment, an arrangement that was not only lucrative but allowed them to keep tabs on who was using answering machines and how many were in service. The FCC approved the mandatory installation of a coupling device that would isolate the phone lines from any potential damage caused by the recorder, an unpopular move widely interpreted as outright resistance on the part of AT&T. The device seemed unnecessary, and customers resented the fact that local companies charged the customer a monthly fee for it.

Although AT&T had lost the lead it had once had in the manufacture of answering machines and was compelled to supply devices made by others (such as the Peatrophone and later the Code-a-Phone) to the local operating companies, ownership of the equipment remained with the Bell System. A lease arrangement provided further opportunities to maintain a degree of influence over answering machine use. For example, AT&T's influence over FCC policy making led to regulations about the maximum permissible length of recorded outgoing messages. By insisting that such messages were limited to less than a minute, the company limited the uses for an answering machine. The machines that local operating companies supplied to customers came from only a few suppliers, limiting the customer's selection to a narrow range of models. These restrictions set important precedents for answering machine technology in later years, even after AT&T's influence had largely faded.[38]

The high cost of leasing an answering machine and its accoutrements from the telephone company virtually ensured that AT&T's existing customers, still mostly professionals and small-business people (including prostitutes) in the 1950s, remained the primary users of answering machines. However, these high costs also spurred more and more customers to install the devices without notifying their local service provider. AT&T's domination of telephone set manufacturing made it easy to control channels of distribution, and telephone sets were not generally available for sale. Answering machines, however, were built by outside firms that made them available to radio and television distributors, retailers, and individuals, so that anyone could order an answering machine from the manufacturer or purchase one at a store. Growing sales of the "Electronic Secretary," "Telemagnet," the "Notaphon," and the "Telemaster," four early answering devices, prompted another FCC hearing in 1951, which confirmed the suspicion that many customers were not following the rules about using coupling devices or submitting to telephone company supervision. Surveys undertaken in 1954 and again in 1965 indicated that far more answering machines were in use than couplers, where if all the machines had been legitimate there would have been an one-to-one ratio. The appearance of several new manufacturers of answering machines in the 1960s, including Robosonics, Record-O-Phone, R.S.V.P., and Phone Mate, also suggested that the market was continuing to expand. Still, the total number of answering machines in use remained small well into the 1970s. In 1957, for example, AT&T estimated that it had only 40,000 customers leasing its Peatrophone, compared to about 200,000 customers for live answering services. The number of legitimate users had grown little as late as 1965.[39]

By contrast, the unauthorized use of the machines was growing rapidly. It did not take customers too much longer to discover that enforcement of AT&T restrictions regarding the leasing of answering machines and the use of couplers was nearly impossible. Manufacturers of the equipment steadfastly refused to take on the burden of enforcing compliance among their customers and sometimes purposefully disguised the real uses of their machines to assuage consumers' fears of being caught purchasing an "illegal" device. In the burgeoning field of home tape recording, the perception that telephone recording was allowable was being encouraged, indirectly, by recorder manufacturers and others. Many "general purpose" tape recorders, though not true answering machines, were supplied with telephone recording attachments. Additionally, electronics hobbyists discovered ways to modify general-purpose recorders to transform them into answering machines, and began publishing "how-to" articles in hobby magazines. Often companies trying to sell telephone recorders to eager customers protected themselves by simply transferring to the consumer the burden of compliance with telephone company regulations. Mohawk, a maker of office dictation equipment, introduced a telephone answering machine called the Tele-magnet in 1950, but made it clear to

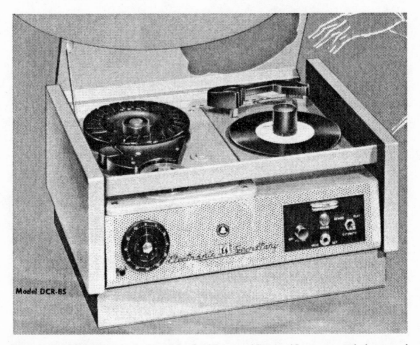

FIGURE 28. The "Electronic Secretary," which combined a 45–rpm record player and a wire recorder, was one of the most successful answering machines of the early 1950s. Ameritech Corporate Archives.

customers that they were responsible for contacting the telephone company and purchasing any additional equipment necessary to operate it legitimately, implying that the recorder was ready to be used for illegal telephone recording. At one point, Mohawk's president George F. Ryan frankly stated that the 750 Tele-magnets in use by late 1950 were "sold with the clear understanding that the telephone company objects to them."[40]

This kind of rule breaking was becoming quite common by the 1970s. John Sunier's 1978 *Handbook of Telephones and Accessories,* distributed by a mainstream publisher, TAB Books, was a virtual cookbook of techniques for outsmarting Ma Bell. Meanwhile, the courts in 1968 had forced AT&T to allow its customers to purchase and use competing brands of telephone sets, rather than leasing Western Electric phones exclusively. Yet many customers were not aware of this change and continued to believe that answering machines and other foreign attachments were still illegal. Local operating companies allegedly encouraged this belief or took it upon themselves to threaten

FIGURE 29. The "Peatrophone," an early answering machine sold by Gray Manufacturing Company, used two phonograph disks. Property of AT&T Archives. Reprinted with permission of AT&T.

noncomplying customers with termination of their service. It was too late. The floodgates were open.[41]

The economics of privately owned answering machines versus an answering service or a machine rented from Bell began to favor the answering machine more strongly between 1965 and 1975. The monthly rate for an answering service was $30 to $40, plus a per-call charge that varied according the caller's distance from the switchboard.[42] To rent an answering machine from the telephone company cost only about $12.50 per month in the 1950s, plus a one-time fee of $15 for installation. The charges for the coupling device included $10–35 for installation and a monthly rental from $2–8.[43] The outright purchase of an answering machine in the late 1960s ranged from $350 to as much as $800. The lower price of the answering equipment appealed to a broader range of businesses, but up to a quarter of users were still physicians or other professionals. Call girls were also believed to be important customers in some areas, for, as one retailer put it, "They say they're actresses, but I don't know any actresses who could plunk down $800 cash for the newest and the best." Through the early 1970s, the answering machine was still rarely seen in homes. Often though, answering machines appeared in movies, television shows, and magazine articles, and were associated with rich celebrities or other successful people. They were a widely recognized luxury item well before their prices dropped to the level that ordinary Americans could afford.[44]

By the mid-1970s, the use of semiconductors and standard cassette tapes had reduced the price of an answering machine as low as $125, although as late as 1981 $200 was about the average for a basic, good-quality machine. In 1976, the FCC made it possible for makers of answering machines to submit designs to the Commission for approval, and if found satisfactory, customers would not have to rent a coupler from their local telephone companies in order to use them. An important economic deterrent had been pushed aside.[45]

Annual sales of telephone answering machines doubled between 1978 and 1982, from about 400,000 units to 800,000. A combination of factors, including an increase in the numbers of home offices and working women, and the dissolution of AT&T's monopoly in 1984 contributed to the explosion of sales in the 1980s.[46] By the early 1990s, according to one estimate, 60 percent of American households had some kind of telephone answering device installed.[47]

The Culture of Answering Machine Recording

As answering machine use began to spread during the 1970s, consumers (sometimes simply following the suggestions of equipment manufacturers) developed patterns of behavior and practice related to the use of the machine. Early instructional material provided to users of answering machines assumed the users would be business oriented and that callers would be unfamiliar with the recording process. The instructional material for new users was correspondingly sensitive to business needs and the possibility of caller confusion. Code-a-Phone's early instruction manuals encouraged new users to "First, greet your caller . . . then identify yourself and your company . . . explain that the caller is hearing a recorded message . . . proceed with your message . . . invite the caller to give information relative to his call . . . instruct the caller to start speaking after hearing the tone signal . . . and then end your message with the usual 'thank you for calling' type of sign off" [ellipses in original].[48] With the transition to home use and growing familiarity with the devices, users developed their own ways of greeting callers. In contrast to the business-oriented announcements recommended by manufacturers, home users often explained why they could not answer the call, or even apologized for using the device, reflecting the perception that the answering machine was a second-rate substitute for a real person. Interestingly, the telephone company's concern for privacy persisted, in that many users were careful to tell the caller that a recording would take place (although sometimes this was just to make it clear that the realistic-sounding voice on the line was just a recording). For many years rather lengthy, explanatory, and apologetic outgoing messages greeted callers, before the majority of people came to be comfortable with a recorded answer.[49]

Early answering machine users also reported experiencing "mike fright," a feeling of anxiety when faced with the prospect of making a recording, and this may have contributed to the awkward or even negative response many callers initially gave to answering machines. One journalist, exaggerating slightly, wrote in 1979 that "Some people hang up. Others giggle or burst into tears in frustration."[50] Another early user recalled: "What a jolt it was, hearing my very first machine greeting. What was this eerie artifice, this absent presence? Did it actually expect me to say something in return? Over my dead body. I was so boggled by the prospect that I just hung up. Later I was told that hanging up mute is a form of rudeness. . . . How could you be rude to a machine?"[51]

As the use of answering machines spread beyond business owners to the general public, outgoing messages themselves began to address the problem of mike fright. Now machine owners offered incentives not to hang up without leaving a message, such as using entertaining or funny outgoing messages. Many found that if their messages were entertaining enough, people might even call just to hear them. Two comedy writers in Los Angeles released a series of cassettes called *No Hang-Ups,* with recordings of celebrity impersonations, sound effects, and even risqué messages intended for answering machine use.[52]

The ambivalence with which Americans greeted the new devices was still apparent as they came to be installed in millions of households. The producers of *No Hang-Ups* published *Getting Even with the Answering Machine* in 1985, and the book was in its thirteenth printing by 1990. The use of the answering machine at home also posed a new kind of threat. Messages became less revealing and informative as some users began to fear the risks of giving out too much specific information. Admitting that one was out of the house was thought to be an invitation to criminals. Despite these frustrations and fears, the answering machine was becoming a part of American culture.

FIGURE 30. Not all Americans saw the coming of the telephone answering machine as progress. J. Carfi and C. Carle, *Getting Even with the Answering Machine* (CCC Publications, 1985).

Between the rock band Blondie's "Hangin' on the Telephone," X's "Your Phone's Off the Hook, But You're Not," both recorded in 1980, and the Replacements' plaintive lyric "how do you say I love you to an answering machine?" recorded in 1983, the device had found a place in daily life. [53]

The use of the answering machine allowed the development of new forms of communication unanticipated by inventors and telephone companies. A telephone's ring had always been a sort of mystery to be solved, and answering machine owners discovered that the device made it possible to "screen" incoming calls. One could easily avoid calls from direct marketers, prying parents, or other unwanted parties by waiting to hear who left a message, instead of answering the phone. This novel application of the answering machine is interesting because of the way its real use is camouflaged behind the small lie that one is "not home" or unable to take the call. Judith Martin, author of the popular "Miss Manners" etiquette books, pointed out that such practices had been established in the nineteenth century, except that they involved actual visitors to one's home rather than telephone callers. Miss Manners, incidentally, condemned answering machine humor for its propensity to bring out Americans' "worst show business ambitions." [54]

Owners of answering machines also developed special ways of addressing callers, just as callers invented ways to express themselves while being recorded. Sociologists studying answering machine behavior discovered that both incoming and outgoing messages were often conversational, even though both parties realized how one-sided the conversation really was. Callers frequently asked "how are you?" as if their party would actually respond. As people came to expect that their calls are being screened, they began to address directly the person whom they suspected was really there, listening to the machine. Some even used the answering machine for purposes completely unrelated to its recording ability. *Dog World* magazine suggested that absent pet owners call their lonely canines to reassure them. [55]

Conclusions

It took many decades for Valdemar Poulsen's invention, the telephone answering machine, to achieve commercial success, but it is remarkable how many of the basic features of his original machine, its purposes, and its appeal to the public have remained intact. Though the American Telegraphone Company suffered from chronic financial and managerial problems, given the opportunity it might have created a new industry based on the home or business answering machine. By the 1920s, however, the company had failed and its technology had been co-opted by AT&T.

The contrast between the entrepreneurial dynamism of American Telegraphone's endeavor and the cautious plodding of AT&T in later years is quite striking. Where American Telegraphone had aimed to transform the use of the telephone, AT&T sought to preserve the status quo and consolidate its control of telephone use. The reason for AT&T's conservatism had some justification in the company's nationwide technical standardization program, but this was secondary in importance to the belief among top management that the use of the telegraphone would undermine the public's faith in telephone privacy. This was a curious belief, and in retrospect it seems clear that managers did not believe that the public could easily distinguish between the surreptitious recording of calls, which certainly would have led to public distrust, and the automatic recording of messages, in which both caller and callee were aware of the process. AT&T's reluctance allowed other companies to exploit the small but important market for call recorders in the 1920s and 1930s and get a head start on the design of answering machines.

New technologies, market competition, and the growing availability of answering devices contributed to the increased use and falling prices of answering machines in the 1950s and 1960s. AT&T and local Bell companies eventually began to supply answering machines to customers who requested them but made the machines expensive to lease. Customers, resentful of the AT&T monopoly, discovered ways to circumvent the rules by purchasing machines and installing them themselves. By the time AT&T's control over the telephone equipment market began to crumble in the late 1960s, the answering machine market was already achieving a sort of momentum, gathering in new users, generating the sales volume that led to price reductions, and creating additional public exposure in a snowball fashion. While it took the entire decade of the 1970s for annual sales to exceed a million units, sales rose to three million units in 1985 and jumped to over twelve million in 1989.[56]

The 1980s saw many Americans using an answering machine for the first time either in their homes or business. A little startling at first, with practice the act of recording became routine. Once the novelty of the experience wore off, many people came to expect that a recorder would normally be in use in the absence of one's called party, and began relying on the answering machine as heavily as they relied on the telephone itself. The use of the answering machine today is an integral part of telephone culture and one of the most successfully assimilated applications of sound recording in Americans' daily lives.

In historian Claude Fischer's view, the telephone extended and enhanced existing patterns of communication in the United States rather than creating entirely new ones, and surely the answering machine has done the same. The answering machine was inspired by a culture of telephone usage that placed a high value on not missing calls. For many years that culture was only expressed in a business context. As an enhancement of the telephone, the answering machine offered an additional way to achieve the leveling of time and space, and this feature appealed to ordinary users just as much as business users. It furthered Americans' expectations for instant personal communication and always being "in touch." Owning such a machine was a satisfying way to avoid missing important calls and avoid taking unwanted ones, and reaching an answering machine was in many cases more satisfying than the unanswered ring.

The history of the answering machine is important both for what it tells us about the development of new communication technologies and for its contribution to our understanding of the culture of recording. Answering machine use transformed an inherently instantaneous and immediate medium, the telephone, by capturing its perishable messages. In so doing, it actually enhanced the immediacy of the medium for the majority of telephone users, since most could only wait by their telephones part of the time.

During the first half of the century, the scope and content of telephone recordings was closely regulated by AT&T, a company with a near monopoly on telephone technology. For a combination of reasons, some related to business, others to the American fascination with the telephone, customers found ways to evade telephone company rules. Manufacturers of telephone equipment abetted this by offering a steady stream of machines equipped to record calls.

Telephone messages are the only type of sound recording that the majority of Americans seem willing to make of their own voices. What they say on those recordings is a significant aspect of our recording culture. The popularization of answering machines in the 1980s saw the evolution of recording practices unique to the answering machine, a culture of recording that continually and often playfully crossed the boundaries of simple utility. Americans were comfortable circumventing another set of rules with recording technology to make consumer goods more useful or more personalized, as we shall see in the next chapter.

CHAPTER 5

The Tape Recorder, Home Entertainment, and the Roots of American Rerecording Culture

The years between the late 1930s and the late 1960s marked an important transition in the history of sound recording; at the beginning of this period, few Americans were users of sound recording technologies, while at the end, tens of millions were. Beginning in the late 1930s and especially after World War II, manufacturers presented Americans with a range of new sound recorders, and individuals, companies, and institutions invented new ways to utilize them. Hobbyists interested in collecting sounds, historians gathering data, and teachers interested in engaging their students' interest were only a few of the new users. In terms of sheer numbers, however, the most important use of the sound recorder that emerged was the duplication of commercial music recordings. This was a not a practice that appeared suddenly but one that incubated for years. The tape recorder by the 1960s became something of an extension of the recording industry, allowing people to create products that they otherwise would not or could not buy. By the 1970s, its use for rerecording would begin to have enormous economic and cultural significance. Rerecording would also reflect the fact that the products of the recording industry, popular as they had become, did not satisfy all the demands of consumers, who felt they must actively produce their own recordings.

The New Recording Technologies

Much happened between the 1930s and the end of World War II to set the stage for the diversification of sound recording technologies. Engineers and inventors made important changes to the existing technologies of sound recording and came up with some entirely new ones. A remarkable diversity of recording products became available in this period, almost an embarrassment of riches, although most are now forgotten. Home phonograph recording, for example, had a brief resurgence as the U.S. economy began to recover from the Depression in the late 1930s. A few companies offered to consumers an inexpensive version of the disk cutting recorders used in professional studio. These machines typically came packaged in a "console," a large piece of wooden furniture that included a record player and radio, and were often expensive. Makers of this equipment believed that people would want to record radio programs off the air. With the addition of a microphone, these recorders could also be used to make original voice or music recordings at home. A second version of disk recording appeared in the late 1930s in the form of the acetate disk, which was superficially similar to the vinyl disks used earlier in the recording industry. But professional vinyl disk records could be played only a few times before wearing out, so most semiprofessional and home disk recorders used a more resilient plastic and an embossing recording process, rather than engraving or cutting. This provided a record of greater durability, but degraded sound quality. Although the leading manufacturer of disk recorders in the late 1930s, Wilcox-Gay, could claim it had sold 25,000 units in 1939–40, sales declined after that. Disk recorders disappeared almost entirely by 1950, although high-quality studio versions of the acetate recorder remained popular in the recording and radio industries.[1]

Consumers purchasing a sound recorder after 1945 had many other novel offerings to choose from. The new dictation equipment companies, fat from wartime government contracts, sought markets outside the business office and saw home recording as a market ripe for exploitation. Soundscriber Corporation of Connecticut and the Gray Audograph Company, for example, promoted their engraved-disk dictation machines as a home voice recorders and found a significant number of customers. Another product that showed much promise was the Hart Recordograph, which embossed its record onto a long loop of plastic ribbon. Recordographs were used extensively during World War II, and the company made much of the fact that reporters had carried them ashore during the invasion at Normandy. The company continued to produce the machines at least until 1950, but they never caught on.[2]

Another entirely new home recording technology that appeared in 1945 was the magnetic wire recorder, so named because it used a very fine stainless steel wire about the diameter of sewing thread as the recording medium. These small, inexpensive recorders were developed by the research institute of the Illinois Institute of Technology, which hoped to earn royalties by licensing its designs to manufacturers. Several dozen companies located in the United States, Europe, and South America produced wire recorders between 1945 and 1955. In the 1940s, before it was clear that the tape recorder (still an expensive studio machine) would be redesigned to suit the home market, the wire recorder was not only the cheapest and simplest but also the most promising form of home sound recorder available. The wire recorder was a flashy technology with a great deal of "high tech" appeal, and its sales seemed to be taking off in 1946 and 1947, when Americans purchased tens of thousands of them. Yet the tape recorder proved to be an even flashier technology with several important technical advantages. Wire recorders were difficult to use, partly because the wire was so fine that it snarled and tangled with frustrating regularity. Typically, the wire would snarl during rewinding, either forming a hopeless snarl on the reel or spilling off the spool entirely, winding itself into the guts of the machine or all over the living room floor.

Marketers of home tape recorders cashed in on the sterling reputation of the studio tape recorders designed by firms like Ampex, although the home machines were in reality comparable in quality to the typical wire recorder. After 1952 and the first big jump in sales of home high-fidelity equipment, the tape recorder ran the wire recorder out of the market and remained the only form of home sound until the 1980s.

Creating Practices of Recording

Sound recording was clearly not a novelty in 1945, but despite the growing number of products on the market, it was still not widely practiced outside of a few specialized businesses. Over the course of the next three decades, a range of firms, institutions, and individuals sought to popularize sound recording activities, promoting practices that to today's consumer may seem unfamiliar. The current popularity of the tape recorder and the way it is used are the result of a long period of development during which Americans tried many different ways of recording.

Many Americans were first exposed to sound recording in the 1940s through the advertisements and sales drives of the makers and distributors of electronic equipment. Also influential were certain types of institutions such as libraries and public school systems. These institutions acted as important consumers and publicizers of sound recording, and their employees helped invent new practices and applications. Furthermore, there were many individuals who invented (or often reinvented) sound recording practices independently, became recording enthusiasts, and then set out to convert others.

Some, such as managers in companies, tried to impose the use of the sound recorder on subordinates. Others, mostly hobbyists excited by the new machines, developed highly creative ways to employ sound recorders to new ends, and the spreading of the gospel of sound recording became their calling.

The manufacturers, retailers, and other companies that sought to instill in Americans the habit of making their own sound recordings combined the precedents of home phonograph listening and the photography hobby. These were two very different types of activities, however. Listening was a passive way of appreciating culture, mostly in the form of music, while photography, at least the type on which recorder companies modeled their thinking, was an active, creative, and sometimes artistic endeavor. What these two activities had in common was their basis in consumerism, and the primary goal of the early promoters of recording was of course to get people to buy recorders. Sound recorders, the corporations said, would supplant the phonograph by doing everything it could do plus record. Promoters imagined that home recordists would soon find all sorts of novel uses for their equipment, and if record companies could be enticed to jump on the bandwagon, there would also be a catalog of recordings for the pleasure of those content with the passive consumption of audio entertainment. Many phonograph makers bought into this vision even though it threatened their traditional lines of merchandise. The phonograph industry's doldrums of the 1930s had led some to believe that consumers would not return to their pre-Depression phonograph buying habits (an assumption that proved to be quite wrong). Some major phonograph manufacturers, including the Webster-Chicago Company, hedged their bets in 1944 and 1945 by entering into an agreement with the Armour Research Foundation to manufacture wire recorders to supplement their line of phonograph record players. Many of the Armour-designed wire recorders actually were phonographs: part of the wire recorder mechanism functioned as a turntable platter, and the machines were equipped with phonograph pickups. Almost every maker of phonographs offered sound recorders by the early 1950s and seemed ready to give consumers whatever they wanted. Interestingly, though, phonograph-recorder combinations were not good sellers in the 1950s. Americans had not yet become recordists.

As wire- and tape-recorder manufacturers turned on their publicity machines in the late 1940s, Americans were bombarded with information about sound recording and advice as to why they needed it. For two years, 1946 and 1947, the wire recorder captured Americans' attention, as it was virtually the only one of the exciting, long-promised, consumer electronics novelties to appear on store shelves. Even after televisions, FM radios, and other new consumer products became more widely available in the later 1940s, wire (or, increasingly, tape) recorders would remain the focus of considerable publicity. Journalists writing for popular publications such as *Life, Science News Letter, Saturday Review,* and the *New York Times* translated corporate press releases into articles that both informed and proselytized for the new hobby of sound recording. Potential buyers who could resist the impulse to buy immediately could read objective evaluations of the new recorders in *Consumer Reports* as early as April 1947. Wire and tape recorders were showing up everywhere in the late 1940s and early 1950s; on stage in Arthur Miller's *Death of a Salesman* (1949), in numerous B-grade spy movies, and on the new medium of television in the *I Love Lucy* show in 1954.

Many of the Americans who embraced the wire recorder and its successor, the tape recorder, in the late 1940s were the technophilic "buffs" who created the new hobby of sound recording. Others were musicians who hoped to explore, on a budget, the possibilities of sound recording outside the studio system. In fact, a survey of home tape users conducted in 1948 by the Brush Development Company revealed that almost all respondents were either musicians or engineers.[3]

Amateur musicians were among the most enthusiastic early recorder users. For the first time, they had at their disposal a practical alternative to the recording studio. Not only would an inexpensive wire or tape recorder make tolerable recordings at low cost, it had technical capabilities which, at the hands of innovators, surpassed professional disk recorders. It was also at this time that "tape recorder music" and related genres first appeared, where composers assembled bits and pieces of cut-up tapes into musical assemblages. Musicians Les Paul and Mary Ford, who had experimented with homemade disk recordings in the 1940s, purchased the first wire recorder they came across. Its technical features made overdubbing and editing rather simple, and Paul soon used this capability to create distinctive new sounds. But musicians' use of the home tape recorder is part of the story of sound recording in the record industry, which will not be discussed here. It is worth noting, however, that musicians' use of home recording equipment continues to have a great cultural significance.

Only a few years after the introduction of these new technologies, Americans had already turned away from the types of recording espoused by the enthusiasts. One British observer commented in 1958 that in his country, recording enthusiasts treated recording media as an artist would, pushing the technology to its limits in hopes of creating or discovering new kinds of sounds. But many Americans used their wire or tape recorders the same way many of them used their cameras; to document the lives of their families. After the initial novelty of simply being able to record wore off, many recorders served primarily as audio baby books, turned on at yearly intervals to preserve a young child's babbling. Then they went into the closet.

Part of the reason infants were so commonly recorded is that adults found recording and especially listening to their own voices disconcerting. While some people grew accustomed to the experience, others never did. Movie and radio stars had known about this for years. Orson Welles, for example, sometimes admitted that he could not stand to hear himself speaking in the movies. As retailers began to discover this phenomenon, they exhorted their fellow salesmen and store owners to record only their own voices during demonstrations, not the customer's: "I refuse to let a man talk into the mike. . . . For years we went along with the canned belief that a man's in love with the sound of his own voice. Not when he hears it played back he isn't! Part of the time he doesn't even recognize himself. The rest of the time, he listens in shocked horror."[4]

But the sounds of other's voices could be a source of fascination. Tape correspondence clubs began to appear around 1950, extending the earlier concept of the pen pal. By the early 1960s thousands of Americans participated in these clubs, which had become international in scope. The wars in Korea and Vietnam led to considerable growth in the use of taped "voice letters." Tape companies offered tiny reels of tape for this purpose, packaged in boxes with lines for a postal address and a spot for stamps. During the 1960s, soldiers' use of voice letters created an important market for inexpensive, open-reel tape recorders, both in the United States and Japan.

At least through the mid-1950s, when home sound recording still had novelty value, a favorite application of the sound recorder was as a party game. Here was another use of the recorder that manufacturers had been pushing for decades without much success. Edison's National Phonograph Company had lured consumers in the 1890s with visions of "phonograph parties" where hosts recorded their guests speaking, singing, or playing music. Fifty years later, the Audio Devices Corporation (a maker of blank recording disks) published books promoting much the same thing.[5] The early customers for wire and tape recorders in the late 1940s reinvented this party game and took it to new levels. Unlike earlier phonographs, magnetic recorders had a much longer recording time (thirty to sixty minutes verses seven minutes or less), and did not have to be monitored, making it possible for the mischievous to hide them easily. This could lead to a sort of playful surveillance

FIGURE 31. Bird watchers, like this couple photographed by Bill Wilson around 1960, were part of a nascent recording hobby in the United States after World War II. Courtesy of the Atlanta History Center.

of an otherwise private discussion. Manufacturers encouraged their customers to hide their machine at a party under a table, or in a closet perhaps, to capture the candid comments of guests or to listen in on the private whispers of couples who thought they were out of earshot. Then the group could be entertained by a playing of the recording. How many people were publicly humiliated by the use of this new technology one can only imagine. Alternately the recorder came out in the open to be the focus of choreographed activities. One company sold scripts for "radio plays" which, combined with party of young cut-ups, a few drinks, and a tape recorder, would (it was promised) lead to fun.[6]

Individuals found other, often bizarre new uses for sound recording, demonstrating the equipment's versatility and the possibilities of the human imagination. The high sound quality and electronic amplification possible with wire and tape recorders was enough to fool animals into believing that recordings were live. One Canadian exterminator tortured rats, recorded their death squeals, and then used the recordings to scare off the rodents' compatriots in a Vancouver warehouse. Even more dastardly was the recording of the "plaintive cries of a lonesome lady rat," which allegedly brought hordes of male rats running. How surprised the amorous creatures must of been to find themselves being "disposed of" with a pistol. Hunters in the U.S. played similar tricks on deer but were punished by the National Park Service which called this bad sportsmanship.[7]

Sound Recording in Business and the Professions

Prior to World War II, the best known use of sound recording among people in business and the professions was in the form of office dictation systems. These machines had carefully prescribed roles in the process of creating office correspondence and only rarely saw other uses. The promotion of "general purpose" wire and tape recorders encouraged many individuals to invent new business uses for sound recording, such as taking inventory or training. Those whose jobs depended on public speaking were particularly avid users of the new technology. Ministers, who had often bought disk recorders or dictation machines in the prewar years, came to worship the economy and simplicity of the tape recorder for practicing their sermons. Museum staff people were another group who became attached to the tape recorder by the early 1950s. Curators and exhibit designers for museums large and small adopted tape recorders by the early 1950s. The devices added realistic sound effects to natural history exhibits, or addressed visitors with information about what they were seeing. These grassroots uses were widespread but at the same time isolated, depending on the imagination and preferences of individuals. They nonetheless contributed in small ways to the overall trend in sound recording, which was its proliferation.

Perhaps the way recording habits formed is better revealed by cases where individuals within organizations tried to impose the practice of sound recording on other employees. Managers found uses for wire and tape recorders that were as varied as they were ingenious. For example, the sales organizations of companies with geographically remote sales offices issued frequent written dispatches to their representatives in the field. Many of them now began to use tape recorders to distribute batches of training tapes. Salesmen themselves, usually at the prompting of their employers, practiced their sales pitches before a sound recorder so they could hear their own delivery. Managers believed that a sound recording was a more effective "mirror for mistakes" than even the boss's own critique. However, early reports of these

FIGURE 32. Composer Arnold Schoenberg, along with many other composers, writers, and scholars, became avid users of sound recording equipment. Copyright © 1953, 1971 Richard Fish.

kinds of training exercises revealed a problem that dictation equipment salesmen had long struggled to overcome, the phenomenon of "microphone fright." One enthusiastic insurance company vice president seemed confident that fear of the whirring tape recorder would subside with experience. Yet he acknowledged to his colleagues that as soon as he placed it in front of an otherwise confident salesman, the salesman "hesitates, hems and haws, and generally acts and sounds like a novice. He is inclined to stutter and exude discomfort."[8] The level of uneasiness new users displayed killed most of these training programs as soon as managerial support for them cooled. They were, however, reinvented many times in later years. This application did not represent a truly vital culture of sound recording in business, though it was important in sustaining the sale of recorders.

More successful and self-sustaining were applications which used a sound recording device as a portable dictation machine. When some other person such as a secretary made use of the records, users did not have to hear recordings of their own voices. Advertising and insurance agencies recorded interviews with clients and warehouse managers replaced paper forms with oral inventories. Some of the successful business uses of voice recording combined this with an element of surveillance. One insurance company in 1952 used a newly invented miniature tape recorder to monitor the sales pitches of agents. A manager accompanying the salesman hid the recorder in a briefcase and recorded the salesman's pitch without his knowledge, "thus our salesmen are not under the emotional strain they would be if they knew every word spoken was being recorded."

Surveillance Recordings

The making of secret or surveillance records has, in fact, become one of the key applications of sound recording. It was possible to make a secret recording even in the early days of the phonograph, although it required a considerable amount of naiveté on the part of others. A National Phonograph Company publication recounted the tale of making such a recording in 1890, but it was clear that the technique still had major technical flaws. The wily recordist, after hiding his phonograph behind a nearby curtain, had to convince his victim to shout, and to talk as rapidly as possible (because the maximum recording time of the cylinder was only a couple of minutes).[9] Electronics technologies developed in the 1930s made it possible to hide a microphone almost anywhere, allowing the recorder (which was still large and noisy until the 1950s) to be hidden somewhere else. Electronics also made it easier to link a sound recorder to the telephone, the medium through which so many confidential conversations take place. Secret recording activities got another boost with the appearance of tape and wire recorders, which could be smaller and quieter than phonograph recorders. Finally, with the coming of miniaturized electronics, the ease of making a secret recording increased once again, for now a recorder was small enough to fit in a handbag or a pocket.

As early as the 1940s, the courts began to debate the admissibility of secret recording as evidence in trials. The secretly made recording as evidence of wrongdoing was a stock feature in motion pictures even in the immediate postwar years, but in the early 1970s it gained more notoriety during the proceedings against Richard M. Nixon. Nixon, using ordinary dictation machines (one made by the German company Uher), had instructed his staff to maintain records of important telephone and face-to-face conversations, the tapes of which would come back to haunt him during the Watergate investigation. Nixon was not the first president to keep such secret records. Franklin Roosevelt had accepted a prototype voice recorder (similar to the Philips-Miller recorder described in chapter 2) from the RCA corporation which he connected to his telephone lines. Harry Truman used a wire recorder for this purpose, and Kennedy preferred a Dictaphone. Journalists of all sorts regularly made recordings of conversations, particularly telephone conversations, a practice which occasionally raised issues of ethics in the profession. Even though movies, television, and the occasional court trial constantly reminded the public of the existence of secret or surveillance recordings, they probably accounted for only a very small fraction of the recordings that ordinary Americans made.[10]

Scholars Begin to Record

Other new uses of recording emerged from schools and universities. Before 1945, sound recording was a remarkably underutilized technology among the scholars who could have benefited from it the most: anthropologists and historians. Well into the twentieth century, researchers making records of speech and song did so with pen, paper, or camera, but rarely the sound recorder. Gradually, however, scholars found ways to use the new technologies.[11]

Part of the reason scholars resisted sound recording technology for so long was that the technology was so crude. The machines available in the early twentieth century, using cylinders or disks, made the process expensive and difficult. Harvard folklorist Jesse Fewkes takes credit for originating the practice of making field recordings when in 1890 he used a phonograph to record Passamaquoddy Indians in Maine.[12] Fewkes and other pioneers in the field of ethnography who enthusiastically set out to use Edison's contraption discovered that it was a devilishly fickle and unreliable technology. Truman Michelson was a staff member of the Bureau of American Ethnology who borrowed a Dictaphone recorder from the Smithsonian in 1912 in order to record the "gambling song" of the Blackfoot Indians. When the moment came, the balky cylinders refused to cooperate, and a frustrated Michelson shouted out that the phonograph was "of no use whatsoever . . .it simply will not record properly, and I think that it's time to send it back, collect, c.o.d.!" True to form, the little machine at that moment worked perfectly. Perhaps Michelson did not realize that his tantrum would be faithfully captured on the cylinder, to be preserved forever in the Smithsonian's collections, but more likely he hoped those in Washington would hear it all.[13]

Early field recording sessions usually lacked any sort of spontaneity, as the technology was obtrusive, fragile, and in constant need of coddling. John Lomax, one of the most prominent folk music experts of the 1930s and 1940s, described in his book *Adventures of a Ballad Hunter* his use of a "large Edison dictaphone" in 1933. The equipment needed to record a simple folk song included a "350-pound recording machine—a cumbersome pile of wire and iron and steel—built into the rear of the Ford, two batteries weighing seventy-five pounds each, a microphone, a complicated machine of delicate adjustments, coils of wire, numerous gadgets, besides scores of blank aluminum and celluloid disks, and, finally, a multitude of extra parts, the purpose and place for which neither Alan nor I had the faintest glimmer of an idea."[14] Most early recording machines had to be set on level ground in the shade and protected from both the elements and the fingers of curious onlookers. Wax cylinders and disks melted when the weather was hot, but they became too hard when it was cold. Those making recordings had to be placed close to the recording horn or microphone and instructed not to move. They had to speak or sing at a nearly constant volume and especially avoid shouting, which could overwhelm the recording stylus and distort the recording. Loud musical accompaniment sometimes had to be minimized, but quiet instruments would surely be lost. Frances Densmore, a leading collector of folk music recordings, advised a colleague contemplating a field trip to substitute "A short stick on a pasteboard box" for real drums. A more subtle instrument like an Indian rattle, she added, "does not record at all."[15]

Because of the difficulty and expense of making field recordings, and because the final product was not a publishable text, most folklorists and apparently all historians before the late 1940s completely ignored sound recording. The massive interviewing missions undertaken by the Works Progress Administration in the 1930s, for example, were to document the lives of former slaves and preserve local myths and songs. While the WPA's *Manual for Folklore Studies* emphasized the art of ferreting out an interviewee's "characteristic speech rhythms," folklorists were expected to record them with pen and ink.[16] Although the total number of field recordings made before 1945 preserved in various U.S. libraries seems large, amounting to thousands of cylinders and disks, they are the result of a small group of prolific researchers. The most important collection of these recordings in the United States is held by the Library of Congress, which describes its "core" collection of Bureau of American Ethnology recordings as the work of only twenty-four individuals over the course of about half a century.[17]

The new technologies available after World War II did not compel scholars to change their methods; they simply offered an easier, more reliable, cheaper way to make the kinds of sound recordings that some of them had long hoped to make. Wire and tape recorders were not on the market for very long before researchers discovered them. In 1948 Columbia University historian Allan Nevins contemplated a research program aimed at preserving the memories of prominent New Yorkers. With $6,000 from the University library, a graduate student, and a pen, Nevins set out to interview a number of the city's prominent politicians and intellectuals. He found note taking unsatisfactory because he could reproduce "only 60 percent of what the man interviewed had told us, and part of that reproduction was inaccurate." He apparently tried an office dictating machine, but then his graduate assistant introduced him to the wire recorder. While it represented a marked improvement, the wire recorder's chief foible soon became apparent, and Nevins occasionally became frustrated with "coiled or snagged" wires. He nonetheless used it fairly heavily for a few years before purchasing his first tape recorder, a machine he found even more delightful.[18]

At Columbia Nevins in effect invented the oral history archive, a new type of collection consisting of interviews gathered with the help of the tape recorder. At almost the same time, the idea was occurring to others who were already engaged in systematic interviewing, particularly the Bancroft Library at Stanford and the U.S. Army. Soon, oral history programs were popping up all over the country, and historians began wondering why they had waited so long to initiate them. It was a means of archival record gathering that suited an age where people had stopped writing diaries and the telephone had replaced a great deal of written correspondence. Interviewing was also a "real world" history that made sense to a public increasingly suspicious of the academic enterprise, and it got broad support from many quarters. Although it was not until 1966 that the Oral History Association called its first conference, by that time dozens of institutions had embarked on ambitious programs of interviewing.

Nevins' oral history campaign, like many in the early years, focused on high-profile individuals such as judges, senators, newspaper editors, and captains of industry. In concentrating on these great men of American history, Nevins was out of step with many of his colleagues, for it was at this time that the new labor history, social history, and other subfields were beginning to explore what practitioners called "anonymous" history. Here was an area where oral history techniques could be applied with enormously profitable returns. Arguing that the lives of society's elites were already fairly well-documented in newspaper articles and in the paper trails they left behind, historians explored the lives of the rest of society in one of the only possible ways: through the personal interview. The lives of ordinary people, captured on tape, could illuminate the important events of recent history. Hebrew University, for example, began to collect the otherwise unrecorded experiences of Jews who had lived Europe during the turmoil of the 1930s and 1940s. The portable tape recorder was a major factor making this possible, not because it created the desire to undertake these projects, but because it was the most powerful labor-saving device historians had ever encountered for the gathering of large volumes of spoken information. Its monopoly in oral history gathering has been unchallenged since the 1950s.[19]

Taping an interview became quite a bit easier by the end of the 1950s, as transistorized tape recorders became available. The tape recorder was one of the first nonmilitary devices to use transistors, because manufacturers believed that enthusiasts and professionals would embrace the lightweight, battery-operated designs that transistorization made possible. Although rather expensive, early transistor portables fulfilled expectations. Oral historians, journalists, and amateurs carried their miniature recorders into places where sound recording had not been possible before. Because these devices were often unobtrusive "black boxes" with no visible moving parts, they made interviewees feel more at ease. Authors such as Studs Terkel, who relied heavily on interviews, frankly admitted that the tape recorder had become an essential tool for interviewing.[20]

Oral history, however, never quite lived up to its disciples' expectations. Partly for practical reasons, almost all oral history archives strove to transcribe taped interviews into typewritten documents. The argument ran that the transcripts were easier for researchers to use than the recordings. Edison had insisted that the phonograph's virtue in historical documentation would be the preservation of men's memories "in their own voices," but through the early 1960s Columbia University among others routinely destroyed the original recordings following their transcription. Evidently, historians of the day saw little value in preserving the information that a transcript could never transmit, such as the sound of the interviewer's voice, intonation, and cadence. Cultural anthropologists they were not. It is also worth noting that Nevins and his followers had their own good reasons for treating the transcript, and not the recording, as the authentic historical "document." It became a standard practice in professional oral history programs to allow interviewees to edit their transcripts, but there was no practical way to do the same for the tapes themselves. This, combined with the fact that interviewees were normally given the right to restrict public access to all or part of the transcripts, made the printed form of an oral history the focus of a collection rather than the tape. Many libraries saved only snippets of interviews for the purpose of preserving the interviewee's voice. Perhaps in the long run the wisdom of archivists may shine through, since it has become clear that some of the tapes sold in past years disintegrate with age.

Historians never completely broke free of the their commitment to text, or found ways to utilize recorded evidence directly. Oral history has not faded away, however. It continues to be the basis of many academic studies. The tape recorded interview is also the basis of much journalistic news gathering, though a great deal of it is combined with motion picture images in the form of videotape recording.

Teachers and Students Begin to Record

The sales chart that accompanies this chapter conveys a sense of the rate at which consumers adopted the tape recorder. The figures do not, however, reveal why they did so. Part of the rise of home recording came directly from the influence of advertising but also indirectly through familiarity. Institutions such as the oral history programs at universities and libraries acted both as consumers and as promoters of sound recording, introducing the sound recorder to many historians and interview subjects. This impact was small, however, compared to the familiarity and experience that came from the use of the sound recorder by teachers and students in primary and secondary schools. Schools gave many Americans, particularly young people who

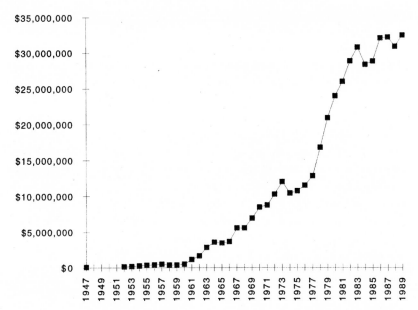

FIGURE 33. Sales of Tape Recorders, 1947–1989. Recorder sales remained low through the end of the 1950s. Sales rose following the introduction of less expensive transistorized recorders in the late 1950s, the introduction of the eight track tape system, and then the cassette. Source: U.S. Department of Commerce.

could not yet buy the devices themselves, their first hands-on experiences with sound recording technologies. As the children of one decade grew to be the consumers of the next, the effect of classroom sound recording would be to stimulate the market for home recorders.

Some sound recording had taken place in schools since the early 1930s, perhaps even the 1920s, but on a very limited scale. Speech and elocution teachers discovered that a sound recorder in the classroom could help students, particularly those with speech impediments, retrain their voices more quickly. It was this small pedagogical market that AT&T sought in the late 1930s, when it unsuccessfully tried to market an early form of the tape recorder called the Voice Mirror. The Brush Development Company, which would briefly become famous in the postwar years for its pioneering role in the consumer tape recorder market, also made a specialized voice training tape recorder in the late 1930s. Arguments for the virtues of these machines, whatever they may have been, fell on deaf ears in the late 1930s, when schools systems everywhere were cutting back on expenses. Acetate disk recording, which appeared at about the same time, generated considerable praise from speech teachers, but few sales resulted. Harvard's Frederick Packard in 1944 envisioned a Utopia where every English class could have a listening room called a "Vocarium" equipped with phonographs and sound recording equipment.[21] Many teachers felt a desire to use sound recording in the classroom, but few administrators could countenance the cost, expense, and inconvenience of the available equipment.

With the end of the war, the return of prosperity, and the appearance of new, low-cost wire and tape recorders, teachers all across the country took up sound recording in the classroom. Many of them did so at the urging of recorder manufacturers, several of which were already in the "audio visual education" field, and by 1954, about one-third of tape recorders sold in America went to schools or the government.[22] Some teachers recorded their own voices as a way to check their performance and improve their lecture skills but discovered how unnerving the experience could be. George Scherer of the University of Colorado described self-recording in 1947 as requiring "considerable courage . . . for the first efforts are sure to be somewhat disappointing."[23]

School systems were also among the most important early purchasers of the wire recorder when it appeared in 1945. At around $150, the wire recorder was easily affordable for almost any school, though teachers who used it soon got frustrated by the propensity of the wire to snarl. Its mechanical shortcomings made it too difficult for younger children to use themselves, which was one of the major aims of many teachers. One former student recalled that around 1955, he and "a couple of other designated geniuses were permitted to try the [wire recorder] out. Despite trying to be careful with it, the wire got tangled, probably when switching from rewind to stop or the like. It got under a hub and jammed the transport, and the teacher decided to rescue the machine."[24] The substitution of the wider, more mechanically stable tape medium, made classroom recording much easier. A junior high teacher gushingly reported in 1949 that she "was amazed at the ease of operation. It was fun to teach my pupils how to operate it, and I taught any number. They were soon teaching others, and each day there were happy children's voices singing and chattering into the mike after school." Her students used the tape recorder to practice recitations of portions of the Declaration of Independence, the Star Spangled Banner, and "historical talks." Yet even children experienced mike fright when making recordings of themselves, and uneasiness when listening to them. One teacher found that students were at ease when simply reading into the microphone, but they showed discomfort when they heard their voices on tape: "There was a good deal of giggling on the replay." Asked to recite a memorized passage, some of the students froze, and even with familiarity mike fright never completely disappeared. The shock of being recorded even led to a number of students developing a permanent "dislike for the gadget." Probably this was a dislike for self-recording, not the recorder itself.[25]

The early school systems that used tape and wire recording heavily were concentrated near the great centers of electronics manufacturing: New Jersey/New York, Chicago, and Los Angeles. To that list we should add Minnesota, where the largest tape manufacturer, 3M Corporation, had its headquarters. These companies influenced local educators first, who reported their findings in professional journals. By the early 1950s, sales of tape recorders to schools were spreading across the country to places like Mississippi, South Carolina, and Idaho.

The growth of the educational market for tape recorders in the 1950s was no isolated phenomenon. Manufacturers had long played the central role in making audio visual instruction a part of American lesson plans. Makers of tape and tape recorders in the early 1950s were simply extending marketing strategies pioneered by manufacturers of filmstrip and motion picture projectors, phonograph players, and educational films and recordings.[26] These manufacturers had in the 1940s successfully lobbied for the creation of several agencies to promote the use of technologies in the classroom, including the National Research Council's Committee on Scientific Aids for Teaching and the Office of Education's Radio Section. Advertisements and promotional literature flooded scholastic journals and the mailboxes of school administrators, and paved the way for carefully choreographed demonstrations by salesmen.[27]

The negative reaction of many teachers and students to the making of voice recordings of themselves sometimes dampened enthusiasm for the new technology. Further, many teachers frankly admitted that the making of recordings in the classrooms required considerable effort and had only a short-lived novelty value, after which students quickly lost interest. "Such short-lived motivation," wrote one Brooklyn College instructor in 1948, "is hardly worth the cost of the equipment."[28] Manufacturers, commercial record companies, publishers, and other firms reacted to increasing evidence that tape recorders were, more often than not, left in the equipment room by encouraging their use for other purposes. Educational programs delivered by radio had been available since the 1930s, but teachers could only use them when they aired at convenient times. The appearance of low-cost tape recorders made such programming more valuable by eliminating the need to schedule classes around performance times. Students in Union City, New Jersey, for example, in the early 1950s created an audio library of radio programs that could be played in the classroom. Opportunities to do so lasted only as long as educational programming on radio was widely available, which was perhaps through the mid-1950s, after which promoters again had to find exciting new educational applications for the tape recorder.[29]

Commercially produced educational tapes soon followed. The first was a taped version of the Gregg shorthand course. The Gregg Publishing Company, an arch enemy of sound recording in the form of the dictating machine, embraced the classroom tape player as a potentially lucrative marketing opportunity.[30] Tapes on other subjects, such as history, social studies, and literature, began flooding the educational market by the early 1960s.

Marvin Camras of the Armour Research Foundation hinted in 1952 that the tape recording might even replace the lecture, but few professors or teachers were ready to relinquish their podia.[31] Instead, the most common and persistent use of sound recording in schools after 1950 was in conjunction with language instruction. An experimental program using wire, disk, and tape recorders was underway as early as 1948 at Wayne University, followed by a similar program using tape recorders at Georgetown in 1949. Georgetown was one of the first to use the concept of the "language lab," in which students sat in cubicles and used individual tape recorders, first listening to a recording and then practicing by making recordings of themselves. This type of installation became a major market, and by the 1950s most U.S. tape recorder firms sold specialized language lab equipment. Curiously, language laboratories succeeded despite the ample evidence that students disliked hearing their own voices. Perhaps this can be attributed the students' lack of choice in the matter. But manufacturers were also careful to design the language lab as a solitary, isolated, and semiprivate experience. Students usually sat in private booths and listened via headphones. If they had to listen to their own voices, at least their voices could not be heard by others.[32]

Hi-Fi and the Tape Recorder

Between 1945, when the first consumer wire recorders appeared, and about 1948, sound recording was the sole province of the recording enthusiasts. As reconversion caused the economy to dip, wire recorders disappeared from the market and even tape recorder sales sputtered. Then, in the early 1950s, television sales skyrocketed and many consumers had to choose between these two fascinating new toys. Most chose television. Television's success also had

FIGURE 34. The RCA 45-rpm record system introduced in 1948 was aimed squarely at the largest market in the country; popular music. Norman Crowhurst, "Stereophonic Sound" (1961).

a second, indirect effect on sound recorder sales stemming from its devastation of radio programming. The transformation of radio into a primarily talk-, news-, and music-oriented medium undermined its attractiveness as a source of program material that consumers could record at home, and hence made the tape recorder less useful. Under different circumstances, a self-sustaining culture of home recording might have emerged (as it would later for the VCR) around the practice of recording broadcast programs. Without many traditional radio shows to record after 1950, tape recorder owners had to find their own fun.

The relatively small hobbyist market for portables, and the market for more expensive semiprofessional recorders (some costing $1000 or more) would continue to generate significant sales, but manufacturers after 1950

sought a true mass market for the tape recorder. They thought they had
found it when the high-fidelity movement appeared. High fidelity emerged
independently and somewhat unexpectedly, and advertisers wasted no time
transforming the image of the tape recorder from a "sound camera" for
recording enthusiasts into a musical instrument that could be integrated into
a hi-fi system. The tape recorder already offered much that manufacturers
believed would endear it to the new hobby, particularly its association with
professional sound recording. By 1950, all the major record labels had
switched to tape for making master recordings. The tape recorder's pedigree
(as presented in ads) appeared to show a direct line of descent from the
machines audiophiles treated as icons, such as the famous Ampex recorders,
directly to the more affordable consumer offerings. In reality, consumer
tape recorders delivered less than that. They were usually more expensive
than phonograph players, but only the machines in the $1000 and higher
price range could exceed a good record player or make recordings that
sounded as good as the original program. Still, in hi-fi, image and mystique were at least as important for sales and owner satisfaction as actual
performance.

The hi-fi movement of the early 1950s upon which manufacturers
hoped to graft tape recording did have some things in common with the home
recording hobby. Both were movements led by technophiles, and both offered
ample opportunities for conspicuous consumption and the display of arcane
knowledge and skills. Yet the two hobbies, often conflated in the press, had
a more fundamental difference: people involved in the hi-fi movement sought
better ways to reproduce musical recordings, not to make them. For this reason, most of the hi-fi "how to" books of the 1950s treated the tape recorder
as a optional piece of equipment rather than a necessity. The phonograph and
radio receiver remained the essential sources of musical entertainment. Even
television as a sound source figured more prominently in early hobby books,
hi-fi magazines, and kit catalogs than the tape recorder.[33]

Record companies did not reject the possibility that the tape recorder
might someday replace the phonograph, but neither were they willing to become
converts to the tape recording cause. In 1948 and 1949, RCA and Columbia
introduced two important new phonograph disk formats, the long-playing record
and the 45-rpm disk. Both these companies were involved in the making of
record players and had a vested interest in seeing this business continue. But
they were willing to supply the demand for recorded tapes. RCA entered the
field in 1954 with a small catalog of classical and pop albums on 7-inch reels
of tape. These tapes cost considerably more than a record album, but offered

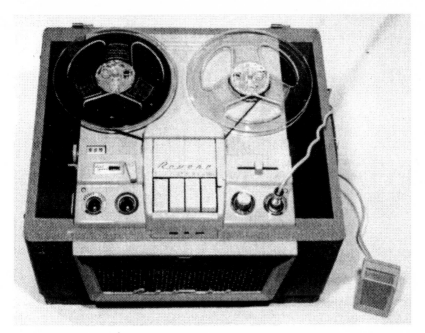

FIGURE 35. The Revere tape recorder of the late 1950s was designed to be a "stand-alone" unit, and had its own amplifier and speaker. Tape remained merely an adjunct to hi-fi systems through the 1960s. Special Collections and University Archives, Rutgers University Libraries.

only marginally better sound quality (or sometimes no discernible improvement at all). The tape market was inherently smaller than the disk market because no company seriously pursued the possibility of tape singles, which constituted the bulk of the record market until the late 1950s. In fact, no tape singles were marketed by a major record company until the 1980s, when "cassingles" appeared.[34]

There was little to distinguish tape and LP versions of recordings until about 1953, when the first stereo recordings appeared. Consumers willing to convert their monophonic tape recorders to stereo operation (at considerable expense) could now enjoy this new sound at home. Many radio stations were also experimenting with stereophonic transmissions at this time, giving owners of stereo tape recorders a new reason to record off the air. In 1958, however, RCA entered the stereo LP market with much fanfare. The possibility of stereo was apparently not enough to drive many consumers toward the tape recorder, and even stereo disk sales took many years to outnumber monophonic disk sales.

FIGURE 36. Much of the marketing of tape recorders in the 1950s attempted to associate the new technology with "serious" music. Ekotape ad, 1954. Author's collection.

Some of the consumer resistance to the tape recorder must be attributed to the actions of manufacturers, who continually upgraded the technology through the 1950s and made expensive equipment obsolete before its time. There were, for example, at least four incompatible stereo tape formats before RCA introduced the four-track tape in 1958. Soon Ampex (1959),

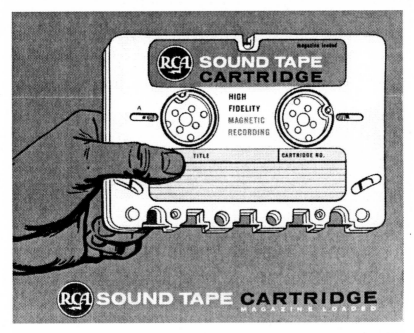

FIGURE 37. The ill-fated RCA cartridge tape system was one of several failed cartridge products of the 1950s. Author's collection. Reprinted with permission of Thomson Consumer Electronics, Inc.

Columbia, Capitol (both in 1960), and others adapted this format for open-reel tape and stuck with it to the end of the open-reel era in the mid-1980s. Manufacturers also tried several times in the 1950s and 1960s to interest consumers in new types of tape recorders. Most of these designs employed some sort of cartridge housing the tape itself. Ever since the introduction of open-reel wire recorders in 1945, manufacturers believed that widespread consumer acceptance would be guaranteed with such a cartridge arrangement, which was easier to use. It was not until 1958 that a major equipment manufacturer was ready to introduce such a machine, but when RCA did so the product almost immediately flopped. Cartridges themselves were not the key.[35]

   The first real measure of mass-market success for audio tape technology came in 1965 with the introduction of the Learjet "Stereo 8" cartridge system (also known as the eight track). Learjet's William Lear had personally led the campaign for the eight track, building it around an existing endless-loop cartridge for background music applications, the Fidelipac. After modifying the cartridge enough to win a set of patents on it, he wisely

FIGURE 38. Based on machines originally designed for commercial background music, endless loop tape system for cars began appearing in the late 1950s. The "Wayfarer" played stereo four-track cartridges sold by the Muntz Stereopak Company. Special Collections and University Archives, Rutgers University Libraries.

combined his company's resources with those of several other top firms: the manufacturing capability of the Motorola corporation, the record catalog of RCA-Victor, and the marketing organization of the Ford Motor Company.

The Ford eight track player, at $128, was an instant hit, and other U.S. auto manufacturers and third-party equipment retailers offered it as early as 1966. Ford sold about 60,000 of them in the first six months of production, marketing them as high-technology gadgets and symbols of status. RCA's initial eight track catalog of 250 titles expanded and other companies entered the field as tape sales grew rapidly. This growth occurred despite the fact that the price of a recorded eight track in 1967 was $6.95, several dollars higher than an LP. In contrast to open-reel tape sales, which had only reached 4 percent of total record sales in 1966, eight track sales by 1970 were about 30 percent of the total.[36] The eight track's main markets shifted as the product grew more successful. The initial catalog and early advertising clearly reflected an orientation toward middle-class, middle-age Americans. An eight track player was a popular option in the most expensive cars of the late 1960s, such as the Lincoln and the Oldsmobile Toronado. By the mid-1970s, record company catalogs contained all varieties of music on eight track tapes. The biggest sellers by far were rock and roll titles, and most ads targeted teens and young adults.

While eight track recorders were available from 1965 onwards, the most popular use of the eight track was for the reproduction of recorded music. Consumers responded enthusiastically to the device in part because they could use it in their automobiles or in portable players, avoiding the annoyingly commercial AM radio stations which were virtually the only other option. The eight track was no breakthrough in high-fidelity listening and *High Fidelity* magazine barely acknowledged the medium's existence, but even aficionados admitted that its shortcomings mattered little in an automobile. What was more surprising about the eight track's success was the number of consumers who bought home players. Consumer purchases gave a clear signal to record companies that portability and compatibility between home and portable systems, not high fidelity, were becoming major factors in tape purchases.

Audio portability was possible even in the early days of radio, but portables blossomed only after the introduction of the transistor. Transistor radios of the late 1950s were expensive novelties, but by the early 1960s they had become the medium of choice for teens, who often used them to listen to rock music beyond the earshot of adults. Transistors revolutionized portable audio, making tiny, lightweight, inexpensive, battery-operated tape recorders, radios, and even record players possible. Sales of transistorized automotive audio products also began to shoot upwards in the 1960s. High-power stereo amplifiers for the car, as well as improved FM radios, tape players, and auto accessories such as reverberation units (which promised to deliver that "concert hall" sound) all benefited from the introduction of the transistor and the popularity of portable audio.[37]

This penchant for portability also represented a turning point in home recording, bringing not only the tape recorder but the practice of sound recording into the mainstream. One indicator of the shift was blank tape sales, which by 1970 already accounted for about 125 million units. The blanks could be had for as little as $1.50, compared to the four to seven dollars that an album or recorded tape cost. Yet sales of blank tapes also suggested that ever-larger numbers of Americans were using their tape recorders for a new purpose, one with dark implications for the record industry. Blank open-reel tapes had traditionally been available in lengths such as fifteen, thirty, sixty, and

120 minutes. These lengths had been derived from the approximate amount of tape that would fit on a seven-inch diameter tape reel in 1945, which was about fifteen minutes' worth. When the plastic tape bases were made thinner and recording speeds got slower, manufacturers simply offered lengths that were a multiple of this. The top selling blank open-reel tapes suitable for music recording had a duration of at least two hours. As home recording on eight track tape began to take off, manufacturers found that their top selling blank tapes were the 45- and 90-minute sizes—in other words they were keyed to the length of the LP record. One 45-minute tape could hold about as much music an LP. This trend was duplicated in the blank cassette market by the late 1960s.[38]

Music Piracy

While home recording slowly increased in the late 1960s, illegal commercial duplication quickly rose up and briefly overshadowed its growth. Small-time music pirates were quick to exploit tape's capacity to make high-quality, low-cost copies of commercial record albums. The cost of a professional tape duplicator capable of making hundreds of copies a day was only a few thousand dollars in the late 1960s: well within the reach of individuals bent on piracy. As eight track sales boomed, so did the market for pirated tapes. Illicit duplicators rerecorded albums, often from a disk purchased in a record store, and transferred them to blank eight track cartridges at a cost of less than a dollar each. They sold them through gas stations, convenience stores, and sometimes even record dealers well below the cost of the legitimate item. Though marred by cheap-looking labels and often by poor audio quality, pirated tapes were considerably less expensive for consumers to buy.

Ampex Corporation, which had become the largest tape duplicator in the United States in the late 1960s, led a campaign in congress to end tape piracy. The company estimated that piracy amounted to $100 million in lost sales in 1970 alone. A new copyright law, passed in 1972, created stiff penalties for unauthorized duplication and led to threats of sanctions against countries where pirates were known to operate.

Even though the industry had eliminated some of the worst offenders by the late 1970s, by that time it faced the more insidious problem of widespread duplication by consumers. The experience of dealing with the pirates and their methods drove home the point that tape would always be a serious threat to record company profits, and that the record companies' enemies were equipment manufactures and consumers themselves.

Home copying by the late 1970s became the anathema of the record industry. It was a problem that seemed unsolvable because some of the same factors that had contributed so much to rapid growth in recorded eight track sales now threatened to turn the tables and cut deeply into the record industry's profits. The eight track tape system's great achievement was its contribution to the expansion of the market for recorded music through the introduction of battery-operated and automotive sound equipment in the 1960s. Some consumers would buy both disks and recorded tapes, and others would buy tape systems that allowed them use the same recordings in the car and in the living room. However, a growing segment of the population began using the tape recorder to copy the recordings owned by others, or to create a low-cost second copy of a purchased album for portable use. Soon 40 percent of consumers, according to one 1965 poll, were using their recorders primarily to make copies of purchased or borrowed LP records.[39]

The practice did not emerge simply from the availability of recording equipment. It was linked to factors such as the relatively high cost of LPs, improvements in other sorts of portable audio electronics, and the economics of home taping. Recorded eight tracks cost up to several dollars more than LPs, so consumers who had both a home audio system and a portable or car eight track player were tempted to copy albums onto blank tape for a few dollars rather than buying both. The widespread perception that the eight track was an inferior-sounding medium seemed to discourage tape-to-tape copying, and no "dubbing" eight track decks appeared. Instead, the use of the LP as source material for eight tracks appealed to people who treated their expensive albums as the "real" product and saw inexpensive tape copies as "expendable," but also to people who did not buy albums at all, but borrowed them only in order to make a copy.

The economics of home copying on the eight track system soon began to look less attractive to consumers than copying on new technology, the Philips "Compact Cassette." The cassette was introduced in Europe three years before the eight track and arrived in the United States in 1965. Launched with little fanfare, it was marketed as an all-purpose, very low cost portable sound recorder. Norelco (North American Philips) had been marketing similar open-reel machines since the late 1950s, and hoped to grab the very low end of the home market the way its earlier cartridge dictation machine had taken a portion of the market for low-cost office recorders. The Norelco "Carry-Corder," a handheld, battery-operated, tinny-sounding cassette recorder, cost $69.95 in 1967, and a blank tape long enough to hold two full albums only $3.75. Teens enthusiastically greeted the cassette and appreciated the low purchase price of both the recorders and the blank tapes. Mercury records began offering recorded cassettes as early as 1968, but in 1970 sales were still only a fraction of eight track sales. The cassette's main use was the making of recordings at home. Even though home cassette "decks" soon appeared, through the mid-1970s 80 percent of cassette recorders sold in America were still battery-operated portables.

The cassette equipment of the 1960s was a harbinger of change in the U.S. audio equipment market. It was inexpensive, "low fi," and usually imported from Japan. It was neither the first nor the last inexpensive tape system to appear in America, but for several reasons it enjoyed the greatest success. An important factor in its acceptance among manufacturers was Philips' liberal licensing policies, which made it available to many different firms; General Electric, Wollensak, and Magnavox already had battery-operated cassette recorders on the market in 1966.[40] Further, it proved to be more adaptable to different uses. Higher-quality home cassette decks began to appear, which broadened the format's appeal to include older and wealthier groups of Americans. Later upgrades were usually compatible with the previous generation of tapes and players. Philips, for example, wisely designed the stereo recorders that began to appear in the later 1960s so that mono tapes could still be played on them.

The format got the endorsement, cautious at first, of many of the most important enthusiast and consumer-protection oriented magazines. In 1967, *Consumer Reports* favored the cassette over the eight track systems it tested, mainly for reasons of convenience in recording.[41] Makers of eight track systems rested on their laurels in the 1970s, but cassette boosters worked furiously to improve its sound quality. One consumer version of the Dolby system of noise reduction, for example, was created specifically to overcome the high levels of tape hiss inherent in the cassette system. The eight track, with much lower levels of hiss, did not seem to need such a crutch.[42] However, the Dolby name became much more important than the technology itself, symbolizing to consumers the cutting edge of technology rather than just a quick fix for an inadequate recording system. Yet Dolby and other innovations like high-bias tapes were not mere gimmicks. By the mid-1970s, top-quality home cassette decks could boast measurable sound quality that not only topped the eight track but rivaled the ponderous open-reel decks.[43] Through a combination of flash and technical innovation, the cassette system soon outperformed the eight track in almost every category.

The pleasure the cassette system provided came not merely from the sound itself, but also from something vaguely defined as "convenience." It

FIGURE 39. The "Maxell Guy," an advertising campaign begun in the 1970s by Maxell Corporation. Tape and recorder manufacturers transformed the image of the cassette in the 1970s from low-fi to high tech. Maxell Corporation of America. Reprinted by permission.

combined new technologies with known elements to provide something that had not been readily available before, and it came along at a time when a younger group of consumers was beginning to exercise a greater level of spending on music and electronics. Teens proved to be the best customers for the lowest cost battery-powered recorders (those costing $50 or less); 20 percent of the girls surveyed by *Seventeen* magazine in 1967, for example, owned tape recorders (almost twice the national average for recorder ownership). Teens, unburdened by habit or large libraries of recorded eight track or open-reel tapes, shifted effortlessly to the use of the cassette, especially as prices for recorders dropped below $30 by 1968.[44]

Sales of recorded cassettes took much longer to catch on. Audiophiles rejected many of them on the basis of their poor sound quality, but a stronger disincentive for younger consumers was the price. At $5.95 in 1968, cassettes were more expensive than LPs (though equally as or less expensive than eight tracks). A significant but temporary factor limiting recorded cassette sales was the lack of titles compared to other formats. Most U.S. record companies maintained their loyalty to the eight track system through the late 1970s, partly because of the home recording problem. At first, RCA, Columbia, and Capitol announced that their cassette offerings would be minimal until "substantial demand was present." Major record-label executives, who admitted to being terrified by the possibilities of the cassette system even in 1969, also chose not to issue some of the most popular albums on cassette in an effort to encourage album sales. In fact, the record companies were much less supportive of any form of tape than they were of the LP. The Columbia Record Company actually listed reasons not to buy a tape on a Bob Dylan album's inner sleeve. The most open hostility, however, was reserved for the diminutive cassette. A Columbia official in 1968 remarked that the company would not help the equipment manufacturers by "telling the public they can play our music on cassettes." Unsure of how to deal with tape, they took a hands-off attitude toward the recorded tape market into the 1970s, particularly in the case of the cassette, preferring to transfer responsibility for duplication and distribution to outside firms. Ampex, with no commitment to the LP (and as a manufacturer of eight track and cassette recorders) jumped at the chance to sell tapes, and offered a catalog of five hundred titles by late 1967.[45] The recording division of Ampex experienced a meteoric rise as a music manufacturer in the late 1960s, mostly through the production of tapes (although it declined just a few years later).

The eight track held its own through the mid-1970s, but sales of cassette recorders and blank and recorded cassettes gradually crept up. When recorded cassette sales finally exceeded those of eight tracks in 1982, several major record companies unceremoniously dropped the older format. The move may have been justified in terms of cost cutting, for record sales were in a slump, but it only intensified what was becoming a disaster for the industry: unauthorized recording on cassette. By now, the installed base of cassette recorders numbered in tens of millions. Not only had the technology been improved to the point where even high-fidelity purists fully accepted it, the portable market had seen yet another burst of growth. Beginning with a craze for battery-operated "boom boxes" in the late 1970s, the rise in portable sales was given an additional spur from the appearance of the Sony Walkman and its competitors. Most of the Walkman-type devices were players, not recorders, but by this time many people owned both home and portable cassette equipment, with the home machine used for duplication. For those who did not own a home recorder or collection of albums, the Walkman still provided an economical way to listen, and soon recorded cassette sales exceeded LP sales.

Now record companies took their case against home taping to Congress. The first round of hearings took place in 1982, shortly after Warner Communications and an industry group, the Home Recording Rights Coalition, had independently sponsored major surveys of home-taping practice. The authors of these surveys, who took nearly opposite positions on the propriety of home taping, concurred with the record companies' accusations that home taping was a widespread and economically significant practice occurring among nearly every category of consumer. Only a quarter of recorder owners never used their machines for recording while many home recordists were using cassette decks to put together "mixes" of their favorite songs, either from borrowed albums or from albums they already owned. A large percentage of home recordists also made tapes of complete albums. These two activities had different economic implications and elicited different responses from the record companies. Home recording of complete albums was, to the record companies, lost revenue, while the making of "mix" tapes did not necessarily compete with commercially available products. Even taping of complete albums was acceptable as long as consumers first bought the album themselves. Record companies probably preferred that the low-cost, second copy be purchased rather than homemade, but they did not subsequently choose to offer products to compete with home rerecording. Instead, they continued to push for its curtailment.

These congressional hearings revealed how deep the record company's concerns were regarding home taping. Warner was considering the adoption of anticopying technology built into its LP records, but the general thrust of the industry was toward some kind of economic penalty to be imposed on consumers and/or equipment manufacturers. Taxes on tape recorders had been imposed in Germany in the 1960s following just this sort of debate, but equipment manufacturers in the U.S. lobbied hard against them. In the end, Congress upheld the right of consumers to make recordings but encouraged he equipment and recording industries to cooperate on a new, anticopying technology.

The failure of record companies to stem the tide of home taping must have had some effect on their decisions to support the new technology of the compact disc after 1982. The aural merits of the new digital recording medium have been debated by audiophiles since its introduction, but its other technical features clearly endeared it to record companies and consumers alike. It was a format that combined high-quality audio, the convenience of operation of a phonograph record, a package small enough to be used with miniaturized portable players, and durability, but no recording capability. The digital recording process, the stylish appearance of the players, and the disk's small size gave it the cachet of high technology, and after only a few years of production the cost of the average player was comparable to phonograph or tape equipment. However, if record companies hoped that the new format would deter home recording they were wrong. As sales of compact discs rose in the 1990s, so too did sales of blank tapes.

The record industry has opposed or ignored most new recording technologies since the introduction of the compact disc, which is remarkable given the fact that several major equipment manufactures have been affiliated with record companies during this time. The most prominent of these was the Digital Audio Tape, a smaller, recordable digital medium introduced in 1987 and capable of meeting the performance of the compact disc. The DAT met with strong opposition, generating another round of congressional hearings and demands for some sort of technological anticopying solution.[46]

Yet it is also true that consumers have not been seen to clamor for DAT or other recordable digital media. The Digital Compact Cassette, a compatible analog/digital medium introduced in 1992, died a quiet death just a few years later. The Minidisc, a two-inch, recordable digital disc, has been on the market since 1993, but it has not displaced either the compact disc or the cassette tape. Journalists continue to report that DAT and other digital media are not readily available in the United States, but the fact is that they simply have not caught on. Perhaps consumers do not want to pay the high costs of obtaining this equipment, since it does not seem to offer them much they do not already have with the combination of the compact disc and the cassette tape.

Conclusions

Many Americans regularly make sound recordings today, but even in the recent past, it was unusual for ordinary people to act as anything other than consumers of the recordings made by the phonograph record industry. In a few specialized professions before World War II, some people tried to make use of the recording technologies available but found them lacking in many ways. The introduction of new sound recording devices after 1945, particularly the tape recorder, overcame some of the technical difficulties of sound recording, but the widespread adoption of the technology was by no means assured. Relatively small numbers of musicians, businessmen, teachers, historians, and others revived interest in sound recording, and even found exciting new ways to use the technology. Sales figures for the open-reel tape recorder in the 1950s probably exaggerate its real impact, for many of these machines quickly went into the closet, where they became dust-gathering reminders of lost enthusiasm and impulse buying. Americans discovered that sound recording demanded more creativity than they were willing to invest, and that they did not like the sound of their own voices. Even at the end of the 1940s, some manufacturers believed they had saturated the market and began looking for a more appealing design to capture a true mass audience.

Tape recording, which was not originally part of the high-fidelity movement, seemed imminently suited to being grafted onto this emerging hobby, and manufacturers were sure that this would lead to the mass market they sought. Enthusiasts responded half-heartedly, appreciating the technical sophistication of the open-reel recorder but finding little to use it for. It was not the high-fidelity movement but the mobile lifestyle of Americans and the youth culture that pushed the demand for recorded tape to new heights. Transistorized equipment fit neatly into the cultures of automobility and rock-and-roll listening. After numerous fits and starts, tape recording's promoters stumbled on their first really huge success not with a recording system, but with a music player—the eight track tape. The eight track system would see a rapid rise but also a sudden fall. It was the technology that introduced Americans to the idea of using multiple audio systems at home and on the move and of programming their own music to suit their tastes and activities. However, the success of the eight track hastened its eventual downfall. The bastard offspring of muzak and the Detroit auto industry, the eight track was too big, too expensive, and too poorly suited to home recording to satisfy home tapists. Americans, in redefining how they wanted to use tape technology, opted for the cassette, with its lower blank-tape cost and greater convenience.

Record companies supported the eight track only grudgingly and were not sorry to see it go, but they despised its successor, the cassette, even more. Despite the cassette's potential for generating profits from sales of recorded tapes, record companies early on identified in it the threat of the easy duplication of their products. They successfully battled the large-scale record pirates, but could never regain the control over their products that they lost to home cassette recording. For the last twenty years, home duplication of commercial records has become an ingrained part of life for many Americans, but its success as a democratized form of activity corresponds with a failure for the record industry. What the record companies lost to cassette recording was the opportunity to introduce a customized or individualized music product on tape. In choosing to make recordings at home, ordinary people have retaken a role, however minor, in determining the ways they receive commercial musical culture. It would be easy to make too much of this—Americans are still by and large simply consumers of the musical commodities blasted at them by corporations. But in subtle ways they have revised the terms by which they consume those products. The record companies are not unaware of this. Like any aspect of culture, the making of tapes may someday disappear, and perhaps the day is not far away. Having learned a hard lesson from the cassette, the record companies are not likely to sponsor a digital recording technology (which seems the most likely successor to the cassette) without effective copy protection. Whether their efforts will kill or co-opt home recording culture remains to be seen.

Conclusion

Diffusion and Ubiquity

Over the past hundred years, sound recording has become an integral part of communication, business, entertainment, and information-storage technologies, and sound recordings have infused American society. In the same way that high-speed printing and photography revolutionized the production and consumption of written and visual information, sound recording transformed the aural environment. Recording technology became the audible version of the artist's pallet, the advertiser's billboard, the editor's page, and everything in between. Recordings today are heard everywhere, and their content runs a gamut from the sublime to the banal, from high art to audio pornography, from brilliant creativity to mundane utility. So common are recordings today that it is difficult to estimate how often the average American hears them. They encounter them regularly in public spaces, their homes, and their beloved automobiles. In 1996 alone, Americans purchased 1.1 billion recordings for personal use, and listened to them via compact disc players, Walkmans, boom boxes, car audio systems, and even desktop computers. While we are able to count these purchases, they do not begin to suggest the real significance of recordings for American listening. Sound recordings are also a component of the movies Americans rent, the radio they hear, and the television they watch. Even technologies not necessarily associated with sound recording are sometimes laden with recorded material. In the telephone system, for example, automated recording equipment indicates misdialed numbers, provides time and weather announcements, announces voice mail instructions, and performs dozens of other tasks.

Americans make recordings by the millions as well, but it is just as daunting to try to estimate how much recording actually goes on as it is to estimate how many recordings Americans listen to. There were almost 30,000 copyrights registered in 1996 for sound recordings, but this number does not include the tens of thousands of motion pictures and television and radio programs in which recordings are an integral part. The making of recordings outside the studios of the entertainment industry can be measured with even less precision. One estimate of the number of tape recorders in use in 1980 was 98 million machines, or about one for every two people in the country. In 1996 Americans bought $314 million worth of blank cassettes, most for use at home to duplicate commercial recordings, but some for use in telephone answering devices or dictation machines. Americans also bought over $1 billion worth of answering machines that year, representing tens of millions of them added to the tens of millions already in use. Many of the millions of personal World Wide Web sites currently in existence include digital sound recordings of one kind or another. The total number of cassettes, answering machine messages, digital recording on PCs, and other recordings made each year must number in the hundreds of millions.[1]

One significant aspect of recording's diffusion through society is that it calls into question the most generally accepted definition of "the recording industry." Sound recording in American society is the basis of a cluster of familiar products related to musical records, the consumption of which is possible to observe and the economic important of which is easy to appreciate. These records are normally the only sound recordings associated with the "recording industry." But sound recording is also the basis of a variety of other forms of commercial and personal communication, and it is these poorly documented uses of recording which truly pervade life today. Americans spend on average 357 hours per year listening to purchased records, which at first glance seems like great deal. However, they also hear numerous sound recordings during the nearly 1600 hours per year that they spend watching broadcast television; during the 1000 hours spent listening to radio, the 57 hours spent watching videotapes, and the 12 hours spent watching movies in theaters. These figures do not include the snippets of records Americans hear almost every time they pass through public spaces, the background or informational recordings of voice and music broadcast in doctors' offices, supermarkets, bank, lobbies, busses, and elevators. In the music record industry, recording is the basis of a form of mass-produced art, but the wider recording industry produces sound records for a diverse range of purposes. Part of the reason that sound recording has become so widespread is that it is so generally applicable to a range of public, private, and commercial purposes. Its flexibility as a medium allowed it to be appropriated by a range of actors with divergent aims, partly explaining recording's ubiquity in late twentieth-century culture.

Technology Push? Demand Pull?

Recording became so pervasive by presenting new opportunities, but also by building on existing social structures and technological systems. In no case was the success or failure of a particular recording technology due merely to the invention of a new device. Historians of technology have argued persuasively that no aspect of the invention, diffusion, or disappearance of a technology can be divorced from its social context. Inventions embody cultural biases, economic constraints, political ideologies, and other factors, even when their inventors see them only as practical solutions to purely technical problems. The subsequent history of inventions, as they become objects of use, is guided as much by social imperatives as the technical possibilities and limitations of the inventions themselves. Sound recording is no exception.[2]

The story of sound recording is thus one of technology *and* culture, and showing the origins and implications of that relationship has been a central aim of this book. In many cases, the life cycle[3] of an invention has two distinct phases, one involving all the decisions and events leading up to the invention, and the second beginning as customers or users begin to interact with it. The unpredictable nature of the social forces that shape the development of inventions is the source of so many of the wrong turns, misguided forecasts, and outright failures seen in the history of sound recording. Sound recording inventions ranging from shining examples of engineering virtuosity to contraptions bordering on the fraudulent have succeeded or failed not merely on their technical merits but due to factors usually beyond the control of their inventors or corporate sponsors. For this reason, with only a few, temporary exceptions, the story of sound recording inventions in America can be fully understood only by tracking their trajectories after they have entered the marketplace. The individuals that made up the marketplace were consumers of many different sorts, exercising varying levels of demand, the economic power that partly determined success or failure. This book has employed a broad definition of "consumer," so that the roles of corporations, engineers, musicians, and managers could be included as well as consumers of the ordinary sort: individuals purchasing items for their personal use.

Consumers and users determine the course of technological history in many ways, and their influence sometimes turns up in unexpected places. There is not always a neat division between the pre-market, or inventive, phase of technological history and the post-laboratory, production, and marketing phases, where consumers act only in the latter. The role of the consumer or user in sound recording history often had significance before a device entered the marketplace. Consumers, or at least imagined consumers, played a role in the invention process as well. Imagined consumers, for example, were paramount in the mind of Frank Stanton, an inventor who in the late 1960s conceived the Playtape system. Playtape technology was an attempt to recombine the elements of several music systems then popular in the United States. The Playtape cartridge was an endless loop device like an eight track tape, but it was about half the size of the Philips cassette. Playtapes contained recorded selections (a tape held two or three songs) from the most popular artists, and they cost under a dollar. The players were usually battery operated, lightweight portables priced to be competitive with the inexpensive cassette recorders becoming popular with American teens. Playtape thus offered the hits available on 45-rpm records, the portability and low cost of the cassette system, and the operating simplicity of the eight track.

A few years later, after grabbing only a few percentage points of the market for tape recording products, Playtape technology was in the technological junk pile with so many other short-lived consumer audio formats. Even though its designers appreciated the appeal of existing tape systems and had tried to extrapolate what they believed were their most attractive technical features, the result could not compete with either the eight track or the cassette, both of which persisted for many more years. Consumers simply did not find the devices appealing, and sales did not attain the volume necessary to sustain Playtape's ambitious marketing and distribution effort. It is appealing to speculate that the Playtape failed in part because it could not make recordings, as the cassette could. However, it is clear that recording capability is not the only determinant of success for a new audio format. We can learn more about the nature of recording technologies by investigating the perceptions of inventors about how their inventions will be used, or by investigating how they actually *were* used, than by assuming that inventions unfolded in a logical manner or that the "best" technology always won.

Off the Record

It is unfortunate that in the past the recording, distribution, and consumption of commercial music has been the only aspect of sound recording's history that has proven to be of interest to scholars and the public. One result of this focus on the commercial music record is that it suggests that the field of sound recording is the same as the music record industry. This notion oversimplifies the relationships between the sound recording, the economy, and society. This is not to say that the music record industry is unimportant. In 1996 the combined revenues of U.S. record companies nearly equaled those of the television networks, and their revenues were nearly half those of motion picture producers. This segment of the sound recording industry rivals in size the fields of newspaper and magazine publishing. But while the record industry is large, it is only the most visible segment of a remarkably varied set of organizations and activities related to the commercial production and consumption of recorded music.[4]

Because recorded sound, especially music, is part of many other commercial enterprises, the true extent of the "recording industry" is much larger than the numbers indicate. The Muzak Corporation is an excellent example of an enterprise that delivers recorded music to consumers, but that is not part of our conventional definition of the record industry. The Wired Radio Corporation, formed in 1930 and from which Muzak emerged, was essentially a radio network without the radio stations. In Muzak's New York studios, programs recorded on 16-inch transcription disks were carried over AT&T wideband telephone lines to remote locations in a fashion similar to the way NBC, CBS, or Mutual network programs were distributed to local radio stations. Instead of being broadcast, however, Muzak programming was fed into hotel and office sound systems; it was "piped-in" music. By 1937 Muzak had a library of 7,500 transcriptions and provided a "red" service featuring dance music and a "purple" service of light concert music.[5]

Just before World War II, British researchers used empirical evidence to demonstrate that certain kinds of music increased the efficiency of industrial workers, and during the war American war production plants all carried background music. Muzak would spawn a host of imitators in the 1950s and 1960s who all distributed recorded programming to private customers in a way that competed, more or less directly, with network radio. Muzak's management soon decided to stop using existing recordings and to hire their own musicians, arrangers, and recording technicians. A team of industrial psychologists and music arrangers carefully selected and recorded songs, and engineers turned them into programs intended to increase worker attentiveness and alleviate fatigue. Muzak and its competitors became more than just providers of background music systems and programming, but also the producers of a specialized type of recorded music. There are many other such specialized recording firms in the United States, all of which might reasonably be considered part of the broader recording industry. The American system of radio broadcasting itself might be considered a segment of the recording industry broadly defined, given the heavy volume of recordings its networks and stations make and use.[6]

Just as there is more to the music recording industry than we previously recognized, so too is the sum total of sound recording history much more than just music recording. The historical focus on makers of commercial recordings and the record as a commodity has also distorted our understanding of the relationship of recording activity, in all its various forms, to systems of production and forms of business. All recording is a type of production, but not all recording activity results in articles for sale. For example, the cassette tape has changed the recording industry by creating a home-based extension of it. Unlike the eighteenth-century's home-based "putting out" system of textile production, the making of cassettes at home is not orchestrated by companies that collect and process these products. Instead, home taping is comparable to knitting as a hobby, where consumers use raw materials similar to those employed at the factories to make their own products. If the making of recordings is viewed as a form of production, then it is clear that its popularization bucks the trend of modern capitalism toward centralized, automated, factory production of goods previously made by hand or at home.[7]

Unlike hand-knit items, the use of homemade tapes constitutes a second activity with broader economic and social significance, for tapes are also a form of communication. Homemade tapes as a form of communication again represent a countertrend to the dominant pattern of modern capitalism. Unlike forms of communication that began as hobbies or amateur endeavors but were later appropriated by powerful corporations, recording has become more democratized over the course of the century. The oligopolistic media empires in radio, movies, television, and phonograph records lost control over this technology, and recording has been taken up by millions of ordinary Americans.

Authenticity, Accuracy, Control

In order to explore the history of technology, in this book I have adopted a broad definition of culture. To some historians, the word culture implies so-called high culture: fine art, music, and literature. Popular culture, by this definition, refers to popularized versions of these same arts, music, and literature. On the other hand, anthropologists (among others) employ the word culture to describe social conventions, belief systems, and virtually all other nonmaterial aspects of society. In this anthropological view, art, music, and literature are merely subsets of the broader phenomenon of culture.

Published histories of sound recording are laden with debate over high culture and popular culture issues but have not examined what I have called recording culture, or the culture of recording. Working from the assumption that the live performance is the only true expression of musical art, critics of the phonograph (and its successors) have denigrated sound recording as a mere "mechanical reproduction" that degrades music. Sound recording as a medium introduces a delay between performers and the audience, and as such represents a barrier between performers and audience. Scholars continue, interestingly, to debate the issue of the "authenticity" of recorded music, as if listening to recorded sound can somehow approach the experience of hearing an actual performance. No matter how "real" a recording sounds, it is and always will be a recording.

The desire to create technologies of sound recording that can convey a sense of authenticity to the listener enraptured generations of engineers and musicians. For at least the first seventy-five years of sound recording history, the technologies that engineers chose for use in music recording usually advanced that aim, and phonograph and tape recordings inched subjectively closer to "high fidelity," despite the lack of a scientific definition of what fidelity really was. Yet the drive for perfect reproduction would drive engineers and musicians toward technologies that enhanced their ability to manipulate as well as capture sound. Increasingly after World War II, the dominant understanding of what fidelity meant shifted from realism in reproduction to simply a pleasing sound. Different people defined pleasing in various ways, but few of those involved in making these recordings imagined that the final product would accurately recreate some original performance. Thus the drive to achieve "fidelity" in recording involved a clash of cultures, and the combination of science and aesthetics pulled recording technology in different ways. In the end, the use of technology to preserve elite culture became less important than the technological manipulation of sound to produce popular culture.

The use of recording to attain accuracy, and the control and manipulation of sound are also evident in the business applications of recording. Dictation machine advertisements and promotional literature from the late nineteenth century onward stressed the ability of the machine to take down words accurately, and to assure the letter writer that his words would not be lost or forgotten through the more fallible process of shorthand transcription. One of Edison's earliest published essays on the phonograph noted that the tinfoil (the medium he initially planned to use) "is a perfect *record*" [emphasis in original], and suggested that the best way to take advantage of its inherent accuracy was to mail the resulting recording as a business letter rather than transferring it to paper.[8] Railroad companies employed early versions of the telephone answering machine to convey orders to remote switching stations for much the same reason. Railroad managers who employed the machine appreciated the fact that a sound record allowed their employees to double-check telephone instructions and avoid a reliance on handwriting. In these cases, management also had in the sound recording evidence of blame if instructions were not carried out. The incidence of inaccuracy in telephone messages taken by live answering services was a factor in the growing success of answering machines by the 1970s. A survey taken in 1974 indicated that many business users had purchased machines because of their dissatisfaction with live secretaries. Businesses, therefore, appropriated the sound recorder for their own ends.[9] Yet the success of sound recording in business also depended on factors far removed from those espoused in management textbooks. Part of the reason office dictation failed to catch on in offices is that it did not suit the managers who were asked to use it. Besides its technical limitations and the uneasiness it created for some users, it disrupted an important social network of gender and status relations. While such relations were rarely acknowledged, they existed nonetheless.

Appropriation and Subversion

The phenomenon of consumers appropriating recording technology, or redefining the uses and reasons for making a sound recording, is one of the most important aspects of sound recording history. Often the process of appropriation was a transgression of boundaries. Underlying many of the different artistic, commercial, scientific, and engineering applications of sound recording, for example, is a history of subversion. Users and consumers of sound recording consistently broke the rules set for them by inventors, engineers, managers, policy makers, and corporations. As it became easier and less expensive to make a sound recording, especially after World War II, consumers found an increasing number of ways to divert the technology to their own ends, many of which put them in conflict with the companies and institutions supplying the devices.[10]

There is no more infamous example than recordings made from tapped telephone lines. Though wiretapping has been practiced since before the turn of the century (and was preceded by the tapping of telegraph lines), recording devices made exploiting the information a wiretap provided more effective. The ephemeral nature of telephone conversations made a handwritten transcription of information gained via a wiretap mere hearsay as legal evidence until the advent of easy-to-use sound recorders. Almost immediately after World War II, courts began admitting wire- or tape-recorded evidence if the voices on it could be authenticated.[11]

The unauthorized duplication of musical records is another important category of recording activity in which users subvert the intentions of corporations, challenge the legal system, and redirect technology to their own ends. The unauthorized copying of recordings began around the turn of the century in the days of cylinder phonographs. There are several different kinds of illegal sound recordings according to American law. Record piracy, defined as the unauthorized duplication and sale of copyrighted material, is different from the more common practice of counterfeiting, which is the unauthorized duplication and sale of copyrighted material with the intent to make consumers believe that the copies are actually originals. Often these two phenomena are called "bootlegging," though technically this is a distinct category. A bootleg is a commercial release of a recording made surreptitiously or the sale of a studio recording not intended for commercial release. Before World War II, many bootlegs were rerecordings of the 16-inch "transcription" phonograph records used by radio stations. With the advent of tape, many rock concerts have been recorded and distributed on disk or tape. Both counterfeiters and pirates sold hit records in large quantities to otherwise legitimate retailers at a deep discount.

The early postwar period also saw much (mostly undocumented) copying of phonograph disks for use in jukeboxes. One famous incident which came to light because the counterfeiters were brought to court involved a commercially legitimate but Mafia-operated record pressing plant in New Jersey. At night, people at the plant made masters and stampers by rerecording ordinary, purchased copies of hit records. While the sound quality of these second-generation masters was somewhat lower than the original, it was good enough to sell. These low-cost disks were then distributed across New Jersey and played in jukeboxes, which were themselves operated by Mafia thugs. Some of the other cases of counterfeiting that came to light had less sinister players. The famous record retailer Sam Goody was convicted of purchasing and distributing large numbers of counterfeit records in New York in the 1950s. By 1960, the U.S. record industry estimated that it was losing approximately $20 million per year to counterfeiters and pirates, and renewed efforts to force the federal government to enforce copyright laws.

Illegal copying of sound recordings took on a new dimension in the 1970s as the cassette tape became more popular. Counterfeit eight track tapes became a significant problem for record companies in the early 1970s in the United States, since the equipment needed to duplicate these tapes was relatively inexpensive. The record industry was able to put pressure on federal and state governments to close down most of the large illegal copying operations in the United States, though pirating remained a serious problem in most other countries. Interestingly, sound recordings themselves were not eligible for copyright before 1972 in the United States, but revisions to the Copyright Act of 1909 made it easier to prosecute record pirates.[12]

The copyright laws were amended in 1971 to guarantee the right of individual consumers to make copies of broadcasts and purchased recordings for their own use, but the changes were reversed in 1976.[13] In spite of recording-industry consternation with home taping, as late as the 1970s only two major manufacturers of tape recorders, JVC and Philips, had any economic ties to the record industry, and most recorder manufacturers simply refused to eliminate or restrict the recording features of their equipment. In fact by the 1970s, most of the major Japanese consumer electronics companies were selling double-well cassette recorders expressly designed to make high-speed copies of tapes. A CBS study conducted in 1980 concluded that the record industry effectively lost $700 to $800 million per year because of home taping. Several countries began to impose royalties on sales of tape recorders and/or blank tapes in the 1980s, including Argentina, Australia, Austria, Congo, West Germany, Finland, France, Gabon, Hungary, Iceland, Netherlands, Norway, Portugal, Spain, Sweden, Turkey, and Zaire.[14] However, the collusion between electronics manufacturers and consumers continued, spurred on by the additional support of blank tape manufacturers.

In the late 1980s, home copying of audio tapes again returned to the forefront in the United States. A number of Japanese and European equipment makers were pushing for new kinds of digital recorders, either optical or magnetic, which promised to make copies of originals without sound degradation. Congressional hearings in 1982, 1987, and 1990 led to a series of new laws aimed at forcing overseas manufacturers to incorporate a copy-protection scheme into their hardware. This Serial Copy Management System electronically prevented the making of second generation copies. The Audio Home Recorder Act of 1992 also put a royalty on sales of digital audio tape recorders and blank tapes, to be paid to copyright owners and performers.

The inability of corporate sponsors and governmental regulators to enforce their will, along with an American penchant to evade their control, are two of the most persistent features of sound recording history. Even so, the same flexibility and adaptability that allowed individuals and corporations to reshape recording technology to suit their own purposes also allowed recording's "legitimate" sponsors to pursue their ends as well.[15]

Transformation

Subversion and appropriation are good ways to describe the ability of sound recording's inventors and users to transform existing systems of communication. Engineers, businessmen, and radio announcers after World War II used a mixture of old and new technologies to transform broadcasting from an instantaneous, live communications medium into a medium for delivering recordings. Although listeners did not select these recordings, put them on a turntable or tape deck, or perhaps even recognize their existence, radio after 1945 increasingly delivered recorded programming to America's living rooms and automobiles.

This shift to recordings in communication is not unique. During the Korean and Vietnam Wars, soldiers purchased inexpensive Japanese tape recorders in large numbers and began making tapes to send home to their families. CBS television correspondent Morley Safer reported in 1967 that the Vietnam War had "rendered the written word obsolete," and played for the audience an example of such a "letter tape." The subsidized mail service available to soldiers made voice letters instantly popular. In a sense, soldiers had transformed, if only partially, the United States Postal Service into an audio medium through the use of recordings. This elderly communication system, designed for written communication, now transmitted voice.

By using recordings, individuals and institutions could even transform a point-to-point medium into a form of broadcasting. In the mid-1960s a political group calling itself "Let Freedom Ring" placed a series of advertisements in local newspapers across the country. Citizens were invited to call a special number to hear a shocking announcement. The recordings had been left on equipment developed by AT&T similar to an answering machine, except that it could be used for delivering outgoing messages to several callers simultaneously. The messages attacked various local and national organizations, claiming communist infiltration, Soviet collaboration, or other anti-American activities. In Denver, for example, the Parent Teacher Association was accused of "promoting Socialist or Marxist schemes," and in Florida citizens were told that the local colleges were indoctrinating students with pro-Soviet ideas.

The public reaction to these events was so overwhelmingly negative that in congressional hearings local telephone companies were required to make available the names of those who sponsored such services. "Let Freedom Ring" quietly disappeared, but the use of recording equipment to deliver repetitive messages to large numbers of individuals remained in place for many years. The use of the AT&T 1A equipment had transformed ordinary, person-to-person telephony into a form of broadcasting, one that gave a loud voice to a marginalized political group and required action at the top levels of federal government to quiet.[16]

Less controversial examples of the transformation of the telephone into a broadcast medium showed up frequently during the 1960s. One was the use of time-of-day announcing equipment for call-in weather announcements. In smaller towns, where the cost of such equipment discouraged local telephone companies from providing such announcements to customers, AT&T allowed its operating companies to sell advertising time on the machines. Along with the current weather, callers would hear a short recorded message from the sponsor. Increasingly, sound recording's use in telephony seemed more like broadcasting than point-to-point communication. By 1967, New York Telephone had a backlog of requests for its Automatic Announcement Service from companies interested in offering advertising-laden news, sports, and stock quotations.[17]

Marshall McLuhan recognized the phemonemon of media acting within media in his 1965 *Understanding Media.* What he described as "interpenetration" was the theory that the new media take over the roles of the old and extend their reach. Technologies such as sound recording, spliced into other systems of communication, can transform them.[18]

The Future: Digitization and Integration

Despite its widespread diffusion, its established economic importance, and the persistence of certain recording activities in American culture, recording technology today is changing rapidly. There is a clear technological trend toward digitization of the recording process, but the economic and social implications of this trend are not certain. The basic hardware underlying digital sound recording came from the computing field, where engineers developed magnetic tape recorders adapted to record digital data beginning in the 1940s.

As early as the 1960s, Bell Laboratories had developed equipment to digitize telephone signals so that several could be packed into a single channel. As the field of digital signal processing emerged as a discipline in the

1960s, electrical engineers began to believe that digital recordings were inherently superior to traditional "analog" methods, because digital devices did not introduce noise or distortion to the data.[19]

Bell Labs' work was taken up by others who wanted to record sound, and particularly by engineers who were high-fidelity enthusiasts. By the early 1970s Sony and others had introduced digital recording equipment intended for use in professional recording studios. In the late 1970s, a consumer digital recorder based on the Sony Betamax videotape recorder was available for sale through Sony and the Radio Shack chain of retail stores. Neither this technology nor the Betamax format were destined to succeed.

Companies such as Philips and Sony in the 1970s had developed optical digital recorders for use in conjunction with consumer television sets— the precursors of today's laserdisc players. Both of these companies subsequently developed digital optical disks for use with music recordings, a logical progression since television programs themselves have a sound component. The Philips Compact Disc system appeared in 1982, manufactured by Philips and a group of Japanese companies. During the 1980s, the compact disc was not the dominant format, but enjoyed rapidly growing success. It was the cassette, rather than the compact disc, that proved the undoing of the LP record, but then the compact disc bested the cassette by the early 1990s.

Record companies wholeheartedly supported the CD. They liked it because it is less expensive to manufacture and ship than the LP, because it was easy to convince most consumers that digital was better, and because the player itself lacked recording capability. Perhaps they thought the new format would steer consumers away from the home tape recorder/players that had plagued the industry in the 1970s. Consumers, after some complaints about the high price of the discs, evidently also came to like the format. By the late 1980s, home players were cost competitive with home phonographs, and consumers could use the same discs at home and in portable players, a feat that had never been practical with the disk record. The new medium did little to quell home taping, however, and the compact disc simply replaced the LP record as the source of material for homemade cassettes. The appearance of CD player convenience features such as multidisk "carousel" machines even made it easier to create customized tapes to suit the individual's fancy.

Record company resistance to the home taping problem has, some critics have suggested, effectively killed some digital recording media such as the ill-fated Digital Audio Tape (DAT). Only a few companies, mostly hardware manufacturers such as Sony, have offered recorded digital tapes.

Interestingly, the industry sees the availability of recorded programs, even for a technology that both records and reproduces, as a crucial determinant of market success. This theory can be supported by observing the fate of some of the many defunct audio formats that appeared between the 1960s and the 1990s. During 1977 and 1978, for example, several Japanese audio equipment manufacturers introduced the Elcaset home tape system. Elcaset was a "large cassette" (hence its name) intended to combine the convenience of the Philips cassette, which was seen as sonically inferior, with the high fidelity of the older open-reel system, which was considered the standard for high quality. With no commercial recordings available, the Elcaset failed almost immediately, despite rave reviews in the technical press.[20]

More recently, several manufacturers offered a Digital Compatible Cassette [DCC], which could record and play ordinary cassettes as well as identical looking digital cassettes. A small range of recorded DCC tapes were, as in the case of the DAT, available for purchase, but the technology failed to catch on. Capitalizing on the success of the compact disc, Sony introduced its Minidisc in the mid-1980s with great fanfare, and immediately issued a catalog of recorded albums. After a few years, portable Minidisc recorders were widely in use in the field of radio broadcasting, but this unexpected success could not disguise the format's failure to attract significant numbers of ordinary consumers, who were predicted to be the primary market for this technology. In the late 1990s, Sony heightened its marketing effort in support of the Minidisc, but sales still lagged well behind those of ordinary cassette recorders. There are many more examples of this sort, some of them digital optical media that have appeared only in the last few years. What is clear is that there is no obvious combination of technical glitter, recording features, and musical repertoire that will spell instant success for the new generation of media.

However, digitization of other types of recording proceeds apace. Dictation systems went digital in the 1980s, as PC-based centralized dictation took most of the market for office recording. Digital recorders have also become standard equipment in most recording studios. As price of electronic memory and digital-to-analog converters have come down, tapeless digital recorders have made inroads into the answering machine field as well. In the telephone, television, and radio industries, many new recorder installations are digital, although much analog equipment remains. There seem to be no major commercial applications for which conventional recording techniques have significant technical advantages over digital recording. Only the cost of digital recorders and their media has kept them from capturing the entire market. There are important niches in the recording industry where a conservative culture of engineering maintains that high-quality analog sound recorders are better for certain purposes. This aesthetic justification for the use of a particular recording technology echoes the way musicians and recording engineers have for many years used their prerogative in the studio to make crucial technological choices, except that in this instance it is turned on its ear by the fact that they sometimes cling to an older technology instead of embracing the new one. A segment of the general public feels much the same way about the LP record. Sales of record albums have risen to more than two million units per year since the mid-1990s, and the format seems destined to remain viable for some years to come. It is worth remembering that one specialty record producer in audiophile-laden Great Britain kept the open-reel tape format alive through the end of the 1980s, that mail-order record and tape clubs continued to sell eight track tapes until the late 1980s, that the 78-rpm record (and the acoustic phonograph) survived in some countries through the 1960s, and that both the 45-rpm single and the LP disk have been in production without interruption since 1948. Granted, the markets for most of these products was tiny and shrinking, but clearly nostalgia and fashion can create temporary reversals of the trends. In the mid-1990s, for example, some musical groups began issuing recordings on eight track tapes salvaged from rummage sales and flea markets, rerecorded, relabeled and sold to nostalgic fans.

The successor to the Philips cassette in the field of consumer recording may not emerge through the current efforts of manufacturers to develop a system that offers good sound quality in a miniaturized player, with home and portable compatibility. Consumers rightly perceive that all these features are already available in current cassette technology. Nor is the key to success determined by subjective improvements in sound quality. High fidelity has been only one factor, sometimes not the most important one, in the commercial success of previous technologies. Rather, the next generation may be a combination of previously separate devices. Part of the success of tape systems in the 1960s was the combination of features of home systems with portable—specifically automotive—audio technology. Many of the most successful recording products of the post-1945 era have been those that achieved similar new combinations. There are many such examples in the field of consumer entertainment devices. Home radio/phono/recorder combinations capable of making recordings from disks or off radio had been available since the 1930s, but they never sold in great quantities. Small, transistorized, battery-operated portable radio/tape combinations were pioneered in the early 1960s by Philips and became widely available after that, though a variant of this product, the "boom box" achieved much wider success only after 1975. The boom box radio/recorder combination transformed the battery-operated portable, which had always been designed for light weight and compact size, into a more powerful, complex machine more like a home stereo system. In a way, the surprising success of the Sony Walkman in the late 1970s was also a new combination of features, a rather expensive tape player or radio that sacrificed a built-in loudspeaker but offered sound quality comparable to a home unit. While the compact disc system offered consumers new combinations of options, subsequent recordable digital media have had little new to offer other than pure "gadget" appeal.

Another possibility is that some company or inventor will find commercial success by grafting recording onto some unrelated technological system. The telephone answering machine, for example, succeeded partly because of its appealing technique for storing the previously perishable messages of the telephone. Promoters of business dictation systems seem, after more than a century of effort, to be on the verge of achieving their aim of mechanizing the spoken word and making it a part of record keeping and other business operations. They have begun to do so since the 1980s by combining the functions of the dictation machine with digital recording and the personal computer. Because digital recordings can more easily be manipulated and transformed into text or computer commands, it is now possible to substitute the voice for the keyboard and the pen. This integration is not complete, and the technology is not perfect, but it may soon become more common to operate all sorts of devices through voice commands.

The powerful combination of digitization and computers may in fact replace recording altogether, or at least recording onto a permanent medium. A personal computer can already replace a home audio recorder, a videocassette recorder, an answering machine, and a desktop dictation machine. Computers as small and portable as a Walkman may be the technology that replaces all current forms of consumer recorders, rather than any of the new digital media now being touted by the audio equipment manufacturers. Consumer recording media may disappear entirely if portables, downloading music from the Internet (perhaps by a wireless connection), can function with the reliability and sound quality of current miniaturized tape and CD players. If that happens, record companies may finally overcome the home taping "problem," by establishing services to supply music on demand directly to consumers.

Alternately, the proficiency of computer hackers may make digitally delivered music even more susceptible to piracy and counterfeiting. In their own studios, digital audio processing devices with built-in memory may replace stand-alone recorders, while in business, communications, and industrial applications, computer software and digital memory devices will probably replace most of the special-purpose sound recorders in use today. Sound recording activities will continue, but today's sound recorders and tangible sound recording media may well disappear, and the history of the sound recording as a physical artifact will end.

NOTES

INTRODUCTION

1. Edward Johnson to the editor of *Scientific American* 6 (November 1877), reprinted in Robert A. Rosenberg et al., *The Papers of Thomas A. Edison*, vol. 3, *Menlo Park: The Early Years, April 1876–December 1877* (Baltimore: Johns Hopkins University Press, 1994), 615–616.
2. There is apparently no definitive record of the very first recording that Edison was capable of reproducing. Charles Batchelor, an associate who was present on the day of the first recording, recalled some thirty years later that the inventor had said, "Mary had a little lamb." Documents based on experiments at the lab, before the *Scientific American* demonstration suggested that the phrase "How do you get that?" had been recorded and reproduced by December 4, 1877. Rosenberg et al., *Papers of Thomas Edison*, 657, 670, 399.
3. Matthew Josephson, *Edison* (New York: McGraw-Hill, 1959), 171.
4. Edison in late November 1877 had privately noted that mechanically produced "sheet music" entertainment records, talking dolls, and other such devices would be an important application of the phonograph, but the company he later formed to pursue these ends promoted dictation machines primarily. The next year, he also mentioned that experiments were underway to duplicate records in quantity through the use of an electrotype technique. Rosenberg et al., *Papers of Thomas Edison*, 629; Thomas Edison, "The Phonograph and Its Future," *North American Review* 126 (1878): 529–536.
5. Oberlin Smith, "Possible Forms of the Phonograph," *Electrical World*, 8 September 1888, 116. Arthur J. Cox and Thomas Malim, *Ferracute: The History of an American Enterprise* (Bridgeton, N.J.: Cowan Printing Co., 1985), 112–115; an excellent survey of Poulsen's business venture in the U.S. is Mark Henry Clark, "The Magnetic Recording Industry, 1878–1960: An International Study in Business and Technological History," (Ph.D. diss., University of Delaware, 1992), 45–100. Scores of articles of the telegraphone appeared at the time of the Paris exposition. See for example "Poulsen's Telegraphone," *Scientific American* 83 (22 September 1900): 178; "The Telegraphone," *Scientific American Supplement* (25 August 1900): 20616.

6. Jacques Barzun, *Music in American Life,* 3d ed. (Bloomington: Indiana University Press, 1969); Jacques Attali's *Noise,* the title of which suggests a broad scope and which includes a chapter on recordings, is also limited to the analysis of music, a fact given away by its subtitle. *Noise: The Political Economy of Music,* trans. Brian Massumi, *Theory and History of Literature,* vol. 16 (Minneapolis: University of Minnesota Press, 1985); Theodor Adorno, *Introduction to the Sociology of Music,* trans. E. B. Ashton (New York: Seabury Press, 1976); a recent history of recorded music and music recording technology is Andre Millard's *America on Record: A History of Recorded Sound* (Cambridge: Cambridge University Press, 1995); also see Norman Eisenberg's *The Recording Angel: Explorations in Phonography* (New York: McGraw-Hill, 1987).

7. Carolyn Marvin pursues a similar argument for electrical communication technologies in *When Old Technologies Were New: Thinking about Electric Communication in the Late Nineteenth Century* (Oxford: Oxford University Press, 1988).

8. Steve Jones's well-reasoned argument that popular music has driven the development of studio recording technology holds up very well, but only for the post-1960s period that he studies. Steve Jones, *Rock Formation: Music, Technology, and Mass Communication,* vol. 3, *Foundations of Popular Culture* (Newbury Park, Calif.: Sage Publications, 1992).

9. Recent histories of network radio include Susan Douglass, *Inventing American Broadcasting: 1899–1922* (Baltimore: Johns Hopkins University Press, 1987); Susan Smulyan, *Selling Radio: The Commercialization of American Broadcasting, 1920–1934* (Washington, D.C.: Smithsonian Institution Press, 1994).

10. Andre Millard, *Edison and the Business of Innovation* (Baltimore: Johns Hopkins University Press, 1990), 253–268.

11. Claude Fischer argues that the telephone was itself an extension of existing patterns of communication. Claude S. Fischer, *American Calling: A Social History of the Telephone to 1940* (Berkeley: University of California Press, 1992).

ONE. HIGH CULTURE, HIGH FIDELITY

1. Daniel Barenboim, introduction to *Music Makers on Record,* by Suvi Raj Grubb (London: Hamish Hamilton, 1986), ix.

2. Recently, cultural studies have produced works such as Steve Jones's *Rock Formation,* in which the author explains the process of music composition and the importance of digital recording technologies.

3. Historians, musicologists, and others have written extensively about the nature of "serious" and "popular" music. For a brief treatment of this subject see Theodor W. Adorno, "On Popular Music," (1941) reprinted in Simon Frith and Andrew Goodwin, eds., *On Record: Rock, Pop, and the Written Word* (New York: Pantheon Books, 1990); Lawrence Levine, *Highbrow/Lowbrow: The Emergence of a Cultural Hierarchy* (Cambridge, Mass.: Harvard University Press, 1989); Pierre Bourdieu, *Distinction: A Social Critique of the Judgement of Taste,* trans. Richard Nice (Cambridge, Mass.: Harvard University Press, 1984).

4. Walter Read and Leah Brodbeck Stenzel Burt, *From Tinfoil to Stereo: The Acoustic Years of the Recording Industry, 1877–1929* (Gainsville: University Press of Florida, 1994), 87–95.

5. "Will it Pay?" *The Phonogram* 2 (March 1892): 69–71.

6. "A New Process of Duplicating Records," *The Phonogram* 2 (March 1892): 93; Oliver Read and Walter Welch, *From Tin Foil to Stereo: Evolution of the Phonograph,* 2nd ed. (Indianapolis: Howard W. Sams, 1976), 80–81, 84.

7. Read and Burt, *Tinfoil to Stereo,* 87.

8. Ibid., 96–97; 126–127. An additional advantage to the disk process came in the late 1890s, when a number of inventors developed a way to record on a disk with a soft wax surface, then electroplate the master to make a metal matrix. This matrix was then used to make the final stamper for making records. The electroplating process did not damage the recording as the earlier acid-etched process had. Read and Welch, *From Tin Foil to Stereo,* 131–133; Emile Berliner, "The Talking Machine," in *Three Addresses* (N.p.: circa 1888), 33.

9. Ibid., 98, 100.

10. Read and Welch, *From Tin Foil to Stereo,* 404.

11. Hereafter I use "phonograph" to refer to any "stylus in groove" device.

12. Read and Welch, *From Tin Foil to Stereo,* 209.

13. "Edison Moulded Records: How They Are Made," *The Phonogram* 5 (July 1902): 39–42.

14. "The Process of Making Musical Records," *The Phonogram* 2 (November 1892): 243–244; "The Secret of Making Phonograph Records," in *The Phonograph and How to Use It* (New York: National Phonograph Company, 1900; facsimile ed., New York: Allen Koenigsberg, 1971), 152–159; Harvey Sachs, *Toscanini* (New York: J. B. Lippincott, 1978), 145; "Irving Kaufman," in John Harvith and Susan Harvith, *Edison, the Musicians, and the Phonograph* (Westport, Conn.: Greenwood Press, 1987), 55; "Lotte Lehmann," ibid., 71; "Rosa Ponsell," ibid., 81.

15. "The Process of Making Musical Records," *The Phonogram* 2 (November 1892): 243; "Points Pertaining to the Use and Care of the Edison Phonograph," *The Phonogram* 5 (May 1902): 10–11; "Edison Moulded Records: How They Are Made."

16. Emily Thompson, "Is It Real or Is It a Machine?" *American Heritage of Invention and Technology* 12 (winter 1997): 51.

17. Ibid., 54; letter to the editor, *The Phonogram* 11 (June 1901): 29 (emphasis in original).

18. Thompson, "Is It Real?" 56; "Anna Case," in Harvith and Harvith, *Edison, Musicians, and the Phonograph,* 44.

19. Fred Gaisberg, *The Music Goes Round* (New York: Macmillan and Co., 1942), 18.

20. A similar account is C. A. Schicke's *Revolution in Sound: A Biography of the Recording Industry* (Boston: Little, Brown, and Co., 1976).

21. Helen Epstein, *Music Talks: Conversations with Musicians* (New York: McGraw-Hill, 1987), 200; Russell Sanjek mentions a figure of $1000 per recording session in 1947, though this figure may not be reliable since it represents a temporary condition existing shortly before a musicians' strike. The author thanks Susan Schmidt Horning for pointing out this fact. Russell Sanjek, *American Popular Music and Its Business: The First Four Hundred Years,* vol. 3, *From 1900 to 1984* (New York: Oxford University Press, 1988), 229.

22. A concise overview of early "talkie" technology is in Sheldon Hochheiser's "What Makes the Picture Talk: AT&T and the Development of Sound Motion Picture Tech-

nology," in *IEEE Transactions on Education* 35 (November 1992): 278–284; one of the most famous texts in sound measurement and recording was by Harry F. Olson of RCA laboratories, who wrote *Elements of Acoustical Engineering* (New York: D. Van Nostrand, 1940).

23. Roland Gelatt, *The Fabulous Phonograph: From Tin Foil to High Fidelity* (Philadelphia: J. B. Lippincott Company, 1954), 212.

24. Sanjek, *American Popular Music and Its Business*, 160.

25. Peter Dellheim, "The Fine Art of Recording," *Saturday Review* 36 (12 December 1953): 34.

26. "U.S. Record Sales, 1921–1962," *Billboard* 69 (3 August 1963): 13.

27. Decca entered the phonograph business in the United States in 1934.

28. "Phonograph Boom," *Time*, 4 September 1939, 36; "Record Rush," *Business Week*, 20 April 1940, 32; Robert M. W. Dixon and John Godrich, *Recording The Blues* (New York: Stein and Day, 1970).

29. Howard Taubman, "Black Disks by the Millions," *New York Times Magazine* 42 (18 January 1942), 11; The relative importance of jukebox sales dropped to an estimated 18 to 23 percent of all sales by late 1941. "Record Comeback," *Business Week*, 13 September 1941, 49.

30. Gama Gilbert, "Record Renaissance," *New York Times Magazine*, 7 January 1940, 17.

31. For example, the *New York Post* in 1938–39 conducted a promotion selling symphonic albums at the greatly reduced rate of $1.93 per set. Soon similar promotions were taking place in fifty cities nationwide. "Record Record," *Time*, 3 July 1939, 26; "Record Revival," *Time*, 20 May 1940, 41; According to Russell Sanjek, RCA-Victor after 1941 began "one of its most ambitious and expensive advertising campaigns, to stimulate 'the growth of good music in America.' " Sanjek, *American Popular Music and Its Business*, 215; Sociologist Paul Lazarsfeld's research in the 1930s appeared to show that a large proportion of radio listeners preferred classical or symphonic music, yet these findings have to be tempered with the caveat that Lazarsfeld did not report the actual listening habits of these listeners, only the preferences they reported. Similar distortions result from the uncritical review of radio network programs in the 1920s and 1930s, when symphonic and classical music were well represented but not necessarily important to listeners.

32. "Phonograph Records," *Fortune*, 94; Sanjek, *American Popular Music and Its Business*, vol. 3, 141, 144–145.

33. Gelatt, *Fabulous Phonograph*, 228.

34. "In the Groove," *Business Week*, 21 July 1945, 29.

35. The Audio Engineering Society appeared in 1948.

36. Raymond Francis Yates, "The Technician Talks About the Talkies," *Scientific American* 143 (5 November 1930): 384; see the discussion of the shortcomings of engineering standards in Edward Tatnall Canby, *Home Music Systems* (New York: Harper and Row, 1953), 13–14.

37. John Urban, "Stand By, Please . . . Recording Session in Progress," *Musical America* 74 (15 February 1954):158; Recklinghausen, "Electronic Home Music Reproducing Equipment," 765.

38. Howard Taubman is typical of the critics of the 1930s and 1940s who believed that

recorded sound was approaching "realism." *Music on My Beat* (New York: Simon and Schuster, 1943), 200.

39. Gelatt, *Fabulous Phonograph,* 274; this original LP disappeared by late 1932; the RCA two-speed phonographs that went with the Victor 33 1/3 rpm records cost between $247 and $1000 and was clearly marketed to affluent buyers. Sanjek, *American Popular Music and Its Business,* 120.

40. M. L. Alexander, "Home Music Reproducing Equipment Performance and Styling," *Journal of the Audio Engineering Society* 25 (October/November 1977): 774.

41. Gelatt, *Fabulous Phonograph,* 271.

42. Ibid., 272.

43. Ibid.; it is likely that some Red Seal records represented a loss for RCA. Sanjek, *American Popular Music and Its Business,* 248.

44. Post-1945 reissues of recordings on vinyl were known to collectors to be better-sounding than the same recordings issued earlier on 78-rpm disk, not only because the microgroove media had less surface noise but because of changes in the process for making stampers. Stampers before 1945 had to be buffed and replated (or "superplated") before they were used to remove surface imperfections and improve their durability. These processes removed some of the detail from the grooves. Reissues made after the war used the same high-quality master matrices (usually from acetate originals) to make new stampers by an improved process, using solid nickel stampers with such improved surfaces that they did not require buffing or superplating. Many of the reissues also benefited from hours of tedious groove repair undertaken by skilled engravers. Addison Foster, "From Nickel, Tonal Gold," *Saturday Review* 36 (26 December 1953): 50–51; Joseph C. Ruda, "Record Manufacturing: Making Sound for Everyone," *Journal of the Audio Engineering Society* 25 (October/November 1977): 703.

45. The tape recorder's potential value seemed obvious to some in the record industry very early. CBS records, for example, arranged for a German magnetophon to be shipped to the U.S. immediately after World War II, and adopted Ampex tape recorders by 1948. Edward Wallerstein, "Creating the LP Record," 60.

46. Edward W. Kellogg, "History of Sound Motion Pictures," in *A Technological History of Motion Pictures and Television,* ed. Raymond Fielding (Berkeley: University of California Press, 1967), 174–220.

47. One of the first "hit" recordings to use the overdubbing techniques of the same type that Les Paul and Mary Ford used was produced by Mitch Miller using acetate recordings. "Mitch Miller" in Ted Fox, *In the Groove: The People Behind the Music* (New York: St. Martin's Press, 1986), 42–43.

48. Lawrence A. Ruddell, "Miracles of Recording," *Etude* 67 (October 1949): 51; "Mitch Miller," in Ted Fox, *In the Groove,* 41.

49. Edward Tatnall Canby, "Sound Editing," *Saturday Review of Literature* 33 (28 January 1950): 71.

50. B. H. Haggin, *A Decade of Music* (New York: Horizon Press, 1973), 212; the Toscanini recordings reissued in 1963 had undergone many separate enhancements to cover up a badly flawed original recording. RCA engineer John Corbett spent some 800 hours trying to reduce the surface noise and clicks on the original matrices. Sachs, *Toscanini,* 145.

51. E. T. Canby, "Chromium Plated Vulgarity," *Saturday Review of Literature* 37 (25 December 1954): 56.

52. "Natural Sound," *New Yorker,* 17 July 1954, 17–18; Russell Sanjek credits Vaughan Monroe's "Riders in the Sky," as an early big-selling record using the new reverberation technique. Sanjek, *American Popular Music and Its Business,* 235, 246; Peter Heyworth, *Conversations with Klemperer* (London: Victor Gollancz Ltd., 1973), 94–95; Carter Henderson, "How Alvin Chipmunk Hopes to Earn Some $7 Million in 1959," *Wall Street Journal,* 9 March 1959, p. 1.

53. Howard Taubman, "165,000,000 Disks a Year," *New York Times Magazine,* 8 December 1946, 64.

54. "Mitch Miller: Listening for Columbia," *Business Week,* October 1952, 105.

55. Philip Ennis, *The Seventh Stream: The Emergence of Rocknroll in American Popular Music* (Hanover, N.H.: University Press of New England, 1992), 272–273.

56. "Men Behind the Microphones: Makers of Music for the Millions," *Newsweek,* 8 September 1952, 56–57; Emory Cook, "The Man in the Control Booth," *Musical America* 73 (February 1953): 175; John Urban, "Stand by, please . . . Recording Session in Progress," *Musical America* 74 (15 February 1954): 158; "Alchemists Anonymous," *Saturday Review* 37 (27 March 1954): 46; Rose Heylbut, "Back of the Scenes at a Recording Session," *Etude* 72 (April 1954): 26, 56.

57. Sanjek, *American Popular Music and Its Business,* 226–227.

58. Technically, the 45-rpm record was not vinyl like the LP, but it did use a low-noise plastic medium.

59. Wallerstein, "Creating the LP Record," *High Fidelity* 26 (April 1976): 58.

60. Michael F. Wolff, "How Hi is Fi?" *Electronics* 36 (14 June 1963): 33–34.

61. Later improvements to the manufacture of microgroove included the use of a new "wet silvering" technique for plating master disks and a nickel-plating technique for making matrices. Joseph Ruda, "Record Manufacturing," *Journal of the Audio Engineering Society* 25 (October/November 1977): 703; the LP master recording process also benefited from the use of a heated cutting stylus. William S. Bachman, "The LP and the Single," *Journal of the Audio Engineering Society* 25 (October/November 1977): 822–823.

62. Daniel R. Recklinghausen, "Electronic Home Music Reproducing Equipment," *Journal of the Audio Engineering Society* 25 (October/November 1977): 767.

63. "100 Years of Stereo: The Beginning," *Journal of the Audio Engineering Society* 29 (May 1981): 368.

64. John T. Mullin, "Magnetic Recording for Original Recordings," *Journal of the Audio Engineering Society* 25 (October/November 1977): 699; John Culhane, *Walt Disney's Fantasia* (New York: Harry N. Abrams, Inc., 1983).

65. Robert Emmett Dolan, *Music in Modern Media: Techniques in Tape, Disc, and Film Recording, Motion Picture and Television Scoring, and Electronic Music* (New York: G. Schirmer, Inc., 1967), 19.

66. "Bringing the Symphony Orchestra to Moving Picture Patrons," *Etude* 55 (November 1937): 710.

67. Suvi Raj Grubb, *Music Makers on Record* (London: Hamish Hamilton, 1986), 9.

68. Sanjek, *American Popular Music and Its Business,* 363.

69. Epstein, *Music Talks,* 203.

70. The issue of "realism" in recordings has been extensively debated by music scholars. A recent example is Theodore Gracyk's *Rhythm and Noise: An Aesthetics of Rock* (Durham, N.C.: Duke University Press, 1996), 37–67. To his credit, Gracyk avoids getting mired in the debate over whether a recording constitutes a mirror of an original performance, which seemed to trouble so many earlier scholars.
71. Edward R. Kealy, "From Craft to Art: The Case of Sound Mixers and Popular Music," in Frith and Goodwin, *On Record,* 208–220.
72. John Mullin, "Magnetic Recording," *Journal of the Audio Engineering Society* 25 (October/November 1977): 699–700.
73. Steve Jones, "The Intro and Outro: Technology and Popular Music Practice," *Popular Music and Society* 14 (spring 1990): 2.

Two. The End of the "Canned Music" Debate

1. A detailed compilation of information on the use of recordings in network radio is in Michael Biel's dissertation, "The Making and Use of Recordings In Broadcasting Before 1936," (Northwestern University, 1977).
2. Christopher Sterling, *Electronic Media: A Guide to Trends in Broadcasting and Newer Technologies, 1920–1983* (New York: Praeger, 1984), 12–13.
3. Ibid., 630–631.
4. Ibid., 609.
5. James Miller, "Improving the Broadcast of Recorded Programs," *Electronics* 7 (June 1934): 178; "Transmission by Tape: NY Station Uses Innovation for First Time in America," *Newsweek,* 26 September 1938, 27; Craig Walsh, "Photoelectric Tape Recording," *Electronics* 13 (May 1940): 16–18; Russell Sanjek, *American Popular Music and Its Business,* 140; Sanjek also reports that the Muzak network of wired-radio broadcasting also used Millertape in the 1930s. Ibid., 168.
6. Sydney W. Head, *World Broadcasting Systems: A Comparative Analysis* (Belmont, Calif.: Wadsworth Publishing Co., 1985), 347.
7. Clark, "The Magnetic Recording Industry," 43.
8. He traveled to the United States in 1930 to show his system to engineers at Bell Telephone Laboratories, but apparently got an indifferent reception there, too. H. B. Ely, "Minutes of Conference for the Purpose of Hearing from Mr. Mallina as to the Trend of Developments in Europe and Other Technical Information Obtained by Him during a Recent Visit—Cases 32184, 32187, and 34465," 17 July 1929, case 32184, Bell Laboratories Collection, AT&T Archive, Warren, N.J. (hereafter BTL).
9. *The B.B.C. Year Book 1932* (London: BBC, 1932), 101, 367–368, 371; When Blattner went bankrupt in 1932, the BBC arranged the sale of the patent rights to the Blattnerphone to the equipment manufacturer Marconi Wireless Telegraph Company. The BBC continued to purchase Marconi-Stille recorders through the 1930s, as did the radio networks of Canada, Australia, Poland, France, Egypt, and Sweden.
10. Walter B. Emery, *National and International Systems of Broadcasting* (East Lansing: Michigan State University Press, 1960), 295–298.
11. R. F. Mallina to C. N. Hickman, 16 May 1935, case 20872, vol. A, BTL; William Charles Lafferty Jr., "The Early Development of Magnetic Sound Recording in Broad-

casting and Motion Pictures" (Ph.D. diss., Northwestern University, 1981), 111–112 (this title is referred to subsequently as "History"); "Shows New Sound Device," *New York Times,* 25 November 1928, II, p. 6.

12. R. F. Mallina to C. N. Hickman, BTL; Lafferty, "History," 114; "Steel Ribbon Recording in France," *Radio-Craft* 7 (March 1936): 556.

13. Paul A. Zimmerman, *Magnetbander, Magnet Pulver, Elektroden* (Ludwigshafen, Germany: BASF, 1969), 9–10.

14. Ibid., 11–12.

15. Ibid., 13–15.

16. *BIOS Final Report 951,* app. 4, p. 3.

17. *BIOS 951,* xix, 2; Ernst Kris and Hans Speier, *German Radio Propaganda* (London: Oxford University Press, 1944), 54–56.

18. James Wood, *History of International Broadcasting* (London: Peter Peregrinus Ltd., 1992), 75–77; Howard A. Chinn, "Audio and Measuring Facilities for the CBS International Broadcast Stations," *Electrical Communication* 21, no. 3 (1943): 178–179.

19. Theodore Stuart DeLay Jr., "An Historical Study of the Armed Forces Network to 1946," (Ph.D. diss., University of Southern California, 1951), 40.

20. The government conducted other recording-related activities which acted as important markets for phonograph equipment manufacturers and record companies. Mobile recording units traveled around overseas bases to collect from servicemen "voice mail" messages on phonodisk for shipment to relatives in America. Another project related to morale building assembled "buddy kits" comprised of a portable phonograph and a selection of popular records for shipment overseas. DeLay, "Historical Study of the AFN," 77–80, 91–92, 223–226. The process of denaturing involved using two identical sets of master recordings and mixing them down to one denatured recording. In this process, one of the master recordings would serve as the input until the moment before a commercial began. The recording engineer would have cued up the second recording to be started at the point when the commercial was over. At just the right moment, the output from the first master recording would be switched off and the second master would be started. The denatured recording would have thus have smooth-sounding transitions between program segments. Engineers who worked on this project developed a strong sense of pride and craftsmanship, believing that they had perfected the difficult art of editing transcription disks. The advent of the tape recorder in the postwar years had the result of replacing such skills.

21. Ibid., 262; Mayfield S. Bray and Leslie C. Waffen, *Sound Recordings in the Audio-Visual Archives Division of the National Archives* (Washington, D.C.: GPO, 1972); "Recordings Evaluated," *Service Bulletin of the Federal Radio Education Committee* 2 (June 1940): 1; Campbell Lateral, "Naval Research Lab," *Communications* (September 1946); Lt. George Marakas, "Audio and the Armed Forces," *Audio Engineering* 35 (August 1951): 16.

22. Sally B. Smith, *In All His Glory: The Life of William S. Paley* (New York: Simon and Schuster, 1990), 17–20; "The Reminiscences of Hans V. Kaltenborn," Columbia University Oral History Collection (New York: Columbia University, 1972), University Microfilms edition, 1972, microfilm reel 16, 231–232.

23. The Armour wire recorders were not the only new portable sound technology to

be extensively utilized during the war. A phonograph recorder called the Recordograph was purchased in large quantities by the Signal Corps, the OWI, and other agencies for similar purposes. However, it is a technology that did not survive long after the end of the war. The Hart Recordograph, with a military designation, is described in detail in U.S. War Dept., "Sound Recording Sets AN/UNQ-1 and AN/UNQ-1A," *Technical Manual TM 11-2522* (Washington, D.C.: GPO, August 1946); that GE should have been a licensee of Armour Research in order to make wire recorders is ironic, given that the company apparently had patent exchange agreements with AEG through 1941 and presumably could have utilized their tape recording technology. British Intelligence Objectives Sub-Committee, *BIOS Final Report 538: Report on German Patent Records*, by R. Jonas, L. B. Davies, and W. E. Batty (London: HMSO, March 1946); J. Allen Brown, "Transcribed for Broadcasting," *Audio Record* 2 (November 1946): 1–3. GE became a licensee in January 1943. The AFRS also used wire-recorded programs instead of transcription disks to broadcast its show "The Army Hour" in North Africa in 1943. "Wire Recorders for Army," *Electronics* 16 (October 1943): 234; Arthur Grahme, "Recording the Saipan Fight on Wire," *Popular Science* 145 (December 1944): 201.

24. Clarence J. West and Callie Hull, eds., "Industrial Research Laboratories of the United States, 5th ed.," *Bulletin of the National Research Council* no. 91 (August 1933): 153; Bob Swathmore, "The Day Tape Was Born," *Electronics Illustrated* 9 (July 1966): 49–52, 113; another example was Don V. R. Drenner, an engineer with Supreme Headquarters, Allied Expeditionary Forces in Europe, who wrote articles for the trade press about the Magnetophons after World War II but apparently returned home to work at a radio station. Don V. R. Drenner, "The Magnetophon," *Audio Engineering* 31 (October 1947): 7–11, 35.

25. "German Magnetic Tape Machine Brought to U.S.," *Science News Letter* 48 (22 December 1945): 399; "German Magnetic-Tape Recorder," *Electronics* 18 (November 1945): 402, 406; R. A. Power, "The German Magnetophons," *Wireless World* 52 (June 1946): 195–198.

26. Clark, "The Magnetic Recording Industry," 304.

27. Ibid., 314–315.

28. "First Full-Time Spot News Wire-Recorded Program Aired in Chi," *Variety*, 10 April 1946, 34.

29. R. J. Tinkham to W. W. Hansen, "Wire Recorder Proves Success," 4 February 1946. File 792, Marvin Camras Collection, Paul Galvin Library, Illinois Institute of Technology.

30. "Radio Commercials Benefit from New Recording Methods," *Ampex Playback* 2 (January 1956): 2. NBS Collection, Archives, National Museum of American History, Washington, D.C; "Sound Inscribed on Paper Tape," *Business Week*, 26 January 1946, 50; "Sound on Paper," *Scientific American* (April 1946): 156–157; Clark E. Jackson, "Magnetic Tape Systems," *Radio News* 39 (February 1948): 46, 140; Richard S. O'Brien, "Adopting Paper Tape Recorders for Broadcasting," *Audio Engineering* 31 (May 1947): 10–14, 48; Gordon Sherman, "Who Said a Recording Engineer's Life Is Dull?" *Audio Record* 3 (October 1947): 1, 3; Merle Fleming, "Converting a Brush Tape Recorder for Broadcast Use," *Radio News* 39 (February 1948): 59; John B. Ledbetter, "Home Recorders for Professional Use,"

Radio and Television News 41 (February 1949): 47–49; Herbert G. Eidson Jr., "Tricks in Tape Recording," *TeleVision Engineering* (March 1951): 14, 16, 23.

31. Another tradition-breaking recording was a 1946 series called *One World Fight*, narrated by journalist Norman Corwin and consisting of interviews originally recorded on wire. Laurence Bergreen, *Look Now, Pay Later* (Garden City, N.Y.: Doubleday and Co., 1980), 150.

32. "Tom Harmon Spurns Live Offers for Recorded Show," *Audio Record* 2 (November 1946): 2, 4.

33. The venture between Mullin and Crosby was called Bing Crosby Enterprises. Although the firm apparently did not produce tape recorders, it remained in business until 1962 when it was acquired by 3M and became the Minicom division, producing precision instrumentation recorders. "News of the Industry," *Tape Recording* 9 (March 1962): 15; John T. Mullin, "The Birth of Tape," *Billboard* 88 (4 July 1976): sec. MR13, p. 38.

34. "ABC's $300,000 Blueprint to Keep Day and Night Shows on Same Time Schedule via Recorded Broadcasts," *Variety*, 27 March 1946, 39; "ABC Sees Daylight on 300G Solution," ibid., 10 April 1946, 33; "ABC Adopts Daylight Time Disk Plan," *Broadcasting* (1 April 1946): 93; R. F. Bigwood, "Applications of Magnetic Recording in Network Broadcasting," *Audio Engineering* 32 (July 1948): 31–33, 38, 40; Howard A. Chinn, "Magnetic Tape Recorders in Broadcasting," *Audio Engineering* 31 (May 1947): 7–10; "ABC's Daylight Saving Time Plant to Start on April 25," *Audio Record* 4 (April 1948): 1, 2; Byron H. Speirs, "ABC Uses Magnetic Tape for Delayed Broadcasts," *Radio and Television News* (April 1950): 41, 134.

35. "Daylight Saving Snafu Rears Head Again to Set Network Noggins Dizzy: CBS to Copy ABC, MBS Delayed Shows," *Variety*, 19 April 1947, 25.

36. *Magnecord, Inc.* (Chicago: Magnecord, n.d.), in Accession 84401417, no file name, Orr Collection. Magnecord was purchased by Midwestern Instruments of Tulsa, moved into background music systems, and later dropped out of the audio tape recorder business. "Noted with Interest," *High Fidelity* 7 (December 1957): 21.

37. Rangertone recorders were tested in 1947 at stations WASH, Washington, D.C., and KSBR, San Bruno, Calif. "New Tape Techniques," *FM and Television* 27 (August 1948): 40–41.

38. Marakas, "Audio and the Armed Forces," 16.

39. Joseph C. Ruda, "Record Manufacturing: Making Sound for Everyone," *Journal of the Audio Engineering Society* 25 (October/November 1977): 710.

40. Cecil Bidlack, "Some Experiences with Mass-Production Tape Duplication," *Journal of the Audio Engineering Society* 4 (January 1956): 31–37; Martin N. Olson, "Multiple Tape Recording," *FM and Television* 9 (March 1949): 30–31; Detailed comparisons of the difference in costs between tape and disk are difficult. The tape itself was more expensive per minute of recording time than master recording disks, but the need for backup copies of disks was eliminated, and the chance of a ruined recording was minimized, so that in most cases tape was considerably less expensive. *Gates Radio Catalog* (Quincy, Ill.: Gates Radio Company, 1949), Trade Literature Collection, Archives Center, National Museum of American History, Washington, D.C.

41. Sterling, *Electronic Media*, 10, table 370–C, 109.
42. See for example "Unusual Sounds," *Radio and Television News* 55 (February 1956): 67.
43. Interestingly, Philip Ennis calls the transformation of radio in the disk-jockey era "redesigning the machine," but provides little indication of the technological transformation involved. Ennis, *The Seventh Stream*, 131–160.
44. Robert K. Avery and Donald G. Ellis, "Talk Radio as an Interpersonal Phenomenon," in *Inter/Media*, ed. Robert Cathcart (New York: Oxford University Press, 1979), 108–116.

THREE. "GIRL OR MACHINE?"

1. See for example Margery Davies, *Woman's Place Is at the Typewriter* (Philadelphia: Temple University Press, 1982); Gregory Anderson, ed., *The White-Blouse Revolution* (Manchester, Eng.: Manchester University Press, 1988).
2. William Henry Leffingwell, *Textbook of Office Management* (New York: McGraw-Hill, 1932; rev.ed. 1943), 207.
3. "The dictating machine revolutionized office procedure as did the typewriter," writes Alan Delgado in *The Enormous File: A Social History of the Office* (London: John Murray, 1979), 75; "The dictating machine became as commonplace in offices as the typewriter or telephone" claims Millard in *Edison and the Business of Innovation*, 253; see also Angel Kwolek-Folland, *Engendering Business: Men and Women in the Corporate Office, 1870–1930* (Baltimore: Johns Hopkins University Press, 1994), 62. Kwolek-Folland also notes that men rarely used office machines after about 1910, although she is referring to clerical workers, not executives or managers. Ibid., 114; Only JoAnne Yates notes that "dictaphones [sic] never became as universal as typewriters," but she gives no clue as to why that was. *Control Through Communication: The Rise of System in American Management* (Baltimore: Johns Hopkins University Press, 1989), 45; also see Harry Braverman, *Labor and Monopoly Capital: The Degradation of Work in the Twentieth Century* (New York: Monthly Review Press, 1974).
4. Roland Gelatt, *Fabulous Phonograph*, 29.
5. There were quite a few monthlies for students of stenography, many with the word "phonographer" in the title, most published in Great Britain and some dating to the early nineteenth century. Often they were written in shorthand. For an outline of the history of shorthand see Benn [sic] Pittman, *History of Short Hand* (Cincinnati, Ohio: The Phonographic Institute, 1856), 73.
6. See chapter 1.
7. Thomas P. Hughes, *Networks of Power: Electrification in Western Society, 1880–1930* (Baltimore: Johns Hopkins University Press, 1983), 18–23.
8. Gelatt, *Fabulous Phonograph*, 33.
9. Millard, *Edison and the Business of Innovation*, 65.
10. V. H. McRae, "Present Position of the Phonograph and a Resume of Its Merits," *The Phonogram* 1 (April 1891): 83–85; "The Columbia Phonograph Co., Washington, D.C.," ibid., 88–89; Easton was apparently an investor in Volta Graphophone and became its president in the early 1890s. Gelatt, *Fabulous Phonograph*, 48.

11. A number of testimonials regarding the use of the phonograph in court reporting appear in *Testimonials as to the Practical Use of the Phonograph and Phonograph-Graphophone* (New York: n.p., 1890).

12. Millard, *Edison and the Business of Innovation*, 86, 253; Edison Inc.'s Nelson Durand admitted that the new business phonograph offered in 1905 was "practically copied" from the graphophone. Durand to Board of Directors, Thomas A. Edison, Inc., 26 December 1916, Correspondence and Memoranda, Inter-Office 1916, box 2, series 3, Ediphone Division records, Thomas A. Edison National Historic Site, West Orange, N.J. (hereafter TAE); Read and Welch, *From Tin Foil to Stereo*, 493; "How Talking Machines Are Used at the U.S. Capitol by the Official Reporters," *The Phonogram* 8 (January 1901): 102–110.

13. Millard, *Edison and the Business of Innovation*, 255; C. K. Woodbridge, *Dictaphone: Electronic Genius of Voice and Typed Word* (New York: Newcomen Society in North America, 1952), 6, 13.

14. Sales Bulletin #72, 19 December 1916, Sales/Promotional Material, Dealer 1912–1917, box 2, series 2, Ediphone Division records, TAE.

15. Millard, *Edison and the Business of Innovation*, 257, 261; U.S. Department of Commerce, *Census of Manufactures*, (Washington, D.C.: Government Printing Office, 1913), 524–525; ibid., (1914), 824; ibid., (1923), 1012; ibid., (1940), 390.

16. Discussion of the 1911 redesign of the Edison machine are briefly discussed in Millard, *Edison and the Business of Innovation*, 258.

17. "New Start and Stop Device," *The Phonogram* 3 (January 1893): 306; interestingly, the dictators reflected the prevailing middle-class attitudes toward cleanliness—1920s Ediphones employed a metal speaking tube called the "Sanitube," which had an easily cleaned glass mouthpiece and a "germicidal" felt lining.

18. "Dictators and Dictation," *The Phonogram*, 4 (October 1892): 205; see for example, *The Ediphone* (Orange, N.J.: Thomas A. Edison Industries, Inc., 1924). Advertising Materials, Ediphone, box 2, Edison Companies series, Primary Printed Materials Collection, TAE.

19. Millard, *Edison and the Business of Innovation*, 262–264; William Henry Leffingwell, *Textbook of Office Management*, 105.

20. Competitors kept popping up, but the two companies staved them off for decades. One notable example was a German import called the Parlograph, which Dictaphone successfully sued in 1916. Ediphone Sales Bulletin #70, 14 July 1916, Sales/Promotional Material, Dealer 1912–1917, box 2, series 2, Ediphone Div. Collection, TAE.

21. Hedstrom, "Beyond Feminisation," in *The White-Blouse Revolution*, 159.

22. Millard, *Edison and the Business of Innovation*, 256; Virginia Scharff, "Gender and Genius," in *The Material Culture of Gender*, ed. Katherine Martinez and Kenneth L. Ames (Winterther, Del.: Winterthur Museum, 1997), 13; "Bridgeport Says It Pays," *American City* 54 (October 1939): 41; "Keeping Dictation Up-to-Date," *Survey* 61 (15 November 1928): 250.

23. "How to Save Four Days," *Survey* 67 (15 October 1931): 101; R. H. Goodell, "Saving 42% on Routine Work," *System* 37 (June 1920): 1184–1185; "The Municipal Significance of Dictating Machines," *American City* 54 (March 1939): 7.

24. *Dictaphone Annual Report*, 1945.

25. Even the electronic Dictabelt and other postwar systems were very sensitive to improper operation. Robert Dameron, "Care and Feeding of Dictation Machines," *American Business* 28 (October 1958): 14–15.

26. Interview with Catherine F. Scott by William Aspray, 12 June 1991, interview no. 85, Oral History Collection, IEEE Center for the History of Electrical Engineering, Rutgers University.

27. "Bulletin No. 25," 27 December 1912, Sales/Promotional Material, Dealer 1912–1917, box 2, series 2, Ediphone Div. Collection, TAE.

28. Millard, *Edison and the Business of Innovation*, 264.

29. Roger Burlingame, *Endless Frontiers: The Story of McGraw-Hill* (New York: McGraw-Hill Book Co., 1949), 419–420.

30. Ediphone advertisements, n.d. (circa late 1930s) from *Gregg Writer*, in untitled scrapbook, box 5, series 4, Ediphone Div. Collection, TAE. On women and technophobia see John Stimson and Ardyth Stimson, "Time, Technophobia, and the Transition of Gender Definitions," in *The Material Culture of Gender*, ed. Katherine Martinez and Kenneth L. Ames (Winterther, Del.: Winterthur Museum, 1997), 37–52; on designing "men's" and "women's" versions of the same product see Scharff, "Gender and Genius," 137–156.

31. *Now How About My Business* (West Orange, N.J.: Thomas A. Edison, Inc., 1931); Davies, *Woman's Place Is at the Typewriter*, 100; Delgado, *The Enormous File*, 74–75.

32. Other prominent users of dictation equipment included Winston Churchill and novelist Charles King. Thomas Edison even personally presented an Ediphone to the Pope, though he had to hew to Vatican protocols insisting that the letter accompanying the gift be written in longhand. "Col. Charles King Dictates all His Novels on a Phonograph," *The Phonogram* (October 1892): 231.

33. Millard, *Edison and the Business of Innovation*, 265.

34. The early issues of *The Phonogram*, the official publication of the National Phonograph Company, never explicitly suggested replacing male stenographers with women, but the message was hard to miss.

35. Millard, *Edison and the Business of Innovation*, 260; Davies, *Woman's Place Is at the Typewriter*, 53–55.

36. On typing pools see Helen M. McCabe and Estelle L. Popham, *Word Processing: A Systems Approach to the Office* (New York: Harcourt Brace Jovanovich, Inc., 1977), 39.

37. *Managing the Firm's Mail* (West Orange, N.J.: Thomas A. Edison, Inc., n.d. [circa 1925]), 10; "She's Capable of More Than This," Thomas A. Edison, Inc., pamphlet, n.d. (circa 1925), Advertising Materials, Pro-Technic Ediphone, box 2, Edison Companies series, Primary Printed Materials Collection, TAE; *Voice Writing Sales Training Manual*, book 7, *Installation Sale—Stenographer* (West Orange, N.J.: Thomas A. Edison, Inc., 1932), copy from TAE.

38. Kwolek-Folland, *Engendering Business*, 63–69.

39. Senate Committee on Patents, *Hearing Before the Committee on Patents on S. 1301: A Bill to Renew and Extend Certain Letters Patent* 72nd Cong., 1st sess., 10 March 1932, 21.

40. Read and Welch, *From Tin Foil to Stereo*, 290.

41. Woodbridge, *Dictaphone: Electronic Genius*, 14–15.

42. Soundscriber, "Dictating Machine," *Scientific American* 164 (February 1941): 104–105.
43. Charles P. Peirce, "Evolution of Wire Recording," *The Insurance Company, P.A.*, April 1949, 20–21.
44. H. J. Rummel, "Centralized Dictation System," *Office Executive* 34 (September 1959): 42; "Satellite Dictating," *Business Week*, 23 January 1960, 136; "Dictating by Telephone," *Business Week*, 5 September 1953, 95–98; " 'Talk Away' Your Paper Work," *Purchasing* 45 (21 July 1958): 82.
45. Woodbridge, *Dictaphone: Electronic Genius*, 17.
46. Thomas A. Edison, Inc., introduced a spring-driven dictation machine in the 1920s. See Millard, *Edison and the Business of Innovation*, 268.
47. "Dictet Portable Recorder," *Hi-Fi Tape Recording* 4 (November 1957): 40–41; "Note Taking Can be Simple," *Purchasing* 44 (17 March 1958): 136.
48. Minifon tape recorder, L. Hannemann, "Pocket-Size Dictating Machine," *Electronics* 33 (28 October 1960): 73.
49. Aurin Uris and Marjorie Noppel, *The Turned-On Executive: Building Your Skills for the Management Revolution* (New York: McGraw-Hill, 1970), 5.
50. Correspondence with Samuel J. Kalow, 1998.
51. Contemporary accounts of this are in McCabe and Popham, *Word Processing*, 23–30; Samuel J. Kalow, "Word Processing," *Words* 4 (August 1975): 14–15. The direct conversion of voice to text was prophesied even in 1900. See "Who Has Ever Heard of a Phonograph Typewriter?" *The Phonogram* 1 (September 1900): 132–137.
52. John D. Gould and Stephen J. Boies, "How Authors Think about Their Writing, Dictating, and Speaking," *Human Factors* 20 (1978): 495–505; John D. Gould, "How Experts Dictate," *Journal of Experimental Psychology: Human Perception and Performance* 4 (1978): 648–661; personal communication from Samuel J. Kalow.
53. Compare this to Rosemary Pringle's discussion of the use of dictation equipment in Australia. She describes how bosses resisted its use until they realized that it would not threaten existing power structures. Rosemary Pringle, *Secretaries Talk: Sexuality, Power, and Work* (London: Verso, 1988), 182–183.
54. Gould and Boies, "How Authors Think," 505.

FOUR. THE MESSAGE ON THE ANSWERING MACHINE

1. George M. Williamson, "The Poulsen Telegraphone," *The American Telephone Journal* 87 (24 October 1903): 259; John A. Lieb, "The Telegraphone: A Magnetic Phonograph," *The Electrical Age* 29 (September 1902): 346.
2. Clark, "The Magnetic Recording Industry," 63–64.
3. Ibid., 85–87; "To Make Telegraphones Here," *Springfield Daily Republican*, 9 November 1910; Senate Committee on Patents, *Hearing before the Committee on Patents on S. 1301: A Bill to Renew and Extend Certain Letters Patent* 72nd Cong., 1st sess., 10 March 1932, 21.
4. "To Make Telegraphones Here."
5. Emile Berliner, letter to *Electrical World and Engineer* 36 (1900): 210.
6. Hammond Hayes to Alexander Cochrane, 8 March 1901, box 1364, AT&T Corporate Collection, AT&T Archives, Warren, N.J. (hereafter ATT).

7. Jewett to Charles Goodale, 19 July 1921, 09 003 01, box 22, file 390 (T-I) ATT.
8. Memorandum, 2 May 1929, 417 07 03, box 64, ATT.
9. See for example U.S. Patents 1,920,729 (filed 1930); 1,454,157 (filed 1918).
10. Read and Welch, *From Tin Foil to Stereo*, 15; Mitchell Mannering, "The Triumph of the Telescribe," *National Magazine* 42 (July-August 1915): 648–651; The priority of the telephone call was well established by the 1920s, as shown for example by the fictional businessman in F. S. Fitzgerald's *The Great Gatsby*, who regularly accepted telephone calls even when they drew him away from important social events.
11. Public discourse regarding new electrical technologies is one of the main themes of Carolyn Marvin's *When Old Technologies Were New: Thinking About Electric Communication in the Late Nineteenth Century* (New York: Oxford University Press, 1988); Mark Clark, "Suppressing Innovation: Bell Laboratories and Magnetic Recording," *Technology and Culture* 34 (July 1993): 516–538.
12. Ithiel de Sola Pool, ed., *Social Impact of the Telephone* (Cambridge, Mass.: MIT Press, 1977), 213.
13. E. F. Stearns, "A Spool of Wire Speaks," *Technical World* (December 1906): 409.
14. "Miss Robson Laughs at the Bunco Trader," *New York Evening Post*, 26 August 1907.
15. "Uses of the Telegraphone," *Springfield Daily Republican* 15 September 1912; "Gambler Who Defied Police Is Shot Dead," *New York Times*, 16 July 1912, p. 1; "Murder Witness Recants in Fear," *New York Times*, 25 July 1912, p. 1; "Burns Uses Telegraphone," *New York Times*, 2 August 1912, p. 7.
16. *Telephone Recording and Dictating Machine* (Washington, D.C.: American Telegraphone Company, n.d.), "Telegraphone Sales Company," series 1, box 24, Primary Printed Materials Collection, TAE.
17. Fischer, *American Calling*, 70–71.
18. Pool, ed., *Social Impact of the Telephone*, 137.
19. Memorandum, 17 July 1929, case 32184, vol. D, BTL.
20. "Telephone that Registers Calls in One's Absence," *Scientific American* 121 (13 September 1919): 261, 272; "An Automatic Secretary," *Literary Digest* 84 (7 February 1925): 22; Memorandum, 8 August 1929, case 33251, BTL; F. Jewett to W. S. Gifford, 11 December 1930, case 3251, vol. A, BTL; "Telephone Conversation Recorder," *Electronics* 3 (August 1931): 75.
21. "Talking Night Letter," *Electronics* 4 (April 1932): 139; "Some Novelties in Sound Recording," *Electronics* 4 (September 1932): 281.
22. B. F. Craig to C. O. Bickelhaupt, 19 December 1930, 417 07 03, box 64, ATT; Memorandum, 26 December 1930, 417 07 03, box 64, ATT.
23. Elam Miller to G. H. Jess, 12 May 1930, 417 07 03, box 64, ATT; C. Wallace to K. S. McHugh, 22 October 1930, ibid.
24. Memorandum, 26 November 1930, 417 07 03, box 64, ATT; numerous items of correspondence from Bell Operating Companies, all dated December 1930, 417 07 03, box 64, ATT.
25. Memorandum, 30 March 1930, case 33251, vol. A, BTL; Memorandum, 14 June 1932, case 20872, ibid.; Memorandum, 27 February 1934, ibid.
26. Memorandum, 15 May 1935, case 20872, vol. A, BTL; Memorandum, 12 June 1935, ibid.

27. Paul B. Findley, "Voice Number Calls from Dial Phones," *Electronics* 1 (December 1930): 424; O. M. Glunt, "The Call Announcer: A Telephone Application of Sound Picture Ideas," *Journal of the Society of Motion Picture Engineers* 16 (1931): 362–367.

28. C. M. Taris, "New Audio Facilities for Recorded Announcements," *Bell Laboratories Record* 38 (March 1960): 102–105; Automatic Electric Company and others had recording-based time announcers in place even earlier. See E. S. Peterson, "The Automatic Time Announcer," *Automatic Electric Journal* 2 (January 1951): 148; W. C. Tillistrand, "The Role of Recorded Voice Services in Telephony," *Journal of the Audio Engineering Society* 11 (April 1963): 130–134.

29. Jewett to Gifford, 11 December 1930, case 33251, vol. A, BTL.

30. A. E. Joel Jr., ed., *A History of Engineering and Science in the Bell System, Switching Technology, 1925–1975* (New York: Bell Telephone Laboratories, 1982), 554–555.

31. A brief discussion of the use of the telephone by prostitutes is in Harold Greenwald, *The Call Girl: A Social and Psychoanalytic Study* (New York: Ballantine Books, 1958).

32. Memorandum, 22 August 1945, 417 07 03, file 10, ATT; Percy Knauth, "The Ipsophone," *Life,* 12 August 1946, 13–14; Leon Laden, "Robot Telephone," *Radio News* 38 (August 1947): 39–41; "Hot off the Wire," *Science Illustrated* 1 (April 1946): 111.

33. Gerald Kloss, "The First Hello," *Milwaukee Journal* 3 August 1989, n.p. From a copy in reference files, Ameritech corporate archives, Chicago (hereafter Ameritech Coll.).

34. "Eavesdropping in Washington," *U.S. News and World Report,* 9 April 1954, 36–37.

35. Memorandum, 1 September 1949, Lloyd Espensheid Papers, 61 06 01, box 37, BTL.

36. Joel, *A History of Engineering and Science,* 557; Justin J. Murphy, "Now It Can Be Sold," *Bell Telephone Magazine* (spring 1954): 51; "Ohio Bell Offers Answering Service," press release, 2 April 1951, Ameritech Coll.

37. "Phone Privacy," *Business Week,* 19 January 1946, 18; "Recorder Rules," *Business Week,* 17 August 1946, 25; "FCC Sets Rules on Telephone Recorders," *Business Week,* 6 December 1947, 22; "Telephone Attachments and Recording Devices," *Public Utilities Fortnightly* 59 (12 May 1966): 35; the "beep" requirement was discontinued for interstate and international calls in 1960. "New Recording Regulations for One-Way Messages," *Public Utilities Fortnightly* 65 (17 March 1960): 400.

38. Early accounts of answering machine use include "Phone-Answer Device Increases Rx Volume," *American Druggist* 160 (8 September 1969): 79.

39. The Notaphon (an imported machine apparently invented by the developer of the Ipsophon) is described in "New Telephone Recorder," *Radio-Electronics* 29 (December 1948): 56; An announcement for the Record-O-Phone is in Clarence Newman, "New 'In' Phrase: This Is a Recording," *Newsday,* 8 July 1968; *Telecommunications Report* 16 (2 July 1951): 16, 35; Edward L. Sherman, "Modern Equipment for Home and Business," *Bell Telephone Magazine* 36 (spring 1957): 53; Senate Committee on Commerce, Subcommittee on Communications, *Anonymous Use of Automatic Telephone Devices,* 89th Cong., 1st sess., 1965; "Hello, Is Anyone There?" *Time,* 3 September 1965, 27.

40. "New Telephone Answerer Awaits Hearing," *New York Herald-Tribune,* 24 November 1950; "Gray Mfg. Co. Announces Telephone Answering Device," *Wall St. Journal,* 27 December 1952; "How to Build an Electronic Phone Secretary," *Popular Science* (February 1962): 147–151; "New Automatic Phone Answerer Awaits Hearing," *New York Herald-Tribune,* 24 November 1950, quoted in *Daily Digest,* 24 November 1950, Lloyd Espensheid Papers, 61 06 01, box 37, BTL.

41. John Brooks, *Telephone: The First Hundred Years* (New York: Harper and Row, 1975), 299–301.

42. Greta Walker, "No Fate Worse than a Hangup," *New York Times Magazine,* 10 June 1973, 36.

43. Mary Lou Gebhard, "At Last, The Perfect Secretary," *American Mercury* 82 (April 1956): 115–116; "Phone Talks Back, Takes Calls while You're Gone," *Popular Science* 162 (May 1953): 88; "Machines that Answer Your Telephone," *Changing Times* 29 (October 1975): 47; "Telephone Answering Devices," *Consumer Reports* (March 1976): 145.

44. Articles on the small business applications of answering machines began to be much more common after 1965. See, for example, "Must You Answer Your Telephone?" *Graphic Arts Monthly* 40 (November 1968): 56–59; John Sunier, *Handbook of Telephones and Accessories* (Blue Ridge Summit, Pa.: TAB Books, 1978), 63; Walker, "No Fate Worse than a Hangup," 36; Men's magazines carried numerous articles in the early 1970s promoting the use of answering machines. See, for example, "The Private Ear," *Oui,* July 1974, 82–86.

45. Ibid; Yvonne H. Burry, "Answering the Phone Mechanically," *Columbus (Ohio) Monthly,* April 1981, 141.

46. *Statistical Abstract of the United States* (Washington, D.C.: GPO, 1984), 794.

47. Electronic Industries Association, *The U.S. Consumer Electronics Industry in Review, 1994* (Washington, D.C.: Electronic Industries Association, 1994), 69.

48. *Suggestions for Recording Your Code-a-Phone Answering Messages* (Ameritech Coll., n.d. [circa 1965]).

49. Lynn Sharon Schwartz, "Only Connect?" in *Tolstoy's Dictaphone: Technology and the Muse,* ed. Sven Birkerts (St. Paul, Minn.: Graywolf Press, 1996), 135.

50. Victoria Irwin and Lorraine Serravillo, "Telephone Answering Machine Use Flourishes," *(Mansfield, Ohio) News Journal,* 9 February 1979, p. 3.

51. Schwartz, "Only Connect?" 135.

52. Craig T. Feigh, *What Do You Say to an Answering Machine?* (Lawrenceville, Va.: Brunswick Publishing Co., 1985); Jonathan Winters, *Jonathan Winters . . . After the Beep* (New York: Perigee Books, 1989); Nicole Hollander, *Hi, This is Sylvia. I Can't Come to the Phone Right Now* (New York: St. Martins Press, 1983).

53. Code-a-Phone brochure, Ameritech Coll., n.d. (circa 1965); "Telephone Answering Machines," *Consumer Reports* (June 1979): 336; Yvonne H. Burry, "Answering the Phone Mechanically," 148.

54. Judith Martin, *Miss Manners' Guide for the Turn-of-the-Millenium,* rev. ed. (New York: Pharos Books, 1989), 282.

55. Fischer, *American Calling,* 261–268; Celso Alvarez-Caccamo and Hubert Knoblauch, " 'I Was Calling You': Communicative Patterns in Leaving a Message on an Answering Machine," *Text* 12 (1992): 473–505; Silvia Dingwall, "Leaving Telephone Answering Machine Messages: Who's Afraid of Speaking to Machines?" *Text*

12 (1992): 81–101; Robert W. Oldendick and Michael W. Link, "The Answering Machine Generation: Who Are They and What Problem Do They Pose for Survey Research?" *Public Opinion Quarterly* 58 (1994): 264–273; *Dog World* magazine quoted in Susan Jonas and Marilyn Nissenson, *Going, Going, Gone: Vanishing Americana* (San Francisco: Chronicle Books, 1994), 161.

56. *Statistical Abstract of the United States* (Washington, D.C.: GPO, 1991), 764.

FIVE. AMERICAN RERECORDING CULTURE

1. One version of the home disk recorder was the $557 "Callophone," which recorded on aluminum disks. Memorandum by R. Mallina, 30 December 1930, case 33251, vol. A, BTL; "Home Record-Maker Has Arrived," *Business Week*, 18 May 1940, 48–50; *How to Make Good Recordings* (New York: Audio Devices, Inc., 1940). Worth noting, however, is a reference to a small number of "enthusiastic home disc recordists" by C. J. LeBel in 1957. LeBel was a prominent booster of tape recording who worked for the Audio Devices Company, a major tape manufacturer. Audio Devices had in 1940s also sold blank recording disks for home disk recorders. C. J. LeBel, "Tape or Disc?" *High Fidelity* 7 (October 1957): 56.

2. Amertype Recordograph Corporation, as it was known during the war, sold almost $1.43 million worth of Recordographs and tapes to the military between 1941 and 1945. Dept. of Commerce, Civilian Production Administration, Industrial Statistics Division, *Alphabetic Listing of Major War Supply Contracts*, vol. 1 (Washington, D.C.: GPO, 1945), 186; ibid., vol. 3, 1436.

3. Clark, "The Magnetic Recording Industry," 281.

4. "Don't Let Him Touch That Mike!" *Photo Dealer* (1963): 58.

5. *How We Gave a Phonograph Party* (New York: National Phonograph Company, 1899), 9–15.

6. Lawrence A. Ruddell, "Miracles of Recording," *Etude* 67 (October 1949): 52; M. G. Winterton, "Candid Recording," *Popular Mechanics* 93 (March 1950): 206–207.

7. "Wire Recorder Techniques," *Electronics* 22 (January 1949): 161–162.

8. "Electric Recorders Valued as Agent Training Devices," *National Underwriter* 54 (1 December 1950): 8.

9. Mr. Openeer, "A Novel Interview," *The Phonogram* 6 (October 1890): 166; see also a similar story, "Rebuked by a Phonograph," ibid., vol. 9 (January 1893): 304.

10. "On the Record—Literally," *Time*, 15 February 1982, 16; "F. D. R. on Tape," *Time*, 25 January 1982, 31; Gary Wills, "The Kennedy Tapes," *New Republic* 186 (24 February 1982): 11–13.

11. Testimony as to the difficulty of making field recordings before the advent of portable tape recorders is George W. Pierce's *The Songs of Insects* (Cambridge, Mass.: Harvard University Press, 1949); also see Arthur A. Allen, "Hunting with a Microphone the Voices of Vanishing Birds," *National Geographic* 71 (June 1937): 697.

12. "A Contribution to Passamaquoddy Folklore," *Journal of American Folklore* 3 (1890): 257–280.

13. Cylinder 1518, Truman Michelson Blackout cylinder collection, Archive of Folk Culture, Library of Congress, Washington, D.C; descriptions of the holdings in the Library of Congress's cylinder collections themselves document the difficulty of

making usable field recordings. Individual entries are peppered with phrases like "inaudible speech," "distorted program," "much surface noise," and "sound breaks up." Judith A. Gray et al., eds., *The Federal Cylinder Project: A Guide to Field Cylinder Collections in Federal Agencies,* vol. 2, *Northeastern Indian Catalog, Southeastern Indian Catalog,* (Washington, D.C.: Library of Congress, 1985), 15, 81, 179 and *passim.*

14. John Lomax, *Adventures of a Ballad Hunter* (New York: MacMillan Co., 1947), 111.

15. Gray et al., *The Federal Cylinder Project,* ix.

16. U. S. Works Progress Administration, *The Manual for Folklore Studies* (Washington, D.C.: GPO, 1918), quoted in William F. McDonald, *Federal Relief Administration and the Arts* (Columbus: Ohio State University Press, 1969), 709, 714.

17. Erika Brady et al., eds., *The Federal Cylinder Project: A Guide to Field Cylinder Collections in Federal Agencies,* vol. 1, *Introduction and Inventory,* (Washington, D.C.: Library of Congress, 1984), 29.

18. Elizabeth B. Mason and Louis M. Starr, eds., *Columbia University Oral History Program,* microfilm ed., 2d set. (New York: Columbia University Oral History Office, 1979), 238–240.

19. Loel Liebner, "The Tape Recorder as Historian," *Saturday Review* 49 (11 June 1966): 98.

20. Studs Terkel, *Working* (New York: Pantheon Books, 1972; Ballantine Books 9th ed., 1990), xxii–xxiii.

21. Frederick C. Packard Jr., "Learning to Listen," *Harvard Educational Review* 14 (1944): 199.

22. "Industry Fights Tape Recorder Tax," *Electronics Business Edition* 30 (10 March 1957): 100.

23. George A. C. Sherer, "Oral Work with the Wire Recorder," *Modern Language Journal* 31 (May 1947): 264.

24. Michael Knudsen, private correspondence, 28 February 1995.

25. Kathleen McBrayer, "How I Use the Tape Recorder," *Audio-Visual Guide* 15 (April 1949): 19; Sherer, "Oral Work," 262.

26. In fact, the growth of the institutional market, comprising the audio-visual departments of schools, corporations, and the military, proved to be a godsend to the struggling magnetic recording industry during the 1950s. Sales of tape recorders to consumers failed to grow as quickly as expected. Further, consumers were more cost-conscious than institutions, and manufacturers enjoyed higher profits there. If regional school systems or an entire branch of the military could be "sold" on one company's offerings, that could represent ongoing sales for many years. This was particularly true for the many magnetic recording technologies that used nonstandard media. Peirce Wire Recorder Company of Chicago, for example, managed to convince the U.S. Navy to install its unique wire-cartridge machines at air fields beginning in World War II. Thus committed to this oddball format, the Navy remained Peirce's largest single customer until 1960. The cartridge design, which had little success in nonmilitary markets, disappeared only after Peirce sold the business in late 1959. The buyer, IBM Corporation, considered fulfilling the Peirce orders but finally declined. Incidentally, this is not an isolated story. The institutional mar-

ket for the last fifty years has absorbed many of the worst failures the consumer electronics industry has offered up. It was also the very last market for ailing U.S. tape
recorder manufacturers after the early 1960s, when companies that refused to
change with the times continued to offer the sturdy but expensive designs of the
1950s into the 1970s. A perfect example was the Wollensak 1500 series of tape
recorders. This sturdy and compact tape recorder won design awards when it was
introduced in 1955 and had considerable success in both the consumer electronics and institutional markets. The basic mechanical design passed unscathed
through the transition to stereophonic operation and from vacuum tubes to transistor
circuitry. By the late 1960s, the company had pulled out of consumer electronics,
and most people probably assumed that Wollensak had gone out of business,
though it was still half-heartedly assembling tape recorders for schools. As the years
rolled on, prices went up and sales went flat, until by 1980 a flagging Wollensak
cranked out its final model, priced at a remarkably high $495.

27. Blatantly promotional lessons in the use of the tape recorder appeared in dozens
of audio visual "how-to" guides and stand-alone tape recorder promotional publications such as *The Tape Recorder in the Elementary Classroom* (St. Paul, Minn.:
Minnesota Mining and Manufacturing, 1955). 3M was the country's largest maker
of audio tape. Sanford Feld, "Build Your Sound Profits Selling Schools and Government Agencies," *Photo Dealer* 29 (June 1963): 56.

28. William J. Temple, "Magnetic Tape and Wire Recorders," *Audio Visual Bulletin* 1,
no. 2 (1948), n.p.

29. Harold Hainfeld, "Saving Radio Programs with Our Tape Recorder," *Audio-Visual
Guide* 16 (March 1950): 16; Albert E. Harshbarger, "How a Radio-Recorder
Helped Our School," *Audio-Visual Guide* 19 (December 1952): 30.

30. It is also true that the Dictaphone and Thomas A. Edison Companies had earlier
released prerecorded cylinders as part of an educational package for teaching students how to use dictating machines; shorthand courses were, in fact, one of the
first types of phonograph recordings to find a market. "How to Harness up the Phonograph to Business," *The Phonogram* 7 (November 1900): 31–32.

31. Marvin Camras, "When the Professor Can't Be There," *Film News* 12 (September
1952): 26.

32. H. B. Dunkel, "If You're Buying a Recording Machine," *Modern Language Journal* 31 (1947): 253–259; John F. Ebelke, "An Experiment with Recording and Playback Machines in Academic Foreign Language Teaching," *Modern Language
Journal* 32 (1948): 591; Morris Lewis Groder, "New Advances in Language Teaching—The Georgetown University Project," *Journal of the Audio Engineering Society* 2 (April 1954): 65–70; J. Wallace Bastian, "Use of Color Slides and Magnetic
Tape in Teaching Spanish," *Audio-Visual Guide* 20 (March 1954): 18.

33. Edward Tatnall Canby's *Home Music Systems* (New York: Harper, 1953) was one
of the earliest full-length "how-to" books on hi-fi. In it, the tape recorder was relegated to the chapter on "Expanding the Home System," along with television sound.

34. Apparently the first company to offer recorded tapes was A-V Tape Laboratories
of New York. In late 1950, this company announced a catalog of fourteen titles priced
at five dollars apiece. "Music on Tape Makes its 1st Attempt at Commercial Out-
lets," *Variety*, 31 October 1950, 39.

35. The RCA cartridge system was available from 1958 until about 1965 but most sales in later years were to schools and other institutions. It is worth noting that RCA offered a cartridge wire recorder in the late 1940s, although it was not as popular as the open-reel types offered by others. R. M. Warner Jr., "Earl Masterson: A Fresh Slant on Video Recording," *IEEE Spectrum* 33 (February 1996): 51–52.

36. "Stereo Tape Players for Cars," *Consumer Reports* 31 (May 1966): 220–221; "Will Stereo Tapes Bring Music to Detroit's Ears?" *Business Week*, 6 November 1965, 35; Scott Schmedel, " 'Cassette,' Continuous Loop Cartridges Compete for Pre-recorded Tape Market," *Wall Street Journal*, 15 August 1967, p. 32.

37. Michael Brian Schiffer, *The Portable Radio in American Life* (Tucson: University of Arizona Press, 1991); Don MacDonald, "The Car Stereo Boom," *Motor Trend* 18 (April 1966): 58–59.

38. House Committee on the Judiciary, *Home Recording of Copyrighted Works*, 97th Cong., 2nd sess., 1982, vol. 2, 659.

39. "Tape Recorders and Tapes," *Photo Dealer* 31 (December 1965): 75.

40. "Tape Cartridge Players," *Sight and Sound Marketing* 2 (June 1966): 16.

41. "Home Tape Cartridge Players," *Consumer Reports* 32 (November 1967): 602–603; Larry Zide, "Are Cassettes Fulfilling Their Promise?" *High Fidelity* 20 (November 1970): 72–77; Ivan Berger, "Trying to Cross the Country by Cassette," *Saturday Review* 53 (28 February 1970): 93.

42. Dolby-equipped eight track decks and Dolby-encoded cartridges were available from the early 1970s on, but neither were popular.

43. Robert Angus, "What's New in Those New Low-Noise Tape Cassettes," *Photo Dealer* 37 (April 1971): 77.

44. The *Seventeen* survey is cited in "Cartridge Recorders Seen Big Seller for This Year," *Photo Dealer* 34 (January 1968): 43; Fred Petras, "The Question for 1972: Cassette or Cartridge?" *Tape Recorder Annual* (1972), 18.

45. "Music Maker for the Masses," *Business Week*, 24 February 1968, 108; "Cassettes Are Rolling," *Newsweek*, 28 April 1969, 90; Schmedel, " 'Cassette,' Continuous Loop Cartridges."

46. Hank Gilman, "Makers of Digital Tape Recorders Seen Putting Machines on Sale by Christmas," *Wall Street Journal*, 1 September 1987, p. 6.

Conclusion

1. House Committee on the Judiciary, *Home Recording of Copyrighted Works*, 97th Cong., 2nd sess., 1982, vol. 2, 656–657; *Statistical Abstract of the United States* (Washington, D.C.: GPO, 1997), 565, 572, 570, 760.

2. On the social construction of technology see Wiebe E. Bikjer and John Law, eds., *Shaping Technology/Building Society: Studies in Sociotechnical Change* (Cambridge, Mass.: MIT Press, 1992).

3. I'm indebted to Svante Lindqvist and several of his students for the concept of a technology's life cycle.

4. *Statistical Abstract of the United States* (Washington, D.C.: GPO, 1997), 565.

5. "Music Piped to Apartment Houses," *Business Week*, 14 September 1940, 446.

6. Willard A. Kerr, *Experiments on the Effects of Music on Factory Production* (Stan-

ford, Calif.: Stanford University Press, 1945); "Wired Music for Wartime," *Newsweek*, 23 February 1942, 59–60; Wheeler Beckett, *Music in War Plants* (Washington, D.C.: U. S. War Production Board, 1943); wired music had been suggested as early as 1931 by conductor Leopold Stokowski during his collaboration with AT&T in the field of high-fidelity transmission and recording. Robert E. McGinn, "Stokowski and the Bell Telephone Laboratories: Collaboration in the Development of High-Fidelity Sound Reproduction," *Technology and Culture* 24 (1983): 50. A wired music system was commercially available in Holland in the 1930s. By the end of 1937, over 340,000 Dutch homes had the service. "Muzak Music," *Time*, 1 November 1937, 73. By the later 1930s Muzak's competitors included Dow Jones & Company, which began offering a wired news service to business customers. "Wired Radio System Used by Dow Jones Service," *Electronics* 9 (July 1936): 38; Robert Leiter, *The Musicians and Petrillo* (New York: Bookman and Associates, 1953), 69–70; see also Elliot N. Sivowitch, "A Technological Survey of Broadcasting's 'Pre-History,' 1876–1920," *Journal of Broadcasting* 15 (winter 1970–1971): 1–18; Joseph Lanza, *Elevator Music: A Surreal History of Muzak, Easy Listening, and Other Moodsong* (New York: St. Martins Press, 1994).

7. Patrick Joyce, ed. *The Historical Meanings of Work* (Cambridge, Eng.: Cambridge University Press, 1987).

8. Edison, "The Phonograph and its Future," 532.

9. Sunier, *Handbook of Telephones and Accessories*, 60.

10. On consumer appropriation of technology see Michel de Certeau, *The Practice of Everyday Life*, trans. Steven F. Rendall (Berkeley: University of California Press, 1984).

11. New York State Legislature, Joint Committttee on Investigations of Public Service Comissions, *Wiretapping in New York City* (New York: New York State Legislature, 1916; reprint, Arno Press, 1974); Allan N. Kornblum, *Intellegence and the Law: Cases and Materials* (n.p.: Defense Intelligence College, 1985).

12. House Committee on the Judiciary, *Hearings on S. 646 Before Subcommittee No. 3 of the House Judiary Committee*, 92nd Cong., 1st sess., 1971.

13. Senate Committee on the Judiciary, *Copyright Law Revision*, 94th Cong. 1st sess., 18 November 1975, S. Report 94–473, 47–50; House Committee on the Judiciary, *Copyright Law Revision*, 94th Cong. 2nd sess., 1975, H. Report 94–1476, 46–50.

14. House Committee on the Judiciary, Subcommittee on Intellectual Property and Judicial Administration, *Hearing on Audio Home Recorder Act of 1991*, (Washington, D.C.: GPO, 19 February 1992), 101. Home video taping brought manufacturers and copyright holders to court after the appearance of Betamax videotape recorders. *Home Video and Cable TV Yearbook* 1982–83, 131. James Lardner, *Fast Forward: Hollywood, the Japanese, and the Onslaught of the VCR* (New York: Norton, 1987), 268.

15. Internationally, cassettes pose a threat not only to record companies but to centralized control of the media. Peter Manuel, *Cassette Culture: Popular Music and Technology in North India* (Chicago: University of Chicago Press, 1993).

16. "Dial-a-Diatribe," *New Republic* 153 (16 October 1965): 7; Senate Subcommittee on Communications, Committee on Commerce, *Anonymous Use of Automatic Telephone Devices*, 89th Cong., 1st sess., 1965.

17. "Ads Get on Phone," *Business Week,* 13 August 1960, 54; " 'This is a Recording': Phone Messages Tell All Kinds of Things," *Wall Street Journal,* 21 June 1967, p. 1.

18. Marshall McLuhan, *Understanding Media: Extensions of Man* (Cambridge, Mass.: MIT Press, 1994), 51.

19. E. F. O'Neill, ed., *A History of Engineering and Science in the Bell System: Transmission Technology (1925–1975)* (New York: AT&T Bell Laboratories, 1985), 525.

20. Larry Zide, "Will the Elcaset Make It?" *High Fidelity's Buying Guide to Tape Systems, 1978* (New York: High Fidelity, 1978), 28–30; "Elcaset," *Hi-Fi Stereo Buyer's Guide* 13 (January/February 1978): 48, 82.

INDEX

About the Author

David Morton is the research historian for the IEEE History Center at Rutgers University.

Printed in the United States
49911LVS00005B/241-252

9 780813 527475